D0762252

Abnormality and Normality

The Mothering of Thalidomide Children

Abnormality and Normality

The Mothering of Thalidomide Children

ETHEL ROSKIES

Cornell University Press

ITHACA AND LONDON

International Standard Book Number 0-8014-0691-9
Library of Congress Catalog Card Number 70-37757

Printed in the United States of America by Vail-Ballou Press, Inc.

Librarians: Library of Congress cataloging information
appears on the last page of the book.

For Arthur, Jonathan, and Naomi

Preface

This book is about mothers' perceptions of the process of bearing and rearing (or deciding not to rear) a congenitally limb-deficient thalidomide child. The topic is both a very limited and a very broad one. It is limited in the sense that the thalidomide population is small, unique, and, hopefully, one that will never be replicated. It is broad in that most of the issues raised in connection with thalidomide maternity would be equally applicable to the maternity of any handicapped or deviant child. For, paradoxically, the very uniqueness of the thalidomide situation only serves to highlight many of the general problems involved in the mothering of children who are different; because of the dramatic configuration of circumstances, much that is usually passed over or ignored becomes clear and inescapable here. Thus, it is both as an account of a highly unusual form of maternity and as a contribution to the general literature on the mothering of a different child that this work is intended.

The study reported here forms part of a larger longitudinal research project on thalidomide children carried out at the Rehabilitation Institute of Montreal between 1964 and 1969 under the direction of Dr. Thérèse Gouin-Décarie.[1] An earlier and more extended version of the present volume (Roskies, 1969) was presented as a doctoral dissertation to the Université de Montréal. With

[1] This undertaking was a joint project of the Institut de Psychologie de l'Université de Montréal (where Dr. Décarie is Professor of Developmental Psychology), and the RIM and was supported financially by the Canadian Council of Medical Research.

regard to the larger research project, most of the data concerning the children are contained in unpublished theses (Hill, 1966; O'Neill, 1965; Rancourt, 1965; Tremblay, 1967), and in a few published articles (Décarie, 1967, 1968, 1969).

The original impetus for the longitudinal research project came from the clinical needs of the RIM in treating thalidomide children. In spite of the almost universal assumption that thalidomide children had normal intelligence, there were in fact no existing techniques for evaluating the intellectual development of young pre-verbal children with severe motor disabilities. Dr. Décarie was asked to devise ways of evaluating these children. Because it was the limb-deficient children within the thalidomide group who posed the most unusual theoretical and methodological issues, they were selected as the focus of the research project that was begun in January, 1964.[2]

Exploration of the mothers' attitudes took longer to begin, but here, too, the motivation was a mixture of theoretical interest and clinical need. From the outset, clinicians responsible for the habilitation of these children were as concerned about their families, particularly the mothers, as they were about the victims themselves. If thalidomide children were to have a chance for a meaningful existence, then some means must be found to repair or substitute for the mother-child relationship that had been endangered by the birth of these "monsters." But if the mother-child relationship was crucial, it was also difficult to treat, or even to understand, because of the many novel elements contained in this form of maternity. Thus there was considerable motivation for including the mothers in the research project. In fact, according to Dr. Décarie (1969, p. 167), one of the essential long-term aims of the project was to study "what kind of interrelationship might evolve between mother and child

[2] Because the sample is basically a clinical one, consisting mainly of cases treated at the RIM, there has been some fluctuation in numbers between 1964 and 1969. Mongeau (1967) states that the total number of thalidomide children treated at the RIM is 34. At the time of the first evaluation (May-June, 1964) there were 22 limb-deficient cases among these; the second evaluation (February-July, 1966) had a sample of 25 limb-deficient thalidomide children.

in the case of infants suffering from congenital malformations."
Nevertheless, the immediate project began with an evaluation of the
children in May–June, 1964.

As soon as the results of this evaluation were compiled, however,
the importance of the mother was again highlighted. The most
surprising of the findings (O'Neill, 1965) was that regardless of
severity of handicap, length of hospitalization, or method of scoring,
there appeared to be a typical profile on the Griffiths Developmental
Scale for these limb-deficient children, and the profile was contrary to any prior expectation. The area most affected was speech,
while the score was highest for items requiring eye and hand co-
ordination. Considering the fact that this sample was limb-deficient,
but (with three exceptions) had no deformities that should affect
speech, this finding was as paradoxical as it was unexpected. Both
Décarie (1969) and O'Neill (1965), in explaining this paradox,
suggested that it might be due to some deficiency in mothering, even
in a home environment. It was as if the mothers refused to be ignored any longer; and so began a research adventure that was to
last for five years.

Nowhere was the tendency of the thalidomide episode to raise
usual problems in an unusually difficult fashion more evident than in
the area of research ethics. Anyone who chooses to work with
clinical topics and samples is unlikely to avoid some confrontation
with ethical issues, but in preparing this account of thalidomide
maternity the problems seemed to be more numerous and harder to
resolve.

The first issue was that of confidentiality. Because this work contains intimate data and because it concerns a sample in which individual cases are relatively easily identifiable (the sample com-
prises almost a total population within a given geographical region;
this population is small, unusual, and has been subjected to extensive publicity, but, apart from its one distinguishing characteristic,
the population is extremely heterogeneous), it was both more
important and harder than usual to keep the pledge of confiden-

tiality. A number of techniques were used. For one, the emphasis throughout the work was placed on typical problems and common patterns of behavior, rather than on individual case histories. Details about the personal background or unique characteristics of any one mother were kept to a basic minimum. Even the numerous concrete examples and direct quotations used were selected to illustrate typical problems and modes of resolution. A second technique used to hinder identification was the alteration of some details. For instance, all direct quotations of mothers' statements are given in English, regardless of the language in which they were originally made, and no identification is made of those quotations that have been translated from French. And third, the desire to preserve confidentiality led in some cases to the rejection of an otherwise desirable technique. Although code names would have greatly facilitated the continuity and ease of cross reference, they were not used because they also facilitate recognition of individual cases.

These precautions had their price. Although the account given here is, to the best of my ability, an accurate record of the group as a whole, the need for concealment may prevent it from being a completely faithful portrait of each mother as an individual. But this price seemed worth paying for preventing the recognition of individual cases without impairing a frank and detailed exposition of the data.

A second problem came from the fact that this account of mothers' perceptions inevitably touched on many other people who were deeply involved in the thalidomide story but who—because of the nature of the research design—were given no chance to tell their versions of events. Fathers, siblings, relatives, and professional helpers are only a few of the crowded cast of characters who were given no speaking parts. Here I can only emphasize, as I do throughout the work, that the "truth" presented is necessarily a partial one. But in spite of its incompleteness, I believe that the story of how the mothers perceived reality is sufficiently important, and often enough ignored, to be worth telling.

My final concern is with the thalidomide child who, knowing that there is a book about him, may someday choose to read it. The maternity described here is not a pretty one in conventional terms, and it is perhaps inevitable that some aspects of this description will hurt him. But if this record does not present a mother-child relationship neatly tied with pink or blue ribbons, it does contain much that is beautiful and even heroic. I hope that he will see this, too.

My debt to Dr. Thérèse Gouin-Décarie is an unusually large one. As director of my doctoral program, she provided support and guidance while permitting me to develop my own ideas—even when this led me into rather foreign territory. As head of the larger research project of which this work forms one part, she initiated the research project and assumed the difficult task of coordinating the various aspects, obtained financial assistance, and, far from least important, maintained a sufficiently good relationship with the clinical agency involved so that the research work could proceed unhampered. The fact that this study was possible is largely attributable to her efforts at every stage of the project.

My gratitude to the Rehabilitation Institute of Montreal also requires public acknowledgment, because this institution contributed far more to the study than merely serving as its locale. The collaboration of the RIM was an active one in assuring access to patients and documents, providing physical facilities for the interviews, and making the arrangements that permitted the costs of bringing the mothers to Montreal to be included in the government program. Perhaps most important, at no time was any attempt made to exert control on the type of data gathered or on the use made of this data. To single out any specific member of the staff is to do an injustice to the many who contributed freely of their time and effort, but I am particularly grateful to Dr. G. Gingras, who, as Executive Director, established the policies that made this type of research inquiry possible within a clinical setting.

I should also like to thank Mrs. Monica O'Neill-Gilbert and Mme Francine Bonnier-Tremblay, fellow members of the research team, for their cooperation during the experimentation period and for the use that was made of their data. To my husband and to Mitzi Becker, who came to my rescue by reading proof cheerfully and quickly, thank you.

My final and most important acknowledgment should be to the mothers themselves, but here I find myself at a loss for words. The expression of thanks, no matter how heartfelt, is an inadequate and somehow inappropriate manner of recognizing the very personal, and sometimes very painful, aspects of their lives that these mothers shared with me. Instead, it is this book itself that must serve as my acknowledgment. To the degree that it is a good one, I hope that the mothers will feel that their participation was worthwhile.

ETHEL ROSKIES

Montreal, Quebec

Contents

Tables

Abnormality and Normality

The Mothering of Thalidomide Children

Chapter 1

The Thalidomide Background

In the most restricted sense thalidomide refers to a ten-cent pill which, when ingested during early pregnancy, could result in a child manifesting a number of congenital anomalies.[1] But the term thalidomide also characterizes a complex historical event with social, psychological, legal, political, and economic consequences. Moreover, the thalidomide disaster occurred not only in many countries simultaneously, but also at a time when mass communication made it impossible for any one locality or country to react to the crisis without awareness of what was happening elsewhere. The mercy killing of a thalidomide child in Belgium, or the abortion of one by an American mother in Sweden, had a direct impact on the situation of a mother in Montreal. Any exploration of thalidomide maternity, then, must include some account of the historical and social context in which it took place.[2]

The World-wide Phenomenon

Thalidomide was first synthesized in West Germany in 1954 and went on sale there in 1958. It was used mainly as a sedative and as an antidote to nausea in early pregnancy. Between 1958 and 1962

[1] Cf. Glossary of Medical Terms.

[2] Unfortunately, a comprehensive history of the thalidomide experience remains to be written. To date, the best review of the available literature on the history of the drug, the incidence and nature of the resulting malformations, as well as the public reaction to this crisis, is that of O'Neill (1965). The account presented here is largely based on her work.

1

it is known to have been legally available in at least twenty countries.

At the same time that the use of thalidomide was becoming common, there appeared a widespread increase in the number of children born with congenital anomalies. The deformities quickly attracted attention because of their unusual nature; the most characteristic anomaly was phocomelia, a type of deformity in which the hands are attached to the shoulders and the feet are attached to the hips like the flippers of a seal. Prior to the early 1960's this deformity was so rare that most international classification systems did not list it as a separate category, and most doctors had never seen a single case.

Limb-deficiency, though the most common and most striking anomaly, constituted only one element of the syndrome among a host of other deformities. The major external defects were coloboma (a defect in one or both eyes), microtia (smallness of the external ear) associated with partial facial palsy, depressed bridge of nose, and hemangioma (tumor) on forehead, cheek, or nose. The internal defects were found in the cardiovascular system, urogenital system, and intestinal tract; there were also abnormal lobulations of liver and lungs, dislocated hips, syndactyly (fusing of fingers or toes), horseshoe kidney, bicornuate uterus, atresia (closure of a normally open channel in the body), and absence of the gall bladder.

By 1962 sufficient statistical evidence had accumulated to identify thalidomide as the teratogenic agent (having to do with development and birth of a monster). This identification of a drug as the source was aided by the fact that, as a rule, the familial medical histories of these children manifested no other incidence of congenital malformation.

The most readily accepted hypothesis was that the teratogenic effects of thalidomide were due to its interference with the critical determination phases of the mesenchymal derivatives (those embryonal connective tissues which give rise to bone, cartilage, and so on). Consequently, the crucial factor was not the amount of thalidomide ingested, but the time of ingestion. The critical period was considered to be between the 28th and the 42nd day following conception. In most cases the damage was done before the mother knew she was pregnant.

Public reaction to the crisis was intense and complex. Because of the iatrogenic (condition induced by physician in care of patient) nature of the deformities, the immediate horror and shock were soon followed by the belief that society itself was responsible for this disaster. Revulsion and the wish to make reparation were twin facets of the public concern and were linked to the etiology, to the large number of children involved, and, far from least important, to the nature of the deformities. Much effort was directed to the formation of large-scale habilitation programs that focused on two areas.

The primary emphasis assumed normal intelligence (without at first any factual evidence; O'Neill, 1965, discusses this point in detail), and was directed at providing education and habilitation (by the use of prostheses as compensation for the missing limbs) to enable the afflicted children to find their rightful place in society. Secondarily, the firm belief existed that these children should not be segregated but should remain with their families. There was considerable fear that the shocked parents might reject these children (cf. O'Neill, 1965), and urgent measures were considered necessary to preserve the integrity of the family.

It would appear that society itself was ambivalent in its attitudes. As fellow parents, the public could easily understand why these children were likely to be rejected. But as guardians of the children, society confronted this danger by insisting even more emphatically that the children must not be rejected. In this paradox was the first clue to the crucial and difficult role that the parents, particularly the mothers, were to play in this drama.

The Canadian Experience

CHRONOLOGICAL HISTORY

The chronological history of the use of thalidomide in Canada (Webb, 1963) parallels the European history. The major difference is that thalidomide became available in Canada three years later than in Germany and, consequently, the subsequent events were to be compressed into a much shorter time period.

Thalidomide legally went on sale in Canada on April 1, 1961, when the Richardson-Merrell Company issued a pill containing thalidomide under the trade name of Kevadon. On October 23, 1961, the Frank W. Horner Company entered the market with a second pill called Talimol. Both pills were sold by prescription only, and the major official use of thalidomide in Canada was as a sedative.

The first warnings in Canada of the possible teratogenic effects of thalidomide were not derived from Canadian experience, but from the accumulation of cases in Germany. Only four such children had been born in Canada when, on December 5 and 7, 1961, both pharmaceutical companies involved sent letters to physicians reporting on the incidence in Europe of congenital anomalies believed to be thalidomide-induced, and suggesting that these pills should not be prescribed for pregnant or premenopausal women. On February 21, 1962, a second warning letter was sent. Ten days later, on March 2, 1962, the drug was withdrawn. Thalidomide was legally available in Canada for a period of 11 months and one day.

In view of the fact that thalidomide was on sale until March, 1962, and the critical period lay in the first weeks of pregnancy, the full impact of this drug would not be known until nine months later, that is, until December, 1962. Nevertheless, so great was the sense of crisis that a federal-provincial conference was convened on August 17, 1962. This led to the formation of an expert committee which issued its report and recommendations in November, 1962. One of its recommendations was that three special units should be designated in Canada as research, training, and treatment centers for these children. The Quebec Minister of Health subsequently chose the Rehabilitation Institute of Montreal as the provincial government's official agent. Preparations were immediately begun at the Institute for undertaking an active habilitation program, and by the fall of 1963 the first patients were admitted.

The timing of events is particularly relevant. In contrast to the many years required to build up rehabilitation services for polio or cerebral palsy, governmental authorities, impelled by the urgency of the thalidomide problem in Canada, responded immediately. From the date that the pill first went on sale to the date that its victims arrived at the RIM for treatment, barely two and a half years had elapsed. In this sense the thalidomide incident in Canada can be considered as an acute crisis situation. Moreover, the crisis in Canada, as in Europe, lay not only in the number of children involved and in the nature of their deformities, but also in the fear that, unless urgent habilitation measures were to be taken, these children would be rejected by their families.

EXTENT OF THE PROBLEM

Webb, the government epidemiologist, has constantly emphasized (1963, 1964) the difficulty in collecting data, and the unreliability of the figures reported about the incidence of thalidomide-related deformities in Canada. This problem is not unique to Canada; O'Neill (1965) has found the same difficulty frequently mentioned in statistical surveys in other countries. The problem here is a double one. Reliable case finding involves both the identification of the syndrome and a proven history of thalidomide ingestion during the first weeks of pregnancy. The thalidomide incident simply highlighted the serious deficiencies already existing in the classification of congenital anomalies and in the accurate recording of physicians' disposal of drugs.

According to Webb (1964), there were 121 children born in Canada in 1961–1962 with thalidomide-induced malformations; 6 were born in late 1961, the remainder in 1962. Of these 121 children, 8 were stillborn and 33 subsequently died. By 1964, 80 children were listed as the known living thalidomide cases in Canada.

Of the 118 mothers involved (there were three sets of twins), slightly less than half had obtained the medication from the physician providing prenatal care. Fourteen women had received the drug from another doctor, 19 had had professional access to the pill, and 13 women had taken a drug prescribed for someone else.

In the remaining 11 cases the source of the drug was not indicated. Attempts to correlate the incidence of malformation with maternal characteristics, for example with age, parity, previous medical history, and so on, yielded nonsignificant results.

In Canada the thalidomide syndrome manifested the same characteristics as in other countries. The most common deformity was limb-deficiency (98 of 121 cases), and the range of severity varied from a simple syndactyly of one hand to tetraphocomelia (involving all four limbs); 44 of the 98 cases were classified as severe deformities. In addition to or instead of limb-deficiency, there were reports of other external and internal injuries. The most common external deformities involved facial anomalies, including absence or malformation of the external ear and external auditory meatus, partial facial paralysis, and hemangioma on the forehead and lip. The major internal anomalies involved the cardiovascular, gastrointestinal, and genitourinary systems. The high rate of neonatal mortality was attributed mainly to the internal anomalies.

THE HABILITATION PROGRAM

The preparation for a habilitation program began, as noted, as early as August, 1962. The expert committee formulated its general recommendations that were later published in the *Journal of the Canadian Medical Association* (1963). In addition to the general recommendations, there were individual reports on the pediatric (Rathbun and Martin, 1963), prosthetic (Gilpin, 1963), surgical (Hall, 1963), social (Armstrong, 1963), and psychiatric (Lazure, 1963), aspects of the problem. The recommendations fall into two main categories: administration and policy.

The administrative recommendations dealt largely with the sharing of responsibilities between federal and provincial governments. The federal government would provide direct financial assistance and personnel training courses to aid in the formation of habilitation programs. Three specialized habilitation units for research, training, and service would be designated across Canada (these were eventually located in Winnipeg, Toronto, and Montreal). Each province would then be responsible for assessing the needs within its own boundaries and establishing a suitable program for these cases.

If the administrative recommendations delineated the broad framework of the program, it was the policy recommendations that provided its content. Although, inevitably, there was some disagreement and contradiction in the views expressed by the various consultants, the basic policy can be summarized as follows:

1. The emphasis in habilitation would be on the whole child and his family. For this reason habilitation would necessarily involve a team of specialists.

2. No date was given for the duration of the program, but it was assumed that it would be a long-term one.

3. These children would not be segregated into separate centers, but an attempt would be made to integrate them into existing services for physically handicapped children. It was emphasized that the treatment centers should be as close to the children's homes as possible.

4. The children were assumed to be of normal intelligence, and the expectation was that they could be helped to lead almost-normal lives within their family units. Both these assumptions were basic to the habilitation program and were to influence greatly the nature of the treatment offered.

5. The probability of adverse parental reaction was considered to constitute a major threat to the success of the program. According to the psychiatric consultant (Lazure, 1963), the expected maternal reaction would be so severe as to resemble a post-partum psychosis. This was partly because the mothers themselves, by virtue of the fact that they had taken thalidomide, were judged to be a selected group predisposed to emotional breakdown, and partly because the specific etiology of the deformities would lead the mother to blame herself instead of accepting the disaster with "resignation and serenity" (Lazure, 1963, p. 963).

THE REHABILITATION INSTITUTE OF MONTREAL

The RIM became the largest of the three habilitation centers in Canada, and it is with its patients that this study is concerned. By arrangement with the Quebec government, the government would have the final authority for deciding the eligibility of cases and be responsible for paying the costs of treatment,[3] while the Institute would act as a centralized agency for evaluation and treatment. The nature of its functions, however, inevitably enlarged the Institute's role far beyond the medical sphere. In fact, for most of the parents the RIM was the habilitation program.

The RIM is a highly specialized hospital for congenital and traumatic amputees, diseases of the brain and spinal cord and their residual disabilities, and other miscellaneous disabling conditions. It began functioning as a small outpatient unit in 1949. At that time its staff consisted mainly of a few physiatrists (medical specialists in rehabilitation), physiotherapists (paramedical personnel trained specifically in physical therapies such as massage and gymnastics), and occupational therapists. The hospital grew rapidly, and by 1962 it had moved to its own large modern building containing inpatient as well as outpatient facilities. The professional staff, too, had increased to include a number of paramedical services.

As a treatment center for thalidomide children, the RIM suffered from three major difficulties. The first was that as a result of its rapid growth there were still considerable adjustments to be made in integrating the various services into a comprehensive habilitation program. Certain paramedical services (for example, the nurses, social workers, and others) were still peripheral; at the time the thalidomide program was begun, the position of social worker, for one, was unfilled. A second problem was that previous experience with very young patients was limited—from the records, one would estimate that approximately eight children under five years of age had been treated there prior to the thalidomide episode. And finally, the time available to prepare this extremely complex and novel program was relatively limited. The first federal-provincial con-

---

[3] It would appear that the term "costs of treatment" was interpreted broadly. It included not only hospitalization, medical fees, and prostheses, but also transportation, baby sitters, meals, hotel bills, etc. Unfortunately, none of the mothers was aware of precisely what features the government program would or would not cover, and it was not possible to find any document concerning this financial agreement in the files at the RIM.

ference on the problem was held in August, 1962; the RIM received its first thalidomide patients in the fall of 1963.

Nevertheless, the RIM accepted responsibility for organizing a habilitation program and quickly began making plans for receiving these children. Preparations not only included visits by senior staff members to other prosthetic centers, but also involved a review of all its own previous cases of juvenile amputees (Gingras *et al.,* 1964). It is interesting to note that in this review there was considerable attention paid to the role of the mother in the successful adjustment of the children treated.

This, then, was the background against which the drama of thalidomide maternity was played. Many elements are contained in it, but in terms of the mothers' future course a few were particularly important. The Canadian government manifested more concern about and more generosity toward the thalidomide-deformed child than it probably has toward any other category of handicapped child. Moreover, the help offered was not restricted to the child himself but included the family. Indeed, the maintenance of the child in the family was one of the essential elements intended to assure the success of the habilitation program. The mothers, however, were perceived as a group of anxious, guilty women who might react intensely to the trauma of a deformed child; thus, the role of the mother was considered important, but problematic.

Chapter 2

The Research Study

From the outset, this study of thalidomide maternity was conceived as an exploratory investigation of a broad problem, rather than as an attempt to provide a definitive answer to a specific question. But, of course, no single study can include everything about a given problem, and inevitably there is the need to select and eliminate, guided by both internal preferences and external limitations. This chapter is a record of the choices made and the reasons for making them.

Before embarking on a description of the experimental design, however, some preliminary explanation may be helpful. Descriptions of experimental methodology are usually quite boring to all but fellow researchers, and there was no reason to believe that this particular one would be any different. And yet the methodology cannot be ignored; it is the foundation on which much of the success or failure of the finished product depends. As the old adage would have it, "no research data are better than the methods used to obtain them." For this reason, the description that follows represents a compromise. Hopefully, it will give the reader sufficient information by which to evaluate the research without burdening him with unnecessary detail.[1]

The Problem

While the congenitally limb-deficient children and their mothers became a focus of public and professional concern, the mothers

---

[1] A more extensive description of the methodology can be found in Roskies (1969), pp. 29–148.

themselves merited special scientific investigation because their situation contained many novel, unknown elements and posed some painful questions.

ETIOLOGY

The thalidomide disaster provided medical history with one of the rare instances where a group of mothers could have known during their pregnancies that they were likely to deliver deformed children. Janis (1958a, 1958b) has shown that, under certain conditions, the possibility of anticipating and preparing for a stress situation can in itself diminish considerably the impact of the stress. Is it possible that the trauma of giving birth to a deformed baby was different for these women because they could have been prepared?

Unlike many others forms of congenital anomalies, thalidomide-induced deformities could not be attributed simply to the "will of God" or an "act of fate." Instead, the etiology was known to lie in a medication obtained from a specific person. Would this make the mothers guilty or angry or both? How would this etiology affect the mothers' relations to their children?

NATURE OF DEFORMITIES

Deformities visible at birth. For most types of handicapped children, there is a period of "normal" mother-child relationship before the presence of the disabling condition is known. Even when the handicap is congenital—and sometimes even when the handicap is easily diagnosable by professionals at birth (Prechtl, 1963)—the mother is often not told of the disability immediately, nor is she able to recognize it herself.

In the case of the limb-deficient child, however, the presence of deformity is obvious. Thus, unlike most other mothers of handicapped children, the mother of a limb-deficient child is forced to confront the fact of the defectiveness of her child *before* she has established any other relationship to the living child. How will this factor affect the nature of her maternity?

Lack of knowledge about deformities. The most characteristic anomaly associated with thalidomide was a rare form of limb-deficiency (phocomelia). But even the general problem of congenital limb-deficiency constituted a largely unknown area, both medically and psychologically (Webb, 1964). Most of the interest in this form of deformity has arisen subsequent to the thalidomide disaster. For example, the major medium for professional exchange of information on treatment of juvenile limb-deficiency, the *Inter-Clinic Information Bulletin,* appeared first in late 1961, and one of the earliest comprehensive texts in the field was published in 1963 (Blakeslee). The psychological interest is of equally recent origin. If one consults *Psychological Abstracts* for 1960–1961—the years immediately preceding the thalidomide publications—there are but 3 references to any form of juvenile limb-deficiency, contrasted with 330 references for mental retardation, 65 for cerebral palsy, 64 for deafness, and 53 for blindness. With the dearth of professional literature prior to the 1960's, it is not surprising that a popular manual for parents of limb-deficient children, such as those available for parents of blind or deaf children (for example, Lowenfeld, 1964; Myklebust, 1966), did not yet exist.

That so little was known about this form of deformity would have serious implications for the nature of the medical treatment available. Few doctors were knowledgeable in this field, and even the habilitation program established by the experts would have many innovative, experimental, and controversial features. The general lack of experience with congenital limb-deficiency would also affect the daily lives of the mothers, each of whom would have to discover for herself that a limb-deficient child would be more likely to run a very high fever (because of the lesser expanse of body surface), or that external help would be needed in order that a baby with deformed *upper* limbs could learn to walk (because of the importance of arms for balance).

Thus one of the basic peculiarities to the problem of mothering a congenitally limb-deficient child was a high level of uncertainty. How do women live with and adapt to a form of maternity which contains so much uncertainty?

Besides the limb-deficiencies, thalidomide-induced deformities constituted a very complex syndome that contained many unknown elements. In addition to the multiplicity of anomalies diagnosable at birth (some of which were extremely rare; for example, absence of tongue), there were many questions that were unanswerable or unanswered at the time these children were born. Had thalidomide affected their intellectual potential? Had thalidomide affected their reproductive capacity? Was there genetic damage, that is, if these children eventually reproduced, would their children be deformed? In a sense these mothers were in the position of raising a first generation of children. No one could reliably predict future development, because no thalidomide child had yet reached adulthood. How does a mother react to this form of uncertainty?

SOCIAL SITUATION

Unlike most mothers who give birth to deformed children, the mother of a thalidomide child was not confronted simply by a private tragedy. The births had become a public issue that aroused intense feelings and curiosity. Arguments for and against abortion, euthanasia, guilt of the mothers, responsibility of society, and so on, were freely aired. In addition, because of the relatively large number of such births within a short time period, there was a suddenly created thalidomide population. How would this affect the situation of the mothers?

HABILITATION PROGRAM

The parents of thalidomide children in Quebec—the population with which we were concerned—were offered a government-financed, centrally administered habilitation program. Unlike other parents of handicapped children, these mothers would not have to solve the problems of financial costs, or search for professional help on an individual basis. But the habilitation program was not solely a matter of financial compensation or specific habilitation techniques. It was also an expression of a public policy founded on the belief that thalidomide children should not be segregated or institutionalized, but could and should be raised in their own families. Thus, mothers were offered a rather unique group solution that conferred considerable benefits but also imposed equal demands. How would this change the situation?

SUMMARY

Briefly, then, the research study involved a group of women, heterogeneous in terms of age, culture, language, religion, parity, and socioeconomic status (see the description of the sample further on in this chapter), who had given birth to children who were equally heterogeneous in terms of intelligence, extent and type of disability (cf. O'Neill, 1965, pp. 30–57 and 105–110); but because of the common features of thalidomide usage and limb-deficiency, all these women were confronted by a form of maternity that was extremely complex and contained a high level of uncertainty and ambiguity. The problem for the researcher was to determine how a woman would mother a child under such circumstances.

Conceptual Framework

At the time this study was begun, there were no other reports on thalidomide maternity.[2] The virgin nature of the terrain meant that there was no well-established tradition to follow, but it also meant considerable latitude in choosing a conceptual framework through which to view the thalidomide situation. The most obvious source of a theoretical model was the fairly extensive literature on the general problem of the family relationships of handicapped children (cf. Barker *et al.,* 1953; Jordan, 1962; Kelman, 1964; Neff and Weiss, 1965; Wright, 1960, for reviews). Unfortunately, however, the more an attempt was made to juxtapose some of the traditional ways of looking at the maternity of a different child against the "live" data of thalidomide families (these preliminary data were gathered by observing thalidomide children at the RIM,

___

[2] After this project was under way, a preliminary report was received of a similar project in Munich (Strasser, 1965). As part of a larger study of a group of thalidomide children in Germany, some interviews were conducted with the mothers. This work will be referred to in the discussion of results.

through discussions with the clinical staff, and by reading and re-reading the voluminous case files), the more did the conventional approaches appear to be inappropriate and sterile. In fact, the first guidelines for this study were constructed as much in reaction against this literature as in derivation from it.

The first of these guidelines was that the study would be descriptive and nonjudgmental. This did not mean a mere collation of case histories. On the contrary, considerable effort would be devoted to conceptualizing the main challenges faced by the mothers and categorizing their various modes of response. But neither the mothers themselves, nor their reactions, would be judged in terms of "goodness–badness," "health–sickness," or "acceptance–rejection." The categories used would be descriptive, rather than evaluative.

At first sight, given the lack of knowledge of what was involved in the mothering of a thalidomide child, the decision to reserve judgment might seem sensible and even obvious. What makes it worthy of comment, however, is that it is directly contrary to much of the research and clinical practice in the area. If one examines the general literature on the mothering of handicapped children, it is surprising how much of it has been dominated by a single approach.[3] The twin postulates of this approach are (a) that personality distortion in the physically handicapped results more from

[3] In choosing our Goliath at which to cast stones, it is possible that we are not doing full justice to the variety of approaches to be found in the literature. There is some very good sociological work (e.g., Farber, 1959; Holt, 1957, 1958a, 1958b; Roe, 1952, etc.) demonstrating the realistic effects of a handicapped child on family functioning. Even more interesting, and more recent, is the "crisis" model developed by Caplan (1960) and applied very well by Davis (1963). Neither of these approaches, however, was suitable for our purposes. The sociological approach was not developmentally oriented and did not bear directly on the mother-child relationship, while the "crisis" model was so broad that it could not be easily or directly translated into operational terms. And since the basic purpose in turning to the literature was to find a conceptual framework for the study of thalidomide maternity, rather than to provide a comprehensive review, one can dismiss these approaches with no more than the twinge of guilt manifested by a lengthy footnote.

the early family situation than from the specific effects of the handicap itself, and (b) that "acceptance" within the family constitutes
the necessary condition for the optimal development of the handicapped child (Allen and Pearson, 1928; Coughlin, 1941; Denhoff
and Holden, 1955; Kammerer, 1940; Meng, 1938, in Barker *et al.,*
1953; Repond, 1956; Shere and Kastenbaum, 1966; Sherr, 1954;
Sommers, 1944; Worchel and Worchel, 1961). Unfortunately,
however, few parents achieve this goal of acceptance. Instead, the
record is replete with examples of overprotection, rejection, incon-
sistent handling, and unrealistic expectations. In essence, what
one has is a theological system in which a few—very few—parents,
those able to achieve the goal of "acceptance," are granted access to
heaven, a large number guilty of the sin of "rejection" are consigned
to hell, and the vast majority, criticized for "overprotection," "ambivalence," and "inconsistency," hover uncertainly in purgatory.
The role of the professional worker then is to lead the parents,
by the forms of prayer and exhortation known as therapy, counseling, and casework, to the state of grace.

The only problem with this approach is that after thirty years of
trial it has borne remarkably little fruit either in increasing our
understanding of precisely how and why things go wrong in the
mother-child relationship, or in helping to right them. In fact, a
recent review of the literature (Neff and Weiss, 1965) states categorically: "We know less about the actual dynamics of family reactions to disablement than about any other aspect of the problems
of handicapped persons" (p. 797). Even more trenchant have
been the criticisms of the concept of acceptance itself. Wright
(1960, p. 107) questions whether the notion of acceptance is anything more than a meaningless cliché, while Barsch (1968, p. 8)
considers "acceptance" and "rejection" to be subjective labels
which are applied arbitrarily, and even punitively, by the professional worker.

The clinical situation at the RIM reflected this paradox in the
literature. The case records at the RIM, too, used the terms "overprotection," "rejection," and "guilt." The one characteristic com-

mon to this very heterogeneous group of women was that, according to the evaluation made by the clinical staff, none seemed to be able to "accept" her child in an optimal fashion.

When the question was turned around, however, and an attempt was made to delineate how a hypothetical ideal mother would translate the concept of acceptance into concrete behavior, the ambiguities and contradictions inherent in the situation quickly became evident. Was the "accepting" mother the one who acquiesced to the lengthy hospitalizations required for prosthetic training because of their benefits for the deformed limbs, or was she the one who resisted them because of their deleterious effects for normal intellectual and emotional development? Would a "good" mother allow a child with abnormal arms to increase his functional skills by using his feet, or would she be more concerned about the social abnormality of a person who uses his feet to eat? Is it more normal for a handicapped child to attend a regular or a special school? Should a child with phocomelic arms be permitted to take ballet lessons, or should she be steered to other interests? For these, and the many other dilemmas faced by mothers of thalidomide children, there seemed to be no clear-cut solutions, regardless of the mother's willingness or goodness.

It was on this basis that the decision was taken to describe rather than to evaluate clinically. Considerable emphasis has been placed on the reasons for choosing such an approach, because this principle proved the hardest to defend and preserve during the course of the research study. For a researcher trained as a clinician and working in a clinical setting to insist that she did not know who were the "good" or "bad" mothers was interpreted either as coyness or heresy. This deliberate naïveté also made the analysis of data much more difficult and time-consuming. In fact, the only thing that permitted us to hold fast to this point of view was that the further we proceeded the truer it became.

In contrast to the lengthy process of deliberation that led to the formulation of the first guideline, the second one evolved in a spontaneous and barely noticed fashion. This was the decision to adopt a developmental orientation toward the study of thalidomide maternity; neither mother, child, nor mother-child relationship could be understood as a static, unchanging entity, but must be viewed as continuously evolving over time. Confrontation with the thalidomide case files in which rapid complex change was a predominant feature made the introduction of a time perspective appear natural and even inevitable. In fact, it was only the almost complete absence of developmentally oriented studies in the general literature on the family environment of handicapped children that underlined the innovative aspect of this type of approach.

The third guideline, the choice of a psychosocial perspective, was the one most clearly dictated by the nature of the thalidomide situation itself. Regardless of how pure a psychologist one wanted to be, to embark on a study of a mother-child relationship marked by world-wide publicity, legal controversy, and government-sponsored habilitation programs, without paying attention to the social context of this relationship was to make a virtue out of blindness. Like it or not, an understanding of thalidomide maternity would involve some consideration of the interrelationship of psychological and social factors. Once again, however, what was most surprising about this approach was its newness in the literature; remarkably few authors had chosen to treat both the inner reality and the outer reality involved in mothering a different child.

These three guidelines provided the preliminary shape of the study. It was to the work of a group of social psychologists and sociologists (Barker, 1948; Barker *et al.,* 1953; Wright, 1960; Goffman, 1963) that we turned for the concept that served as focus: the concept of marginality. According to this view, the problem of physical disability is fundamentally a social one because both the definitions of, and the meanings attached to, physical normality and abnormality are essentially social judgments. But the basic difficulty faced by the physically handicapped person is not simply that of an absolute deviation from a given social norm. On the contrary, the psychological dilemma of the disabled arises as much from his sameness as from his difference. He is both normal and abnormal, a member of the community and different from it. It is this dual identity that gives rise to both external and internal conflict.

In dealing with his dual identity, the handicapped individual may revolt against the stigma or against community values. Thus a deaf person may attempt to conceal or minimize his hearing loss or, at the other extreme, renounce hearing as a positive value and associate mainly with other deaf people. Most frequently there will be an oscillation between the two depending on the time, the situation, and the place. Although there will be considerable variation among disabled individuals, the common condition of frequent exposure to "new" and "overlapping" situations may lead to fluctuation in perceptions and inconsistency in behavior (Barker *et al.*, 1953, pp. 27–45). Moreover, because the essence of the conflict lies in the individual's marginality between two cultures, the person with an intermediate level of handicap may suffer more acutely than the more severely disabled (Cowen and Bobrove, 1966).

In many ways this viewpoint was an extremely attractive one to apply to the thalidomide problem. Unlike most other theoretical approaches, this viewpoint did not simply deal with the handicapped child's abnormality, but sought to explore the much more complex problem of the relationship between partial normality and partial abnormality. One could explore the effect of the handicap within the context of general development. Moreover, it promised to shed light on one of the basic paradoxes inherent in the social reaction to the thalidomide episode. In reviewing the historical background of the thalidomide phenomenon, we have stressed that public reaction to the crisis contained the dual aspects of horror at the monstrous nature of the deformities, and insistence that these children were intelligent and could be raised in their families. If these children were initially perceived as simultaneously both very abnormal and very normal, the dilemma of marginality might turn out to be a central factor in their subsequent careers.

Although the model of marginality appeared to offer considerable promise for the study of thalidomide maternity, it had never been used in this fashion, and some extensions were necessary before it could be applied. For one thing, marginality is usually conceived of as affecting the handicapped individual directly because it is he who is partly normal and partly abnormal; the extension made here is that this conflict would also confront the mother who bore and sought to rear such a child. Secondly, in studying the concept of marginality, the emphasis has traditionally been placed on the handicapped individual's relationship to the larger social environment. For the study of thalidomide maternity one would have to consider that the impact of this conflict would also affect intrafamilial behavior.

We formulated, then, a working model in which, basically, we hypothesized that the birth of an obviously defective child could create a very specific type of crisis. The essence of the crisis lies not only in the narcissistic injury to the parent, or the need to mourn the wished-for normal child (Solint and Stark, 1961), but also in the fact that the existing child embodies a basic contradiction. To put it in its crudest terms, living children are taken home, cared for, loved, and identified with, while dead children are buried. The child who is living but defective is an unknown combination of the two. Thus, immediately, the mother is confronted by the dilemma of deciding whether her child is normal enough to induce the mutuality of mother and child, or whether he is so defective that he no longer arouses the emotions and responses habitually aroused by a child. In practical terms, this conflict may be expressed in the decision to attempt to integrate the child within the family, institutionalize him, or kill him.

Unlike many other forms of family crisis, however, we hypothesized that this particular form is usually neither resolvable through time, nor terminable by a single decision. Unless the mother is able to kill the child, or consider him as totally dead, she is faced by a growing and developing child who is partly normal and partly abnormal.

In common with mothers of all children, the course of development exacts a continuous process of adaptation and readaptation of a changing mother to a changing child. In this sense the rearing of a disabled child resembles the rearing of a normal child. But for the mother of the disabled child, the normal developmental crises are intermingled with an additional continuous crisis. The unclear and constantly changing amount of normality and abnormality embodied in the handicapped child makes the mothering of such a child an adventure in two different cultures. At times the rules of the culture of normality are most relevant, while at other times the rules have to be taken from the culture of abnormality. Often it is difficult to predict in advance which would be most relevant. And frequently the choice involves an overt conflict between two equally valid but incongruent possibilities.

It was from this perspective that the mothers' perceptions of the process of bearing and rearing (or deciding not to rear) a limb-deficient thalidomide child were traced. The underlying assumption was that, in spite of the heterogeneity of this sample (both mothers and children), there would be certain common characteristics linked to the problem of marginality that could be isolated and described.

In searching for a conceptual framework, the original aim had been a simple one: to find a perspective from which to view and understand the thalidomide phenomenon. Somewhere en route, however, we found ourselves constructing a new and rather different approach to the study of the maternity of a deviant child. If this approach proved fruitful for the thalidomide situation, it might be applicable to a wide range of handicapped children. In a sense, the original research problem had become a double one; we not only wanted to know more about a novel, unique, and hitherto unexplored population, but we also wanted to test a new and hopefully better way of understanding the issues involved in mothering a handicapped or deviant child.

The Sample

CHOICE OF SAMPLE

At the time this study was begun, there were twenty-five cases of limb-deficient thalidomide children known to the RIM. Twenty-three were actively enrolled in the habilitation program and resident in

Quebec. Of the other two, one was a Maritime child sent to the RIM for treatment, and the other was a Quebec child whose family had decided against participation in the habilitation program. It was from these twenty-five cases that the sample was selected.

For the purposes of the larger longitudinal study, it was desirable to have the total sample of mothers whose children were participating in the project. Thus the process of sample selection was restricted to the elimination of unsuitable cases. Only one criterion was established a priori for selection; that is, the family structure prior to the birth should have been of such a nature that the mother would have been able to care for a nonhandicapped child.

Three families failed to meet this criterion and were eliminated on this basis. In one case, both parents were mentally deficient, and their previous nine children had been placed shortly after birth. In the second case, the child was illegitimate; the mother's previous illegitimate children had been placed in foster care or adopted. And in the third case, the mother had a history of alcoholic and narcotic addiction prior to the birth; she died when the child was a few months old, presumably by suicide.

After the research interviews were completed, another case was eliminated on the grounds that, although the handicap was congenital, the mother was not aware of it for some months after the birth. The limb-deficiency in this case was so minor that it had been noticed neither by the physician nor the mother at birth. It was only when the child was eight months old that the mother became aware of a "weakness" in one hand. The psychological process of gradual discovery of a handicap has been well detailed by other researchers, and it is a rather different one from the situation of visible congenital deformities that confronted the other mothers in this sample. For this reason the protocols of this case were not included in the analysis of data. Fortunately, this mother was the first one seen and, consequently, the case served as a form of pre-experimentation.

A fifth case was eliminated for clinical reasons. The mother lived in an isolated Quebec village and, following a previous visit to the

RIM, she had undergone a depression sufficiently severe to raise the possibility of psychosis. Although the mother in question was willing to be interviewed in her home, the lack of any psychiatric facilities in the area for follow-up made us unwilling to risk subjecting her to the stress of the interviews.

Thus the final sample was comprised of twenty mothers of congenitally limb-deficient thalidomide children. Nineteen of these mothers had children who were enrolled in active treatment at the RIM; one did not. The children of all these mothers were enrolled in the longitudinal project. Although the sample contained only 80 per cent of the mothers whose children were enrolled in the larger study (cf. Bonnier-Tremblay, 1967), it should be noted that any elimination of cases was based on the researcher's decision, rather than on the refusal of mothers to participate.

DESCRIPTION OF SAMPLE

The basic criterion for selection was that all these mothers had ingested thalidomide during their pregnancies and had subsequently borne limb-deficient children. The relevant sample characteristics must include, then, a description of the mothers, the children, as well as the reason for, amount, and source of thalidomide ingestion.

Community membership. All but two of these mothers lived in the Province of Quebec at the time of the study (the exceptions were the Maritime case, and one mother who had recently moved back to the Ontario border town where she had been born). However, the families were distributed throughout the length and breadth of the province. About a third came from Montreal and environs, but more than half came from small communities with populations of less than 10,000. No other locality besides Montreal had more than one case. It would appear that there was no particular geographical pattern to the distribution of thalidomide in Quebec.

In line with the general pattern of life in Quebec, these families manifested considerable geographical stability. More than half the sample had lived in their present communities more than ten years, and none had been there less than two years. More than two-thirds were presently homeowners. And when the mothers' present place of residence was compared with their place of origin, it was found that two-thirds of the women continued to live in the same community or vicinity in which they had been born.

The effect of the birth of the thalidomide child on geographical stability is difficult to determine. Only three families had changed communities since the birth of the handicapped child; in all cases this move was accounted for by the father's transfer or change of employment. But at least two mothers mentioned that even a move within the same community was difficult for them, since they did not know how their new neighbors would react to the child.

Socioeconomic status. Only a rough socioeconomic classification of this sample could be attempted, partly because of the vagueness of the information provided by the mothers (for example, by description of the husband's job) and partly because of the differences in background and present status that made it difficult to interpret the social meaning of a given index (for example, the attainment of a high school education may connote a very different achievement in New York, Montreal, rural Quebec, or a small village in Greece).[4] Four indices were used to estimate socioeconomic status: (1) father's occupation, (2) family income, (3) father's education, and (4) mother's education.

(1) *Father's occupation.* Roughly five of the fathers could be placed in the top group made up of professionals, proprietors, and administrators. At the other extreme, seven of the fathers were unskilled laborers or owners of small farms. The remaining eight fathers were in an intermediate category and were employed in such jobs as skilled worker, owner of a small grocery, bookkeeper, and so on.

---

[4] For instance, the large number of parents who did not complete secondary school may seem striking by American norms. But, at the time most of these parents were at school, education in Quebec was neither free nor compulsory and, particularly among rural families, secondary schooling represented a considerable luxury.

(2) *Family income.* The range of incomes for these families varied from under $3,000 per year to over $20,000. Almost half had an income under $5,000 a year, while only four families earned over $10,000. While none would be classified as clearly below the poverty line, few were well-to-do.[5]

(3) *Educational level of fathers.* The range was wide. At least one father had not completed elementary school, while, at the other extreme, one held a graduate degree. The most common level, however, was partial or complete secondary schooling; half of the fathers were in this intermediate category. The other half were about equally divided between "finished elementary school," and some post-secondary schooling.

(4) *Educational level of mothers.* In general, the women had less formal schooling than their husbands. Roughly two-fifths had partial or complete elementary schooling; another two-fifths had attained partial or complete secondary schooling, while the remaining one-fifth had some post-secondary training (for example, the teacher's certificate). Only one had a college degree.

On the basis of these criteria, the families could be divided into three broad categories: four constituted an upper middle class, six constituted a middle class, and ten were classified as working class. While the sample was weighted toward the lower socioeconomic levels, the heterogeneity was striking. Thus, at one extreme was a college-educated senior executive earning more than $20,000 a year, with a very wealthy family background, while at the other extreme was a barely literate farmer who earned less than $3,000 a year from his marginal farm.

Religious and cultural background. (1) *Religious adherence.* The overwhelming majority of mothers (seventeen) were Roman Catholic; this proportion is not out of line with the religious distribution in the Province of Quebec. The remaining three mothers belonged to three different religious groups; there was one Greek Orthodox

---

[5] The one family earning under $3,000 was a farm family. Thus the value of noncash revenue (e.g., food grown on the farm) would have to be added to its income

woman, one Jewish woman, and one Protestant woman. The original religion of the fathers was the same as that of the mothers in all but two cases; one of these fathers had converted to his wife's religion, while in the other family both parents placed little stress on religion.

In terms of strength of religious adherence, four of the women regarded themselves as devout, fourteen as practicing members of their religion, while two women considered themselves to be non-practicing. None of the mothers reported becoming more religious following the birth of the handicapped child. On the contrary, three left the church for a while; two have since returned, but one remains nonpracticing. For many of the Catholic mothers the desire to practice birth control following this birth has been a source of religious conflict.

(2) *Language of home.* Thirteen of the families use French as the family language, six use English, and one uses neither. It should be noted that the English-speaking families are not randomly distributed in the sample. None is rural, and the majority live in Montreal. Socioeconomically they form an elite; three of the four families placed in the top socioeconomic group are English-speaking. In addition, while all the women in the French-speaking families are Catholic, the English-speaking women are distributed among all four religious groups. Furthermore, two of the mothers classified as "English" are immigrants and use other languages in the home. These characteristics, however, would probably be representative of the ways in which the general English-speaking population in the province differs from the French-speaking one.

Family composition. (1) *Stability of marriage.* For all the mothers in this sample, the present marriage constitutes their only one. In only one case was the husband previously married and divorced. Although one of these mothers has been separated from her husband (prior to the birth), none is currently separated.

At the time of the birth of the thalidomide child, four of the mothers had been married for less than two years, and eight had been married for less than five years. And six had been married for more than ten years.

(2) *Age of the mothers.* Half of the mothers were between 20 and 30 years old, but two were under 20, and four were over 40.

(3) *Number of children.* For only three mothers does the thalidomide child constitute the only child in the family. Twelve have one to three other children, while five have at least four other children.

(4) *Ordinal position of thalidomide child.* For three-quarters of the mothers, the thalidomide child is the youngest or only child in the family. In the other five families, the number of subsequent births varies from one to three.

In spite of the fact that three-quarters of the thalidomide children are the youngest or the only children, the effect of the birth of the thalidomide child on subsequent family limitation is difficult to determine. In some cases the age of the mother or size of the family would have made any further children unlikely, regardless of the characteristics of the child. Perhaps more relevant is the fact that ten of these women have had one or more subsequent pregnancies, but only five have borne living children; the other five miscarried. None of the living children, however, is deformed.

(5) *Presence of thalidomide child in the family.* At the time of the research interviews, all but two of the thalidomide children were living with their families. Two of the children who were then living with their families had originally been institutionalized but, following their habilitation at the RIM, had been taken by their families. The two "non-family" children had never lived with their families; they had come to the RIM, where they were currently living, from institutions.[6]

It should be noted, however, that even for the "family" children there have been repeated interruptions in the family care of the thalidomide child. Only in the case of the family which has refused government aid has the child never been separated from his family. The other children who are categorized as never having been institutionalized have undergone from one to eleven hospitalizations, spending from one to eighteen months away from their families.

[6] These children were later placed in foster homes.

(6) *Work outside the home.* The birth of a thalidomide child appears to have exerted little influence on the outside employment of the mothers. Currently none of these mothers holds a full-time job outside the home, and the only one who has a regular part-time job has never had her thalidomide child at home. However, when they became pregnant with these children, only four mothers had regular employment, and in three of these four cases the thalidomide child was the first one. Thus the change in working habits for these mothers could be accounted for by the advent of a child, rather than the specific factor of a handicapped one.

A few mothers would like to return to work, but once again the major barrier appears to be the preschool age of the child rather than the handicap. It should be noted that for these families the government program has eliminated the financial burden of treatment, thus making it unnecessary for the mother to work because of the handicapped child.

(7) *Participation in social, religious, or political groups.* Most of these mothers do not participate in any formal activities outside the home. Only four are members of any group, and, of these, two rate themselves as nonactive.

For most mothers the birth of a handicapped child did not change the pattern of organizational activity. Only one mother has joined an association of parents of handicapped children. Two other mothers report becoming less active following the birth (one temporarily and one permanently), but this appears to be the extent of the change.

Characteristics of the thalidomide child. O'Neill (1965) and Tremblay (1967) have presented a detailed summary in their studies of the characteristics of the thalidomide children in terms of age, sex, length of hospitalization, type and severity of limb-deficiency, associated anomalies, and so on. In spite of the fact that the sample used here is not identical to theirs, the two samples are sufficiently similar to make repetition of this data unnecessary. Here we shall simply focus on some of the most salient characteristics.

(1) *Age*. At the time of the research interviews, thirteen of the children were between three and four years old, and six were between four and four and one-half years old. The presence of one older child (a girl of five) was explained by the fact that the mother had obtained the thalidomide pills in Germany.

(2) *Sex*. Of the twenty thalidomide children in the sample, seventeen are girls and only three are boys. The ratio of girls to boys is thus slightly higher than 4:1. This is in line with the general preponderance of girls in thalidomide samples (O'Neill, 1965, p. 33). For the purposes of this study, the small number of boys will make any discussion of sex differences difficult.

(3) *Nature of limb-deficiency*. The classification of the children's anomalies is extremely difficult. Not only are the diagnoses very complex, and the medical terminology itself variable, but, depending on the perspective of the observer (medical, psychological, or social), the classification of a given case can vary considerably. In classifying the malformations here, the aim is to present a rough picture of the major forms of limb-deficiency involved, rather than a precise description of the total anomalies manifested by each child.

On this basis, fourteen children can be classified as manifesting severe forms of limb-deficiency. Ten of these present the most characteristic anomaly associated with thalidomide—bilateral upper-limb phocomelia; two manifest bilateral lower-limb phocomelia; and one is a case of tetraphocomelia. For the remaining child the malformations are not considered phocomelic, but there is severe involvement of all four limbs. It was for these fourteen children that prostheses were considered necessary; thus, these are the children who were likely to spend longer periods in hospital and be most intensely involved in the habilitation program.

At the other extreme, there are two children whose limb-deficiency is restricted to a dystactyly or syndactyly of one hand. The remaining four children fall into an intermediate category; all have malformations involving more than a single hand, but none has any missing limbs that would require him to wear prostheses.

It should be noted, however, that for almost no child is the major limb-deficiency the sole handicap. The vast majority of children also present other external or internal anomalies or sensory defects (cf. O'Neill, 1965). In fact, Mongeau (1967) states that within the total thalidomide sample seen at the RIM, the average number of handicaps per child was slightly more than three.

Circumstances surrounding ingestion of thalidomide.

(1) *Reason for taking thalidomide.* More than half of the mothers claim they took thalidomide as a sedative (see classification set forth below); this is congruent with Webb's (1963) classification of the major reasons for use of thalidomide in Canada.

Classification of mothers by stated reason for taking thalidomide

Reason	Number
Sedative	12
Antinausea	2
Loss of appetite	1
Heartburn	3
Relaxant	1
Cold	1

The uses of thalidomide, however, were surprisingly varied. Even when taken as a sedative, the circumstances leading to its use were quite different. Thus, two mothers were in the hospital for investigation of other medical difficulties when they were given thalidomide as a routine sleeping pill. In one case, the mother was on a European trip. Eight of the women claim they were not aware of the fact that they were pregnant at the time they took thalidomide.

(2) *Source of drug.* The source of thalidomide for this sample highlights a basic medical problem in the distribution of drugs. Thalidomide was legally available by prescription only, but only twelve of the women obtained the drug from a doctor professionally responsible for their care. In the other cases, three women obtained the pills from a relative who was a physician, three used pills prescribed for someone else, and two women bought the pills in a pharmacy.

The ironies implicit in the source of the drug were many. In one case a woman had had eleven previous pregnancies without prenatal care; at the time of the pregnancy with the thalidomide child, she decided to follow the modern trend and visit a physician. It was he who gave her thalidomide. In a second case it was a doctor husband who gave his wife the pills. And in a third case, a wife sent her husband to the pharmacy to buy her medicine for her loss of appetite. The pharmacist recommended some medication costing $10, but the husband felt that this was beyond his means. Instead he bought the less expensive thalidomide.

(3) *Number of pills ingested.* More than half the mothers claim they took less than five pills (note classification given below). The reasons given for stopping were varied, but in most cases thalidomide successfully alleviated a temporary stress situation, and no more pills were needed. On the other hand, at least three of the women state that they took the pills for months.

Classification of mothers by stated number of pills ingested

Number of pills	*Number*
Less than 5	11
Five to 20	4
More than 20	3
Unknown	2

There seems to be no relation between the number of pills ingested and the severity of the resulting anomalies. Two of the women who claim to have used the pills for months bore children with very minor handicaps, and, on the other hand, the mother whose child was tetraphocomelic claims to have taken only two or three pills.

Summary of sample characteristics. A composite picture of a typical family in the sample would include a three-year-old girl [7] with upper-limb phocomelia in a French-speaking, practicing Catholic, rural, working-class, Quebec environment. She was born when

[7] Although the predominance of girls in the sample makes it correct to refer to the thalidomide child as "she," to avoid confusion with the mothers the more usual "he" will be used in the rest of this work.

her mother was twenty to thirty years old, had been married over five years, and already had two to four children. Her ordinal position is that of youngest. She has always lived at home, but with frequent interruptions for hospitalizations. Her mother is a full-time housewife who belongs to no organizations. The mother obtained thalidomide from a physician during early pregnancy for a temporary discomforting situation and ingested less than five pills.

But although this composite picture describes the majority of families in the sample, it does not describe them all; the most striking characteristic of this sample remains its heterogeneity. For a sample of twenty women, there is considerable diversity in almost all characteristics investigated. In fact, the most basic link between these women remains the primary one, that is, that all ingested thalidomide during their pregnancies and subsequently bore limb-deficient children.

Research Techniques

The basic technique used to gather the data was a series of semi-structured interviews. The element of structure, by means of a series of interview schedules (cf. Appendix A), was introduced to ensure that the material gathered would be comparable from one case to another.

The conceptual framework of the study determined the basic format of the schedules. Each would cover a defined chronological period and, by a series of both direct and open-ended questions, seek to build up a picture of how the mother perceived and dealt with the medical, psychological, and social issues involved in her maternity. In so far as possible, an attempt would be made to obtain behavioral examples for the attitudes and feelings expressed by the mother.

For the section on child-rearing practices, the work of Sears, Maccoby, and Levin (1957) served as a general guide, but, for the most part, it was the case files at the RIM that provided suggestions for specific questions. It should be noted that in many cases specific questions were introduced because of the researcher's "hunch" that they might prove significant. Thus such questions as those about baptism, or choice of godparents, were used because it was hoped that they might provide indices on how normal or deviant the baby was perceived to be at birth.[8]

In arranging the questions, particular care was taken to "bury" emotionally charged questions in more neutral contexts. For instance, there was no separate section on the use of the prostheses (the subject of considerable controversy between parents and the RIM at the time of the interviews), but questions referring to this topic were included in a number of places. In addition, some of the questions were deliberately repeated at several points during the schedule. Often a mother might be quite cautious when a subject was first broached, but when it was raised again, in a slightly different form, she would amplify her statements.

Because the interviews were conducted in two languages, both English and French schedules were required. The schedules were composed in English and translated into French. Verification of correct usage of French terms, in reference to the social and educational level of the sample, was done by experienced French-speaking clinicians.

Because of the unique nature of the sample, these schedules could not be pretested on a different group.[9] Instead, the schedules were discussed both with experienced researchers and with the clinicians who already knew the mothers.

The interview schedules may be construed as an attempt to standardize and objectify the process of data collection. But given the nature of the research study, it was unavoidable that the interviewer

[8] While many of these behavioral indices did eventually prove significant, unfortunately it was not always those anticipated in advance. Thus the mode of baptism showed little relation to the mother's perceptions of the normality or abnormality of the child, while the issue of baby gifts (a question not anticipated in advance) did prove an important indication of social reaction. In this sense the interview schedules illustrate well the exploratory nature of the research.

[9] As it happened, the protocols of the first mother interviewed were later eliminated from the analysis of data (see "Choice of Sample" above). Thus this case did serve, inadvertently, as a mode of pre-experimentation.

would influence the quality of the relationship established during the interviews, the type of data obtained, and the interpretation given to this data. Since it was impossible to eliminate the experimenter variable, it was necessary for the author to train herself to be an effective research tool. (In a sense, we were functioning more as an anthropologist than as an experimental psychologist.) Training was on two levels. The simpler one involved a process of familiarization with children, hospital, and habilitation techniques. Goffman (1963) has spoken of the role of the "wise" person, that is, the person who is familiar with the intimate details of the disability or stigma without being disabled himself. This role was a necessary one for the researcher to assume if she were to speak meaningfully with the mothers about their experiences. Learning in this area did not follow a formal program, but involved a process of assimilation and acculturation through observation and occasional participation in hospital routines. For example, a single attempt to put the prostheses on a child taught the interviewer more about the nature of prostheses than countless hours of reading. Similarly, attempts to feed, dress, or play with individual children provided a rapid course in the nature of their disabilities.

The second level of apprenticeship was far more difficult; it involved the attempt of the researcher to come to terms with her own feelings about the mothering of a limb-deficient thalidomide child. This meant not only that the researcher had to try and become aware of her feelings and behavior toward each child, but also to pose herself the question: How would I feel and behave if I were the mother of this child? Would I have wanted to abort or kill this child if it were possible? Could I have taken him home, or would I have wished to institutionalize him? What would be the deciding criteria for me? Could I tolerate seeing this child using his feet to eat? Would I prefer to hold him with or without prostheses? Could I hope or want to hope that this child would eventually marry? Detachment in the face of such emotionally charged issues being impossible, it was necessary for the researcher to be sufficiently aware of her own feelings and desires so as not to confuse them with those of the mother.

In addition to the formal techniques of data collection, for the five years that this study was in progress, the researcher had continuous contact with staff and case files at the RIM. There were, as well, sporadic contacts with individual mothers following the formal research interviews. (In one case the mother asked to see the interviewer for advice about the problem of "telling" the child about his handicap, a matter that at first appeared irrelevant but six months later had become a central area of concern. In another case, the interviewer volunteered to follow mother and child through a hospitalization for surgery at another hospital, a move prompted by the desire to have first-hand observation of the effects of hospitalization on mother and child.) While most of the data acquired by casual contact were not formally incorporated into the results, they were used as a general background. In certain areas, too, the case files served as an external verification for the reliability of our data.

Research Interviews

The formal research interviews were carried out at the RIM between February and July, 1966, at the time of the second evaluation of the children. The invitation to the mothers to participate in the research project was contained in the letter which set the appointment for the child; this letter was written by the doctor in charge of the program (cf. Appendix B). Because most of the mothers were seen at the same time as their children were evaluated, the government program paid all costs of transportation, lodging, food, and so on.

Upon arrival at the hospital, the mother would be met by the interviewer, while responsibility for the child was assumed by the researchers concerned with the child's evaluation. A separate office was used for the interviews with the mother.

During the short, preliminary interview, the mother was acquainted with the general aims of the project. The fact that participation was voluntary was stressed. It was also emphasized that the interviewer was not a member of the hospital staff, and that all information obtained during these interviews was confidential and not part of the general hospital records.

The timing of interviews was flexible, depending on the fatigue of the mother, and so on. The total number of hours of interviews varied from 12 to 18 hours spread over 3 to 5 days.[10] In all cases the language used (French or English) was the choice of the mother.

The interviews were held in the following sequence: (a) socioeconomic questionnaire, (b) the present, (c) the future, (d) the birth, and (e) the baby's arrival at home. The decision to modify the chronological sequence of events was based on two factors. The present was considered the most factual and immediately relevant aspect to the mother; therefore, it provided an opportunity to build up rapport in a relatively nonthreatening situation. On the other hand, the interviews on the birth and the future were considered potentially the most traumatic ones; it was desirable, therefore, to provide some period of preparation for and recuperation following them.

Financial limitations made it impossible to tape-record all the interviews. Thus on most occasions the interviewer completed the questionnaire as she talked with the mother.[11] Supplementary infor-

---

[10] Although the time period over which the mothers were seen was a relatively short one, the spacing and context of the interviews led to a situation of considerable intimacy. All of these mothers were removed from their usual occupations and many from their familiar surroundings and families. Moreover, the frequent changeover of social work staff at the RIM meant that by the end of a week the mother had sometimes had more prolonged contact with the interviewer than with any other member of the hospital staff.

[11] It is a rather sad commentary on the situation of mothers of handicapped children to realize that these mothers posed few questions about the notes that were being made or about the eventual use that would be made of the material. It appears that most of these women had become habituated to their role as "patients," one aspect of which was the recording of intimate details of their lives.

mation was added later. For the interview on the birth period, however, it was considered desirable to use a less structured form of questioning, one that would permit the interviewer to devote her full attention to the mother. Thus, this interview was recorded with the permission of the mother.

Following completion of the research query form, the mother had at least two clinical sessions with the social worker and with the child psychologist. This constituted an additional safeguard that any problems engendered by the research interviews could be dealt with.

While the procedure described is a relatively simple and straight-forward one, it was neither simple to plan nor, once planned, simple to follow. The difficulties came from two main sources: (1) the clinical status of the sample population, and (2) the fact that no member of the sample was replaceable; if a member of the sample could not or would not fit into the research design, one either had to change the design or risk being left with a smaller, and probably biased, sample.

Since all but one of the families in the sample were patients of the RIM, and it was under the hospital's auspices that mothers were invited to participate in the research project, the clinical context of the study was an important factor. The problem here was a double one in that the dilemma of clinical needs versus research needs was encountered both in relation to the hospital and to the mothers.

From the hospital's point of view, the major concern was that the research study would not harm their patients. At the time this part of the research project was planned, there was considerable anxiety among senior staff members that these interviews might prove traumatic. A preliminary meeting for hospital staff members was held at which the interview schedules were shown and the sequence of interviews was explained. Following this explanation of aims, purposes, and procedure, cooperation was excellent.

From the researcher's point of view, the major requirements made to the hospital were for freedom of access to patients and documents, for independence in deciding the content of the research interviews, and for assurance of confidentiality. In working out these details, the hospital authorities proved extremely generous. The researcher was given most of the privileges of a staff member but bore no clinical responsibilty toward the hospital. Thus the hospital, under the government program, paid the costs of bringing the patients to the hospital, provided a separate office for the research interviews, and gave the researcher free access to all case histories, files, and so on. But in no case was the researcher required to transmit any information obtained during these interviews. A general report, in the form of this book, was the only obligation undertaken.

The dilemma of clinician versus researcher was far more serious in relation to the mothers. A number of problems arose, such as the use of the interviewer as clinical confidante, and as intermediary between mother and hospital. By far the most fundamental one, however, was the issue of potential benefit of the research to other mothers of handicapped children versus potential harm to these particular mothers.

From the research point of view, our interest was in obtaining as detailed as possible an account of the birth period, anticipations of the future, and so on. For most of the mothers, however, these interviews touched on many painful memories and anticipations, and the pain inflicted could not be justified on the grounds that this abreaction was therapeutic. In fact, after a while, the interviewer became convinced that the reverse was true. Whatever the benefits to be achieved by catharsis, these mothers had already experienced it. By the time these interviews were conducted, most of the mothers had already told their stories repeatedly to a variety of psychiatrists, social workers, psychologists, and doctors (though none of the mothers, to the best of our knowledge, had had formal psychotherapy). There had obviously not been a process of working through, and one could question whether, in fact, environmental stresses of this nature can be worked through. Whether the researcher was justified in probing for information under these circumstances was a continual concern.

Surprisingly enough, a number of researchers in this area do not mention at all the effect of this type of interviewing on the subject (cf. Davis, 1963; Ehlers, 1966). Where it is mentioned, the belief is that this form of interviewing is therapeutic (Barsch, 1968). While the therapeutic aspect was present in our interviews, too, we became increasingly convinced that there was as much potential harm as benefit. Thus there was a delicate ethical problem here of balancing clinical versus research needs. Although the interviewer attempted to err on the side of caution, this problem was never fully resolved.[12]

The modifications necessary to adapt the standard procedure to the heterogeneity of the sample took a number of forms. For example, for the two mothers whose children had never been at home, it was obvious that the usual sequence and content of the interviews were inapplicable. To ask a mother who saw her child once a year detailed questions about his daily activities would be ridiculous. Thus for these mothers the format of the interviews was changed. While following the same chronological sequence, the interviews were much less structured and all were fully recorded.

At the other extreme, the one family which was not participating in the government program would permit the interviews only if they were held in their home, a few hundred miles outside Montreal. This home visit proved to be the most difficult, enlightening, and, in retrospect, amusing of all the research interviews. Indeed, at one critical point in the interviews, when the family was quite hostile, the interviewer conducted her talk with the mother under the supervision of the husband, an unidentified male relative, the maid, and two older siblings. A two-year-old toddler clutched at

[12] The problem is not simply one of learning to be more cautious. Some idea of the acuity of this conflict can be gained from the author's experience during a series of follow-up interviews with these mothers in 1969. Possibly because she had only one interview with each mother, possibly because of a residual of guilt concerning the first series of interviews, the interviewer was much more hesitant to probe. While this type of procedure may have left the interviewer with a glow of virtue, it also left her with data containing a multitude of platitudes and little else.

her papers, while a younger child fought for a place in her lap. The only lit lamp in the room was ten feet away, and a radio and television set blared in the foreground. At this point the safety and privacy of the office at the RIM were very appealing.

The heterogeneity of this sample in terms of cultural background also required modifications in procedure. While the research procedure required the mother to be seen alone, in one case the mother spoke very little English (she spoke no French), and the father felt that it was part of his role as the male of the household to be present during the interviews. Since this accorded with the mother's perceptions of correct procedure, in terms of her cultural background, the husband was present during most of the interviews.[13]

In another case it was the middle-class orientation of the interview schedules which created difficulties. The mother in question had a family of ten children and was mainly concerned with eking out a living from her subsistence-level farm. Most of her day was spent in the fields or with the animals, and the care of the child was left to the older siblings. Unlike the typical middle-class child, this particular child was dressed and fed by whoever happened to be available at the moment, and the mother had little interest in or information about these areas. Questions about play activities or friends elicited an equally blank look. Occasionally the mother would counter with the comment: "It's too bad you don't know much about picking corn." This series of interviews aroused a new appreciation of the cultural relativity of many of the "laws" of child-rearing.

In fact, it is fair to say that either the interview procedure or the schedules required some adjustment for almost every mother. In describing these "deviations" from standard procedure, however,

[13] During one of these interviews a nurse in the hospital, whose native language was the same as the mother's, was used as an interpreter. This proved disastrous. The nurse had strong opinions on what questions should be asked and how the mother should reply. Thus, often, following a heated five-minute discussion with the mother, the nurse's translation would be a short phrase: "She says no." The sensation was of watching a foreign movie with very scanty subtitles.

two observations should be made. First of all, in no case was any modification introduced without cause. Moreover, to have attempted to conform rigidly to standard procedure in the face of these differences in the sample would, in our opinion, have been far more detrimental to the validity of the interviews than were the variations in procedure.

Analysis of Data

The process of analyzing the data is almost as difficult to describe as it was to carry out. Perhaps the easiest way of doing it, is to begin by describing the procedures we sought to avoid. At one extreme is the purely quantitative approach. A counting of noses was not particularly useful for our purposes both because we were dealing, for all intents and purposes, with a nonreplicable population, and because many of the answers to individual questions had no immediate or obvious psychological significance in themselves. They became meaningful only to the degree that they could be fitted into a pattern. At the other extreme to quantative analysis is an approach that can be termed the clinical one. Here the author first presents general conclusions, presumably drawn from his data, and then illustrates them by one or more typical cases. For us this approach has always aroused the admiration and the bafflement produced by a magician pulling a rabbit from a hat. How did the author get from raw data to conclusions? Were all the cases typical ones? If not, what happened to the untypical cases?

The technique finally arrived at for the analysis of data involved a combination of inductive and deductive sleuthing. The first step was to block out the three main topics that would serve as chapter headings (for example, prostheses, or social implications) and, within each chapter, the major time divisions (for example the birth period, the present). In this way approximately twenty broad subject areas were delineated. For each of these subject areas there was a process of teasing out from the data what can be termed the predominant theme and the major variations. In essence, the questions we posed were: How could the mothers' statements about what happened during this particular time period in this particular subject area (say, the child within the family) be most economically conceptualized? What dimensions best expressed the issues, conflicts, or challenges perceived by the mothers? And what were the major modes of response?

To cite a specific example of the process, we gradually built up, from the mass of statements made by the mothers, a picture of the birth period as one in which doctors, mothers, and families were the main actors. By the same inductive process, it was possible to categorize the mothers' perceptions of the doctors' behavior under two main headings: (a) affective—how he dealt with the mother's feelings, and (b) instrumental—what he did or proposed to do about the baby. At this point, having conceptualized the raw data along two dimensions, one went back to the data and empirically tried to determine, by means of the mothers' statements, how each doctor rated on these scales. One could then go on to see if the data permitted us to try to explain the variation. Were the differences that the mothers perceived related to urban versus rural hospitals, severity of deformities, and so on? In a sense, what we had done was start with a set of statements about the doctors, gradually organize these statements into a series of concepts or scales, and then return to the data to see if these scales were useful and meaningful in describing, and sometimes explaining, both the common pattern and the major variations.

The difficulties of such a procedure are obvious and deep-seated. For one thing, it was an extremely lengthy and cumbersome technique; each subject area was a miniature research project in itself. Another difficulty was that there were many false starts and much wasted effort. For example, in the chapter on the child within the family, an attempt was made to delineate common practices of child rearing. Weeks were spent constructing charts of eating and sleeping behavior, or patterns of socialization, until we were gradually and reluctantly forced to conclude that the precise details of child-rearing practices were too varied to be meaningful in terms of a common pattern. Fortunately, by this time the common pattern approach had already worked for the other two chapters, so we could afford to change our question and ask instead why the mothers and children had become dissimilar in this area at this time. But the weeks of lost effort still hurt. A third problem was the question of selectivity. Regardless of the attempt to objectify the process of analysis, only a portion of the 80 to 150 pages of data collected for each mother could be analyzed. To what degree the most fruitful questions were asked of the data still depended, to an uncomfortably large extent, on the skill and honesty of the researcher.

But if the advantages of this technique are less obvious, they are equally deep-seated. Most important, this approach permitted us to deal with the total sample in a meaningful manner. We could go beyond presenting a collection of individual case histories and, at the same time, had no need to sweep embarrassing exceptions into a dusty corner. Similarly, this technique, in our opinion, offered a happy compromise between presenting masses of undigested, and consequently meaningless, raw data or emitting conclusions at a high level of inference with little empirical support. A disinterested observer need not necessarily agree with the conclusions drawn from the raw data, but he should be able to follow the process by which they had been arrived at.

Chapter 3

The Social Normalization
of Abnormality

It is obvious that any attempt to separate the child's status in the family from his social role in the community is an arbitrary one. In the case of any child, and particularly in the case of the handicapped one, there will be a continuous interaction between the two. Thus the mother's perception of society's view of the handicapped child may strongly influence her feelings concerning her capacity to love and care for this child in the family (Mead, 1952). Conversely, the attainment of a developmental milestone within the family may vastly modify the perception of the child's social role; for example, the child's attainment of independent toilet care may change the perception of his social horizons considerably in that this achievement alone may decide whether he is to be admitted to a regular school or be sent to a special one. Nevertheless, in spite of the artificial nature of this distinction and the inevitable overlap, a careful consideration of the child's social role in the community apart from a view of the child within the family provides a helpful technique in managing a large mass of unwieldy data. Consequently, this chapter will deal with the mothers' perceptions of the social implications resulting from the birth of a thalidomide child, while the subsequent chapter will deal more specifically with the mothers' perceptions of the child within the family.

Anticipations, Presentiments, and Preparations

The thalidomide disaster resulted in one of the few exceptions to the general rule that for most women the birth of a defective

44

baby is necessarily a sudden, unanticipated crisis. Not only was it theoretically possible for each of these women to have had certain knowledge that she had ingested a possibly teratogenic agent, but the relatively large number of such births within a short time period conceivably might have led each pregnant woman in Canada in 1962 to explore the possibility that she, too, might be affected.

The first question then is whether the women in this sample had prior knowledge, and, if so, from what source; at what time during their pregnancies they knew; and how this knowledge was communicated or acted upon. And the answer is a surprising one. Only three women knew definitely before they gave birth that they had ingested thalidomide and of its possible teratogenic effects, and even these women experienced great difficulty in gathering the information, communicating it, or acting upon it.

Only one of the women knew definitely both aspects at a stage of the pregnancy where abortion is usually considered possible. As a medical secretary, she had had access to samples and had taken the pills on her own initiative; when two and a half months pregnant, she heard the news about thalidomide over the radio. We do not know the motivation that led her to conceal this, but she did not tell her husband until the end of her fourth month. At no time did she tell her doctor, and by the end of her pregnancy she says that she was convinced that she had not harmed her baby because she had taken too few pills.

The other two women reached the stage of "certain knowledge" much later in their respective pregnancies, but here, too, there seems to have been considerable conflict about knowing. One of these women, who had managed a pharmacy for a number of years and had considerable knowledge of drugs, knew that she had taken thalidomide at the beginning of her pregnancy. Her husband discovered the possible teratogenic effects a month later upon their return from Europe. According to her, he managed to conceal this knowledge from her by burning all newspapers or articles containing references to thalidomide. She does mention that she was "very disturbed" throughout the pregnancy and unable to prepare any clothes for the forthcoming baby. But it was only in her eighth month that, by chance, she read an article about thalidomide and realized its implications; she reveals her conflict about this knowledge by recalling that she felt "if your neighbor's house burns it doesn't mean that yours will," and then adding, "even if it's very close to yours." She delivered precipitously, one month prematurely, but remembers being "surprised" when told that her baby was deformed.

The third case of "certain knowledge" also manifests the same difficulty in seeking and obtaining information. This woman had been given thalidomide by a doctor she had consulted for marital problems prior to and early in her pregnancy; at two months she read reports of thalidomide and suspected that this was the drug she had been taking. Throughout her pregnancy she questioned her psychiatrist who denied it; she did not believe him, but she did not seek information from any other source. At the beginning of her ninth month, according to her account, her doctor told her that in fact she had taken thalidomide, and he then discharged her as his patient. At this point she claims to have wished vehemently for an abortion but she realized that it was "too late."

These cases illustrate well the psychological and social complexity of the process of knowing about a possible disaster. However, before analyzing the issues involved, it is necessary to consider the situation of the remaining seventeen women in this sample. Davis (1963), Wolfenstein (1957), and others have shown that the process of acknowledging crisis is a slow one even when there are many signs along the route to open acknowledgment of both illness and disaster. Although it is difficult to quantify or categorize these subtle phenomena, there were at least four possible sources of realistic anxiety. Two are common to all pregnant women: first, a previous medical history of abnormal births, or factors at the time of conception that might lead these women to consider themselves in the high-risk group, and, second, some unusual feature in the pregnancy itself that might serve as a warning signal. Two were specific to thalidomide itself: the general knowledge about thalidomide available to the public, or the presence of some significant person in the environment who knew that the woman had taken thalidomide and could have communicated his concern in a more or less disguised fashion.

Of the seventeen women involved, sixteen [1] had at least one possible warning sign, and a few had as many as four, that all might not be well. But, regardless of the medical point of view that places certain women in a high-risk group, none of these women mentioned that she attached any significance to the fact that her previous difficulties with childbearing, or her age or health at time of conception, might indicate a cause for concern. Nor did any mother's ill-health or threatened miscarriage during pregnancy serve as a signal for alarm. Retrospectively at least, the most anxiety-provoking of the general clues were abnormal movements of the baby, but of the seven women who claim to have felt them, only three complained to their doctors, and they were quickly reassured.

Knowledge about other thalidomide babies had little emotional impact in that the implications were denied. Six mothers stated that news of these events did not register or else commented that "this happens in Europe, not here." Two did give some thought to the possibility that they, too, might be involved. One of these women went so far as to discuss her anxiety with her husband, but he advised her not to ask her doctor, claiming that he wouldn't tell her the truth. Thus none of these women discussed this knowledge with her doctor. But in at least two cases the women's reactions, when told of the deformities, would indicate that this denial was not completely successful. Both recall that their first comment upon being told that their babies were deformed was: "It's thalidomide."

The category that "somebody else knew" (for example, the doctor or the pharmacist) is an interesting one because it illustrates some of the possible collusion underlying the denial of knowledge that could involve both doctor and patient. In one case a doctor strongly

[1] The one exception is also an exception to this group in a number of other respects as well. A young healthy primigravida, she had taken thalidomide in Germany in 1960, and her baby was born a year before the others. This was before there was any general concern about thalidomide in Canada.

advised a patient to stop taking thalidomide (she had been using pills prescribed for her husband), and in another case the doctor changed his own prescription (telling the woman that the former pills were no longer on the market). In the case of a third woman, a pharmacist, filling the thalidomide prescription, asked her why she was taking it and mentioned that this medication might not be good for her. None of these women either sought or was given further explanation. The other two cases where the women believe that their doctors knew are more ambiguous. They attribute their belief to some sudden change in the doctor's behavior. For instance, one woman claims that her doctor suddenly left town in the midst of her pregnancy, although he was in the process of building a house; according to her, he told her of his impending departure only a week before he left, did not recommend a replacement, but advised her to have another blood test because he had broken the test tube.

Thus it appears that the women were not able to use the clues particular to the thalidomide situation. Most did not believe that this could happen to them. They showed extreme reluctance in asking questions and, even when they did, had difficulty in obtaining answers.

In contrast to this general picture of nonexpectation, there were three women among these seventeen who had strong premonitions that their babies would be deformed. In these cases, however, this belief stemmed as much from inner needs or anxieties as from external evidence. In one case a woman recalls having recurrent dreams that her child would be "beautiful but infirm." Two of these women based their fears on their intense desire to have these babies; one remarked that to have had a whole baby would have been "too close to heaven on earth." The other woman presents a constellation of severe neurotic problems, but the basis of her expectation of a retarded child appears to have been both the need to punish an errant husband and insecurity in her own capacity to bear a child.

In analyzing these findings, certain cautions concerning the limits of this type of data must be mentioned. First of all, the information given here is retrospective and subjective; all retrospective case histories are likely to manifest some degree of distortion, but, depending on the area, the reliability may vary considerably (Smith, 1958; Wenar and Coulter, 1962). In this area we are discussing feelings rather than facts, and these feelings are so "loaded" emotionally that considerable distortion may be present. Secondly, while our sample is derived from a known population of mothers of living deformed thalidomide children, we do not know the extent of the total possible thalidomide population. Thus we do not know how many mothers knew they had taken thalidomide and actively prepared for this crisis, but bore normal babies. Nor do we know the number of women whose preparations consisted of terminating their pregnancies by abortion.

From our data, however, it would appear that in this sample the "knowers" and the "non-knowers" did not form two distinct and separate groups. Instead there is a continuum, ranging from those who knew more to those who knew less. In all cases, however, there was some difficulty in recognizing, interpreting, and communicating information. Davis (1963), in his study of polio, has commented on the lack of a "rightful place" for the death of a young child in our culture; on the basis of this sample one can state that there seems to be an equal lack concerning the possibility of delivering a living deformed child.

In trying to understand the barriers to knowledge, three possibilities come to mind. Psychological preparation for the birth of a deformed baby may be difficult precisely because the dreaded event is neither certain nor inevitable. Because the rate of risk associated with thalidomide is below 100 per cent,[2] mothers and doctors who suspected the possibility had some basis for hoping that a normal child would be born and that there would be no need to face the issue. Even more important psychologically in fostering denial may be the fact that for a certain period of the pregnancy the birth is not inevitable; the baby can be aborted. Five mothers spontaneously mentioned that, had they known early enough in their

---

[2] There are no reliable statistics on the rate, but it has been estimated to be anywhere from 20% (McBride, 1961) to 60% (Franz, 1962).

pregnancies, they would have sought or been tempted to seek abortions. One wonders whether the process of preparing for a deformed child necessarily involves some consideration of the wish to destroy this child, but, considering the religious, emotional, social, and legal problems that abortion poses in our culture, knowledge that raises this possibility may lend itself to denial.[3] Doctors, too, may not be eager to communicate their fears to their patients if they raise the specter of abortion. A third possibility is that the nature of the potential deformity may in itself have fostered denial. It is possible that a child without arms or legs may be more dreaded than other forms of handicap and, consequently, may be more difficult to prepare for.

Powerful as these motives may be, they are not sufficient to explain completely the time lag in the dispersion of knowledge. By 1962 most people had accepted, at least statistically, the link between ingestion of thalidomide and the resulting deformities. The only task remaining then was to establish which of these mothers had taken the drug during a critical period of her pregnancy.

And yet, the process of "knowing," for these mothers, took up to sixteen months. Prior to birth three knew; by one month after birth eleven knew; six months later seventeen knew; and at the end of a year eighteen knew. For the remaining two mothers, this process took four months longer. The difficulty is not unique to this sample; Webb (1964), in her report on the statistical incidence of thalidomide cases in Canada, emphasizes the difficulties involved in collecting data. She also notes that there are forty-two cases of congenital bilateral limb malformations, similar to the thalidomide syndrome and born during the same time period, where it has been impossible to confirm the ingestion of thalidomide. Speirs (1962) also notes the difficulty in ascertaining the truth about the ingestion of thalidomide.

---

[3] There has been such a rapid and radical change in Canadian public opinion concerning abortion in the last 10 years that this may no longer be true. But it certainly was true at the time of these women's pregnancies with their thalidomide children.

In some of these cases this lag may be ascribed to the general problem of defining, recording, and communicating relevant medical knowledge. Three of the doctors, for instance, asked the mothers whether they had taken any pills during pregnancy. They seemed to have forgotten that they themselves had prescribed the pills for the mothers. In two cases, it was the mothers' bringing the pills or the prescription to the doctors that made them remember. Sometimes, particularly where the physician had not been the one to prescribe the pills, the difficulty lay in the mothers' inability to report this knowledge, or in the type of questions asked. One mother was asked a number of times by her pediatrician if she had taken any antinausea pills during her pregnancy. She replied, honestly, that she had not. She had, in fact, taken thalidomide, but as a sleeping pill. In another case the mother was repeatedly asked if she had taken Kevadon; she answered, again truthfully, that she had not. It was only when the child was a year old that she read in *Life* magazine a list of pills containing thalidomide and realized that the pill she had taken (Contergan) was among them.

Another difficulty lies in the aura of fatalism that seems to be aroused by medical accidents. A number of mothers reported that following the birth they were advised to accept it as the "will of God" by relatives, priests, and doctors. This attitude can have many roots. The search for knowledge can be discouraged because it is considered futile. It may also be seen as dangerous because the question "How?" may soon lead to the question "Why?" At least three mothers mentioned that this episode undermined their traditional religious beliefs; they refused to accept that they had sinned badly enough to warrant this form of punishment. In at least two other cases, the mothers believed that the doctors discouraged knowledge because they sought to protect the mother, or one of her relatives, from the guilt associated with being the agent responsible for the ingestion of the fatal pill.

Nevertheless, there are at least six mothers in this sample who remain convinced that the doctors' main concern was to protect themselves by deliberately withholding knowledge. They feel that many of the doctors' actions at the time of the crisis were motivated by their guilt and their fear of social consequences rather than by concern for the patient's welfare. As the government program for thalidomide children became available, the stakes for knowing became high ones (for financial compensation, and for participation in the habilitation program), but some of the mothers believe that considerable pressure was necessary in order to force the doctors involved to testify that they had prescribed thalidomide. There is, of course, no way of verifying how correct the mothers' perceptions are, but many of the stories told are bizarre.

Here we shall limit ourselves to one story only; it is not typical, but each of these stories is atypical. This mother believes that she was given thalidomide by a physician substituting for her own obstetrician during an early stage of her pregnancy. According to her, shortly before the birth of her child she noted that this doctor avoided her at Christmas mass. Following the birth, she asked the attending obstetrician what had caused the deformities; he told her it was better not to ask. The pediatrician attributed it to a "nervous shock" of the mother during pregnancy, the village priest to the "will of God." When her baby was four months old, the public health officer of the area questioned this mother about her ingestion of pills during pregnancy. She became suspicious and began to search for the source of the harmful pills. She asked the doctor who had given her the pills whether he had given her thalidomide; according to her, he denied it. But a few months later the dog belonging to this doctor bore limbless pups; she believes that he gave thalidomide to his pregnant bitch in order to test its effects. In the interval, her husband had learned of the existence of another of the thalidomide babies and was shown both the deformity and the pills. She returned to the doctor, and this time he agreed that he had given her thalidomide but denied that these pills could have caused the deformity. A pitched battle then ensued in the village; the mother claimed that the pills were responsible, while the doctor maintained that the deformities were due to a hereditary defect in the mother or to shock during pregnancy. The doctor moved from the area shortly afterwards.[4]

In seeking to answer a rather short question—about the possibility of prior knowledge and psychological preparation for the birth of a deformed baby—the answer has become a long and complex one. This problem has been treated in considerable detail for two reasons. As the first area of results to be discussed, it serves as an illustration of the inherent complexity of much of this material. In order to keep this work within reasonable limits, it will not be possible to repeat this process with much of what is to follow. But it may be helpful to remember that if at times the analysis is rather brief, and appears superficial, it is not due to the limits of the material, but simply to the necessity of choosing to emphasize certain aspects and, consequently, neglecting others.

The other reason for choosing to analyze this problem at length is that it provides an important historical framework for much that is to follow. Our conclusion is that, in the traditional sense of the term, these mothers were not able to or did not prepare psychologically for the advent of deformed babies; the crisis or shock was as severe for them as that habitually described for this event. Nevertheless, the circumstances surrounding the dispersion of knowledge concerning the etiology of the deformities did have two important consequences:

1. The problem of "knowing" does not end with the mothers. At the time of the research interviews, many mothers were concerned with how they would explain to the children the reason for their deformities. But for at least five mothers this "telling" will have to conceal another secret: had the mother known early enough, the child might not have been allowed to survive until birth.

2. The other consequence is far more general. It involves the

4 The doctor described here is not the same one whose precipitous move has been mentioned previously. According to the mothers' statements, more than half the doctors involved in this episode have left the communities in which they practiced at the time of the thalidomide incident.

effect of this particular doctor-patient relationship on subsequent ones. As a result of the trauma, all these women require a great deal of medical help for their children, if not for themselves. And yet, because of their perceptions concerning the doctors' part in this tragedy, many of the mothers are extremely mistrustful of doctors and medical treatment. Here there is a severe conflict between present need and perception of past experience.

The Birth Crisis

A common view in the literature on physical handicaps (Blakeslee, 1963; Hall, 1961; Michael and Shucman, 1962; Roe, 1952; Solint and Stark, 1961; Strasser, 1965), would indicate that the period immediately following the birth of a defective child constitutes a severe crisis period. In general, this crisis has been considered from two main aspects: (1) the emotional reaction of the parents (from shock to bewilderment, hopelessness, hope for a miraculous cure, mourning, and so on), and (2) the crucial importance of the early days after birth as the time for determining the fate of the baby. Particularly where the deformity is visible, evident, or known at birth, there is the fear that the child may, as Winnicott (1956) puts it, "fail to release the early maternal feelings and may therefore be a greater risk of institutional placement." And yet, in spite of the importance placed on this period, we have almost no detailed studies of what are the dimensions of this trauma and what is the psychological and sociological process that leads to some form of resolution or decision concerning the baby. To cite only one glaring omission, we find scattered references in the literature to the emotional impact that an event of this nature may have on the professional and hospital staff involved, and some awareness that the actions of the doctor at this point may be very important (Blakeslee, 1963; Franklin, 1963), and yet there is surprisingly little writing in this area.

In attempting to study this crisis in our sample of mothers of thalidomide limb-deficient children, the omissions in the literature quickly became more understandable. Beyond the limitations of our data—in studying mothers' perceptions of what happened the account is inevitably retrospective and subjective—the nature of the crisis itself immediately plunges us into complexity and confusion. In a very short time period, a few hundred people—mothers, fathers, physicians, siblings, nurses, priests, friends, family, neighbors—were involved in a very unexpected event that had a strong emotional impact and raised some profound questions (for example, about euthanasia and institutionalization). Thus, as soon as one ventures beyond broad generalizations such as "shock" or "confusion," ordering the material becomes very difficult. How can one remain faithful to the oscillation, change, and confusion so evident in the data, and, at the same time, make this material coherent? Davis (1963, p. 19) has stated the dilemma of the crisis researcher extremely well: "The . . . paradox of ordering reality versus the unreality of order taunts the investigator who wishes somehow to describe objectively the course of events." Particularly in this area, the effort to categorize inevitably deforms.

And yet, even with all the limitations inherent in such a study, the subject is worthy of analysis. Evidence of its importance was obtained not only from the theoretical literature, but also from the reactions of the mothers themselves. The interviews with the mothers that focused on the birth period were extremely difficult ones. In spite of the fact that considerable effort was made to cushion the impact, all but three of the mothers collapsed into violent sobbing during the interview, and the general impression of the interviewer was that the mothers were reliving rather than recalling the trauma. Regardless of the present "adjustment" to or "acceptance" of the child, even three to four years later this period remained, for most of the mothers, an unhealed wound.

As is obvious, the complexity and implications of the totality of this trauma are beyond the scope of this work. Here we shall limit ourselves to a description of certain selected aspects of events that occurred within a defined time period. The specific topics are the mother's perceptions of professional reaction to the birth of the baby, of the general environmental reaction, and of her own reactions to herself as the mother of a deformed child, and to this child. The time period chosen is an arbitrary one: the length of the mother's stay in the hospital. While the duration of the crisis certainly extends beyond this period—in fact, the basic assumption made in this study is precisely that of a continuous development— the departure of the mother from the hospital usually marked a preliminary crystallization of her perceptions of the baby, for example, whether the baby was to be taken home or institutionalized.

MOTHERS' PERCEPTIONS OF PROFESSIONAL REACTION TO THE BIRTH OF THE BABY

While professional reaction is usually the least-studied aspect of the crisis, it nevertheless constitutes an extremely important part of it. Chronologically, it is the doctor who is usually first aware of the deformities; it is from him that the mother usually receives the first "news" of the event, and it is his and the hospital staff's reaction that may provide the first clues concerning the social meaning attached to this event. The physician also assumes unique importance because of his professional status; in contrast to the mother who is an amateur in dealing with such an event, the doctor, in his professional role, is expected to be endowed with the authority, knowledge, and experience to manage such a crisis.

In some ways the physicians' behavior, as perceived by the mothers, would indicate that the doctors themselves viewed their role as including some form of professional management of the crisis. Thus, in all but four cases, it was the doctor who assumed complete or partial responsibility for telling the mother about the deformities. Most doctors, too, made some attempt to provide support for the mother and family, and to offer a preliminary diagnosis of the baby's condition. Almost all believed it was part of their role to counsel whether the child should be kept at home or be institutionalized, and in at least two cases the physician assumed the responsibility of placing the child.

But at this point the model breaks down. The clearest finding to emerge from our data is the lack of a defined ritual surrounding the birth of a deformed baby. In tabulating the data, we attempted to investigate whether there was any relationship between the physician's behavior and other factors, such as, for example, the nature of the deformity, the extent of the deformity, whether the doctor who delivered the baby had prescribed the thalidomide pills himself, whether the reaction was different in rural and urban hospitals, and so on. None of these categories provided us with a constant pattern. If there is a pattern, it is one of confusion and contradiction in terms of when the mother was told, what she was told, and whether she was urged to or prevented from seeing the baby. All these babies were born in hospitals, but, in institutions devoted to life and death, the birth of a living deformed baby appeared to constitute a "no man's land" for which no definite pattern existed. In essence, what follows is the description of how twenty individual doctors reacted to this crisis.

Many examples could be used, but here we shall illustrate the uncertainty permeating the atmosphere by considering the process by which the mothers were informed that their babies were deformed. Three mothers were told of their babies' deformities in the delivery room or shortly afterwards, while, at the other extreme, two were not told until three days later. In a few cases, the mother was the first one told, but in most cases it was the husband or another family member who was told first. Sixteen women were told either by the doctor alone, or by the doctor in combination with the husband, while in four cases the task was left to priests, husbands, or others. Some women were told very abruptly, while others were told very gradually. Thus, in one case, the doctor simply motioned with his hands to indicate that the woman had delivered "half a baby"; in another case the deformity was exposed by degrees. First the mother was told that one finger was deformed, then all the fingers of one hand, then the fingers of both hands, then the hands and finally the arms. Some doctors cried when they told the mothers; others exhibited no visible emotion. In all cases this telling was accompanied by some form of implicit or explicit prognosis or recommendation, but, as we shall see, this varied from complete hopelessness (for example, the child is dying, or is a monster never to be taken home), to strong assurances of normal intelligence and insistence that this child particularly needed and deserved a home.

For the twenty doctors involved there were at least twenty possible combinations of the elements that composed the process of telling the mother. And yet, even with this bewildering diversity, it is possible to establish certain broad categories, if we remember that each category involves some omission of individual features.

Thus, while there was considerable variation in the time at which the mother was told, the modal pattern was one of initial denial of abnormality, followed by a period of uncertainty and delay, until the mother's rising anxiety, or the doctor's inability to hide the baby any longer, produced an open confrontation of the mother with the fact that this baby was deformed. Eleven of the mothers were initially assured that their babies were normal. In three cases, at least, this stalling for time could be understood on the basis that the child was expected to die shortly. But in at least three other cases where stalling occurred, the child's handicap was classified as minor.

As perceived by the mothers, the pattern followed a common form. A mother might wake up in a delivery room, perceive that there were tears in the doctor's eyes and that the nurses were acting strangely, but when she asked questions might be told to rest quietly, that everything was fine. For the next day or so she would be refused permission to see the baby (hospital regulations, baby weak and placed in incubator, and so on); people would question her about hereditary abnormalities in the family, or about the medications she had taken during her pregnancy; visitors would look sad; a nurse would be extra sympathetic or avoid her eyes as she handed her a food tray; but again she would be reassured that all was well. Finally, the doctor, or the doctor and the husband or the priest would arrive, a curtain would be drawn around her bed or she would be removed to a separate room, and then she would be told. While this description is a composite one, rather than one derived from an individual case, it does represent a fairly accurate picture of the experiences of a number of these women. At least two mothers interpreted the anxiety they perceived in the environment as implying that they themselves were very sick or dying.

The doctors' behavior, after they had communicated the news either to the husband or the mother, also varied considerably. Four never returned at all to see either the baby or the mother. In twelve cases, the doctors chose to focus their interest either on the baby or on the mother. Thus, in the eight cases where the treatment was "baby-focused," possible medical procedures were discussed with the mother, examinations were ordered, consultants were called in to clarify the diagnosis, and indications for possible operations or future prostheses were mentioned. As a group, however, the "baby-focused" doctors were extremely uncomfortable with any manifestation of shock or grief on the part of the mother. A few mothers mentioned that they wanted to cry, but they soon stopped because it made the doctor "uncomfortable." In the other four cases, the focus was "mother-centered"; these mothers were treated as afflicted women to be consoled, but the babies were classified as dying or hopeless. In fact, out of the total sample of twenty doctors, only four chose to deal both with the affective needs of the mother and the instrumental needs of the baby. Thus here again, while the variation was considerable, a pattern does emerge. For most of the doctors it was difficult to help the mother mourn the wished-for normal baby and, at the same time, treat the living deformed baby. In over three-quarters of these cases the choice was "mainly mother" or "mainly baby," and for the remaining doctors it was neither.

Some understanding of the dilemma that the birth of a deformed baby may pose to the doctor who delivers the child can be gained by an interesting sidelight. In the search for common patterns we tabulated and retabulated all the data we had, even those factors that at first sight appeared irrelevant. Eventually it was two of the "irrelevant" factors that provided the most consistent pattern of physician behavior we could find. Although no direct questions were posed in this area, our attention was caught by the fact that many of the mothers would follow their account of the telling by mentioning, "and then I was given a needle," or, "I was moved to a private room." When we tabulated these responses, it was found that approximately three-quarters of the mothers believed that they were heavily sedated during their hospital stay, and about the same number either had been originally in a private room or were moved to one. It seems that in dealing with this difficult and unclear situation, the doctors retreated to a much safer medical model; as in infectious diseases, the indicated treatment was isolation and alleviation of the symptoms.

The general atmosphere in the hospital reflected much of this uncertainty and ambiguity. All the mothers, regardless of diagnosis or prognosis for the child, remained on the maternity floor. But the nurses' and religious authorities' handling of these mothers varied considerably. In some cases it was the nurses, in contrast to the doctor, who were most willing to talk about the baby, while in other cases the reverse was true. It is impossible to cite all the verbal and nonverbal contradictions in the hospital environment, but two cases will be used as illustrations. Thus one mother received extremely strong affective and instrumental support from her doctor, and, after two days of indecision, with the doctor's encouragement, decided to take the child home and raise him as a "normal" child. At this time she became very involved with the baby, started to feed and dress him, and began to adopt an attitude toward the baby as being very handsome, special, and bright. Superficially, all the hospital staff strongly recommended and encouraged this. And yet she still remembers her consternation when she discovered that she was the only mother on the floor who was not invited to a class on baby care offered to all the new mothers. In another case, the nurses used to smuggle a baby to his mother, contrary to the doctor's orders that the mother was not to be left alone with the child.

If the mothers' perceptions of the doctors' behavior toward them reveals a situation of uncertainty, confusion, and contradiction, the babies themselves provoked even more disorganization. The difficulty here does not lie in the absence of clear diagnoses. All the doctors, without exception, considered it part of their role to furnish some form of diagnosis and prognosis concerning these babies, if not to the mothers, then at least to the husbands or families. All the mothers, too, appear to have retained clear memories of this initial diagnosis. But the term "diagnosis," as used here, was anything but "a careful investigation of the facts to determine the nature of a thing" (*Webster's New World Dictionary,* 1958). Instead, to the degree that the facts were unknown and in some cases unknowable at this period, it became a complex moral-social judgment that reflected both the level of the physician's disturbance by the handicap, and his need to make reparation. In short, these judgments were much more a measure of the physician's own balance of hopefulness and hopelessness about the baby than of anything inherent in the baby himself.

Nevertheless, these initial judgments are important because in many cases they constituted the decisive voice in the disposal of the baby; fifteen of the mothers followed the doctors' recommendations to keep or place the baby. Each of these judgments had many idiosyncratic elements, but we can group them into three broad categories (see list below).

Mothers' perceptions of physicians' initial diagnoses

Diagnoses	*Number*
Baby is hopeless or dying	7
Baby is healthy but severely deformed	8
Baby has only minor handicap	5

Of the eight babies who were classified as healthy but severely deformed, six were judged to be of normal intelligence, while in the other two cases this factor was not included.

The hopeless babies. The seven cases in the hopeless category represent babies who, according to the mothers' perceptions of what the doctors said, were so deformed as to be judged in imminent danger of actual physical death or to be considered socially dead. In all cases the doctor either judged it unnecessary to consider placing the child because it might soon die, or else recommended immediate placement. It would be interesting to further subdivide this category into those babies who were physically dying and those who were considered healthy but monsters. We were unable to make this distinction. The term dying was used very loosely in this context, and it could express an actual judgment of the child's physical condition, a feeling of hopelessness, or a wish.

In terms of present diagnoses, these seven cases are a very heterogeneous group. While the deformities in all these cases would presently be classified as severe, only two of these children manifest extreme degrees of deformity compared to the rest of the sample.[5] Superficially, anyhow, the other five are not particularly different from the six children who were diagnosed as being severely deformed but healthy, intelligent, and able to live at home.

What is fairly consistent within this group is the reaction of the physicians. The level of disturbance would appear to be high for all these doctors, though their overt behavior varied. It is in this group that we find the four doctors who, according to the mothers' accounts, never returned to see the mothers or the babies. Two, however, appeared to regard the family's tragedy as theirs, too; for example, one of these doctors took the father home with him the evening of the baby's birth, and both doctor and father spent the night crying. In the remaining case, although the child was more than a month premature and under four pounds, he was not placed in an incubator. The justification was that if the child were to live it would have to be by his own effort.

None of these doctors had anything to do with the mothers' seeing their babies. In three cases, according to the mothers, the doctors recommended that the babies were too deformed to be seen by their mothers. These mothers, in fact, did not see their children until months later. In the other four cases the doctors said nothing,

[5] One of these cases is a child with tetraphocomelia and a rectovaginal fistula; the other child manifests deformities of all four limbs and absence of tongue.

and it was either the initiative of another member of the hospital staff, or the mother's own desire, that led to the meeting of mother and baby.

The minor handcaps. At the other extreme, there were five cases where the initial diagnosis was of a relatively minor handicap. On the basis of Webb's (1963) classification of the severity of the handicaps, these children would currently be placed in the "least severe" and "intermediate" categories. But compared to the rest of the sample, the handicaps of these children can be considered minor; none of these children manifests the typical phocomelia, and none has subsequently required prostheses.

Professional reaction to these mothers and children reflected the greater degree of hopefulness about these children. None of the doctors manifested the degree of conflict or disturbance apparent in the "hopeless" group; the doctors neither avoided the mothers, nor offered them much emotional support. The general hospital atmosphere, too, reflected little anxious commotion. In many cases, the other mothers on the floor and many of the nurses were unaware of the handicaps. In short, professional reaction to these mothers was much more casual.

Instead, the focus here was on the treatment of the child's handicap. Because the doctors tended to view these babies as "children with handicaps," rather than as "handicapped children," much that was explicitly stated for the other children was here implicitly assumed. Thus, as in the case of normal children, there was little or no discussion by the physicians about whether the child was intelligent, or whether he should be taken home. Instead, the emphasis was on how the condition itself should be treated. All these doctors were quite hopeful that operations could greatly improve or correct the deformities, and in one case treatment was started immediately.

And yet, surprisingly enough, here, too, there was considerable uncertainty in telling the mother about the handicap, or in showing the baby to her. For instance, two of these mothers were told only after three days. One of these mothers was told on the first day that the child was normal, on the second day that the child was sick, and on the third day that the child was handicapped—but that the handicap was minor and that there was no reason to be upset. She then went to the nursery and asked to see her child but was told that this was against the doctor's orders. In another case, a nurse first showed the mother the baby's face, and only five days later the deformed hand. And one mother was not shown the handicap at all during her hospital stay; the baby was brought to her a few times but always completely wrapped.

The overt message, then, given to these mothers was of a "minor" handicap, and the attitudes of the doctors tended to discourage emotional outbursts or open mourning. And yet, from the uncertainty with which these mothers were told about their babies or shown them, one wonders whether some of them did not receive a rather contradictory covert message.

The severely deformed yet healthy babies. But it is the remaining eight cases—where the doctors described the babies as being seriously deformed, but neither hopeless nor dying—that manifested the greatest potential for what we call the birth crisis. For it is with these children that the parents most acutely faced the decision of whether to take the babies home and raise them as "normal" children, or whether to consider them as sufficiently deformed or "monsters" to be institutionalized for life. It was for these parents, too, that refinements in the diagnoses (for example, whether the child was intelligent or retarded) and possibilities of future help were most relevant.

For six of these cases the diagnoses were remarkably similar. At about the same time that the mothers were informed of the deformities, they were told that the children were intelligent and should be taken home. This compound diagnosis of "severe physical deformity—normal intelligence" led to a perception of these children as embodying the most nearly even balance of normality and abnormality in the total sample. As Smithells (1963) has pointed out, severe retardation is the most salient reason for rejecting or institutionalizing a child in our culture. Once the child is presumed to be of normal intelligence, it becomes much more difficult to view him as a "monster"; instead the dissonance he embodies becomes much more acute. He fulfills the criterion of normality mentally but still remains very deviant physically.

Because of these factors, the physician's motivation for this particular type of diagnosis becomes important. Once again, it appeared to have little relationship to any known facts about the baby. Only one of these children was subject at that time to even a cursory neurological examination to rule out the possibility of brain damage, and in terms of current intellectual functioning (cf. Tremblay, 1967) these children range from retarded to superior.

In four of these cases one can speculate that this form of magical compensation arose from the physician's desire to help both mother and baby. These four doctors were the only ones who chose or were able to deal with both the feelings of the mothers and the instrumental needs of the babies. They spent long hours talking to these mothers, and, although their knowledge of habilitation techniques was generally vague, they all mentioned the possibility of prostheses some day. As a group, too, they strongly encouraged the mothers to see their babies.

In the other two cases within this "severely deformed but intelligent" group, the doctors' reactions are less clear. At least one of these doctors, according to the mother, suggested to the father that, if he felt unable to care for this child, the baby could be helped to die. The father refused this solution and insisted that he could and would raise this baby; the diagnosis then became "deformed, but intelligent." In the remaining case, though the doctor himself was noncommittal, he called in neurological and pediatric consultants to examine the baby. Here it was the neurologist's opinion that the baby had not suffered brain damage that proved decisive.

Whatever the motivation for the physicians' diagnoses in these six cases, the result was clear; all these babies were taken home. And yet, six weeks later one of these healthy babies was found to have a severe congenital heart defect. Three years later it was becoming more certain that another of these children was retarded. For these mothers an important part of the birth crisis was simply postponed.

There are two remaining cases where the diagnosis was of healthy, severely deformed babies. Neither of these doctors included any statement regarding the child's intellectual functioning. In one instance the mother was told that the child's physical condition was hopeless but that he should be taken home. In the other case the doctor said nothing.

In discussing professional reaction to the birth of a deformed baby, our constant emphasis has been on the lack of a defined professional role for the doctor in this situation. One is immediately confronted by the questions: (1) How is the doctor supposed to act? and (2) How would the mothers like him to act? One must consider whether there is something specific to the thalidomide incident that provoked this professional anxiety, or whether there is in general some medical difficulty in coming to terms with the complex problems posed by congenital anomalies.

Consultation of standard obstetrical textbooks (Danforth, 1966; Eastman and Hellman, 1966; Lacomme, 1960; Reid, 1962) provided little help, because no explicit reference is made to this problem. Two (Danforth, 1966, and Reid, 1962) do not mention congenital anomalies. One (Eastman and Hellman, 1966) devotes 17 pages to describing different forms of congenital anomalies, including thalidomide-induced phocomelia. The only suggestions concerning management of the parents are contained in the final two pages where discussion is restricted to comment on genetic counseling. The broadest treatment is found in a French textbook (Lacomme, 1960); here one chapter is devoted to congenital anomalies, and the section on parental management includes suggestions on how to handle the parents' questions on etiology, as well as advice on genetic counseling. But even this textbook goes no further. The medical ethics section of the *Index Medicus* did not provide greater clarification; for the years 1962–1966 there were only two articles which touched on the moral and social problems posed by the birth of a congenitally deformed child.

We could find only one article written by a doctor which dealt with some of the problems posed in this section. This was the work of a pediatrician and appeared in the *Lancet* (Franklin, 1963). While one could argue with some of his premises (for example, he neatly avoids the problem of mental retardation associated with severe physical deformity), this article does tackle such thorny problems as the obstetrician's frustration and anger when confronted with this type of birth, whether the child should be killed or allowed to die, how the mother should be told, and so on. The *Lancet* in general has been one of the major medical forums for the discussion of problems related to thalidomide, and the controversy, particularly in the Letters to the Editor column, has been rather lively. Although this article was written about one year after the height of the thalidomide controversy, at a time when a few hundred doctors in England had recently had the personal experience of delivering a limb-deficient child, only two letters were received in response to the article. One, by a social worker, lamented that the author had not placed more emphasis on the role of the social worker. The other, by a pediatrician, dealt exclusively with the social worker's letter; he insisted that the job of leading the team belonged to pediatricians and not to social workers. The obstetricians themselves remained silent.[6]

The essential point here is not that the doctors behaved well or badly, but that they were expected to act as professionals in a situ-

[6] In view of the dearth of written material, some attempt was made to gather information by personal contacts. Three obstetricians were contacted: a French Catholic, an English Protestant, and a Jew. One doctor claimed that he had received no formal lectures on the subject during medical training and that this topic was never discussed openly. However, during residency training the attitudes of his superiors were clear, though never explicitly referred to. A second doctor simply replied that he knew of no information about when the doctor was supposed to tell the mother. The third doctor attempted to keep the discussion on the level of cleft-palates. This doctor had been prepared for the call and provided a rather well-thought-out answer, e.g., tell the mother immediately, show the child, and so on. However, when a direct question was posed about babies born without arms or legs, the situation changed dramatically. He recalled that he had delivered such a child. Had the mother seen the child? He didn't know. "Fortunately," the child had died a few days later.

ation where the professional role was very unclearly defined. Nor can one blame the medical profession for failure to assume the task; these doctors simply reflected the fact that the society in which they lived, and of which they formed a part, had not clarified the underlying moral values. The Hippocratic oath may exhort the doctor to do good; it does not tell him how to act in a situation where the baby's needs, the mother's needs, and society's needs may have to be balanced against each other (cf. McKeown, 1967, for a discussion of this point). And yet, the fact remains that, regardless of the human frailty of an individual doctor, his initial diagnosis was usually treated as a considered professional opinion.

One additional insight into why the task of handling the birth of a deformed child is so difficult for the doctor may be provided by these mothers' feelings on the subject. The mothers were asked how they felt the doctor should act; what would be the ideal? There was considerable variation in their answers; most wished that more detailed knowledge had been available about prognosis and habilitation, while a few wished the doctors had been better able to deal with the mothers' feelings. But almost all emphasized that there was little that the doctor could do to prevent shock, grief, and anger. At the time of birth the only really acceptable help would be to cure the baby magically. Since current medical knowledge is insufficient for this purpose, the ideal doctor in this situation would have a doubly difficult task. He not only would have to treat mother and baby under very difficult circumstances, but also he would have to tolerate the frustration of accepting that even his best efforts were perceived as not good enough.

MATERNAL REACTION TO THE BIRTH OF A DEFORMED BABY

Chronologically, the discussion of professional reaction should not be followed directly by a consideration of the mothers' reactions. Usually before the mother herself was told of the deformity, the husband or some other relative was notified, that is, the environment was usually involved before the mother herself was involved. And yet the mothers' perceptions of the logical sequence of events does not follow the chronological sequence. While all report some awareness of confusion, horror, shock, and uncertainty in the environment, only nine mothers out of the twenty considered the environmental reaction a salient factor in the birth crisis period. The other eleven were aware of some confusion, but society's reaction to their problem did not really impinge on them. It appears that the mother's perception of environmental reaction, particularly its ambivalence, tended to correlate with the acuity of her own conflict concerning the child. Therefore, we shall deal with initial maternal reactions first.

The message that was transmitted to each mother was an extremely complex one composed of who told her, when, what she was told, and so on. And yet we were able to categorize the physicians' diagnoses under three broad headings. Seven mothers were told that their babies were hopeless or dying; five mothers were told that their babies had minor handicaps; and eight mothers were told that their babies were severely deformed but healthy (six of these mothers were also told that their babies were intelligent). How did these mothers react, and to what degree were their perceptions concordant with those of the physicians?

The most common reaction pattern reported by these mothers, when told that they had given birth to a deformed child, was an immediate sensation of shock—a feeling of not being able to register or understand the news—followed by a retreat from the external world. Almost all mention this need to be alone and to assimilate gradually what they had been told. But although this initial experience of shock and withdrawal was universal for the total sample, it could be followed by one of three categories of reaction pattern.

Intense shock. The physicians had told seven mothers that they had borne hopeless or dying children. Five of these mothers responded by a sense of shock so intense that it led to a state of emotional paralysis. Two of the women, however, were unable to accept the physicians' diagnoses completely; in both cases another doctor in the hospital disputed the original diagnosis. For these two mothers there was not this experience of global disorganization. Either these women were originally less shocked and thus more open to conflicting opinions, or else their recognition that medical opinion was not universal permitted them the possibility of more hope. In any case, for them total hopelessness was replaced by conflict and, in terms of categories, their future development can be discussed below in the "conflicted" group.

In addition to the five women who, in a sense, confirmed the physicians' diagnoses of total mourning, one mother joined the intense shock group in spite of her physician's diagnosis. Her child had a simple syndactyly of the right hand, and the physician considered it minor and operable. But because of this woman's cultural background, this minor handicap was perceived as a major disaster. By her standards, the handicap reflected shame on the total family and ruined any possibility of even a semblance of normal living for the child within her cultural group; for example, she believed the child would never be able to marry. Thus this mother was not in doubt about the normality–abnormality inherent in her child; she considered the child totally abnormal. Whatever conflict existed here was not in the mother's perception of the handicap, but in the manner in which two different cultural groups can perceive the same handicap.[7]

Thus the group of six mothers with intense shock reaction was

[7] Unfortunately we could find no published literature on this problem. Thus, in order to ascertain whether this mother's reactions were indeed culturally influenced, the case was discussed with a child psychiatrist of the same cultural origin. The psychiatrist knew neither mother nor child, but was simply asked whether it was customary in this cultural group for a mother who had borne a child with this type of handicap to react as if total disaster had befallen, to refuse to consider institutionalization and, instead, literally to shut herself up in a room with the child for a period of two years. According to the psychiatrist, the mother's interpretation of the social consequences of the handicap (e.g., inability to marry) was very realistic in terms of her cultural milieu. The refusal to consider institutionalization was also in line with her cultural norms. What the psychiatrist did find unusual, was that the mother was able to arrive at some form of adaptation after two years. According to the psychiatrist, had the mother remained in her place of origin, she and the child would probably have remained physically isolated and publicly stigmatized forever.

composed of five who shared their physicians' judgment of total abnormality, and one who considered her child as totally abnormal in spite of her physician's opinion. As can be seen, the doctor's original diagnosis played an important role in influencing the mother's perceptions but was not in itself conclusive.

These six mothers report such intense shock during their hospital stay that they were unable to think much about themselves or their babies. One of the mothers recalls that her only thought was the hope that both she and the baby would soon die. Another remembers that she was "asleep" during the three days she spent in hospital. One does recall that she asked the doctor to kill the baby; when he refused, everything became a "fog" for the next year. Another had a phantasy of a "long, long tunnel with a black band on one side; as far as the eye could carry it led to nowhere." Three of these mothers hemorrhaged severely when told the news and were seriously ill for some time. All report being heavily sedated. The intensity of feeling was high, but it was much closer to the mourning phenomenon than to conflict about a living, deformed baby. In a sense, these women became and were treated as mourners and patients, rather than as mothers of handicapped children.

In such circumstances it is not surprising that for these mothers there was very little consideration, at this point, of the etiology of the deformities, or of the future of the babies, beyond the general hope or expectation that they would soon die. Nor did the environmental reaction make much impact upon them; they were aware that the birth of these babies had aroused intense feelings in their families, and even, in some cases, in the total community, but this reaction was at some distance from them. Thus a mother might note that "hordes" of people had come to the hospital to see the "freak," or that the community was buzzing with the news of the monster. Even more precise details could be remarked on. One mother, on her arrival home after three days, discovered that the baby clothes she had previously prepared had disappeared; she didn't ask what had happened to them, and nobody told her. On the whole, however, these mothers didn't talk very much about their babies, and nobody talked to them about the children. Only two had visitors in the hospital; the others either didn't want any, or friends and relatives were reluctant to intrude. Whatever the intensity of the environmental response in these cases, the mothers perceived it as relatively unambiguous; it only confirmed their own feelings of horror and mourning.

For these mothers the actual sight of the baby made little difference. Three didn't see their babies at all. Of the three who did, two have no memory of what they saw, and for one it only confirmed her feelings about the disastrous nature of the handicap.

In spite of the common feelings about these babies, the disposition reflects the very different ways in which a commonly perceived problem may be handled. Four children were left in the hospital to die. Two were taken home immediately, not because the parents were more hopeful, but for very individual reasons. In one case, the father wanted his child to die at home. In another case, the mother's cultural tradition did not allow for institutionalization.

These six mothers, in a sense, manifested the most extreme reaction in the total sample. And yet, it should be noted that, while their situation was painful, it was one of initially low dissonance. They were mourners at a funeral awaiting the arrival of the corpse. It was only when their children did not die, but instead were transformed into living deformed children, that the potential for conflict began.

Minimal reaction. Five mothers were told by their doctors that they had given birth to normal children with minor handicaps. One of these mothers, as we have seen, was unable to accept the physician's diagnosis and reacted with extreme shock. In another case, the mother accepted intellectually the physician's diagnosis, but rejected it emotionally (the child revolted her); her situation became one of conflict, and she will be discussed in the "conflicted" group. However, three mothers' initial perceptions were concordant with the physicians' diagnoses, and they were able to treat their children as "almost-normal" at this time. In addition, two mothers who were told that their children were severely deformed but healthy manifested little overt reaction. They considered the children abnormal but believed that they were able to act normally toward abnormal babies. Thus the group who manifested an initial minimal reaction consisted of five mothers. Three had children who appeared to their physicians to manifest only minor deformities, and two had children diagnosed as severely deformed, but the mothers themselves felt able to assimilate the deformity.

For these five mothers there was little time spent in introspection. Either the birth of this baby did not pose a personal crisis for them, or else they viewed this crisis as an instrumental rather than an affective one; the job was to help the baby rather than to consider their own feelings. Their perception of environmental reaction was also consistent with their attitudes; they either felt that there was no need for intense sympathy, or else that their matter-of-fact attitude toward the event made others react similarly. Thus the mothers in this group report that visitors came as usual, and there was neither reluctance to talk about the baby, nor any particular emphasis on his handicap.

All these mothers, too, manifested little overt reaction at the sight of their babies' handicaps. One didn't see the deformed hand during her hospital stay, and the others make no specific reference to the impact of the anomalies.

But in spite of the fact that the overt reactions of these mothers were similar enough to be able to group them under the "minimal" category, this apparent similarity masked considerable diversity of reaction. In fact, within this group of five mothers who manifested little overt initial reaction, one can distinguish three subpatterns.

(a) Two mothers concurred with the doctors' diagnoses that the children had only very minor handicaps, and they did not really expect that these deformities would have much effect, either on their own future lives, or on those of the children concerned. One believed that the handicap would soon be corrected by an operation; the other was not even aware that an operation might be necessary.[8] There were a few dissenting voices in the environment

[8] This was the mother who didn't even see her child's deformed hand during her hospital stay.

for these women—one mother remembers that her grandmother, who had had both legs amputated, believed that anyone born with a congenital deformity, even a minor deformity of the upper limbs, should be institutionalized. But this was perceived more as an expression of the grandmother's problem than of the child's. In fact, one can say that during this period these two mothers really did not perceive their children as handicapped, nor themselves as mothers of handicapped children. It was only when they took these "normal" children home that their conflict began.

(b) Two other mothers perceived their children's handicaps as relatively serious (in one case the child had a minor deformity of both hands, in the other bilateral upper-limb phocomelia) but felt that attention should be "baby-centered and instrumental" rather than "mother-centered and affective." One of these mothers rejected her physician's attempt to console her and immediately became involved in consultations with orthopedic and plastic surgeons concerning treatment. The other, after a few hours of shock, asked to see her child, and fed and dressed the baby during the hospital stay. In recalling this event, she said, "I probably had more feelings than I showed but I felt I had to keep a stiff upper lip in order not to go to pieces." In short, these were mothers who considered the handicap serious, but who were inclined to view it as a challenge, rather than as a threat, to their maternity. It is interesting to note that these two women were among the very few who did not cry during the interviews on the birth crisis.

(c) The remaining mother in this group also displayed little overt reaction, not because she did not consider the deformities serious (the child had an intermediate deformity of the hands and other internal anomalies), but because this was just one more burden in a life that was dominated by the necessity to eke out an existence.[9] This woman comes from a rather primitive farm where life is dictated by the reality of raising crops, tending the animals,

[9] As Kelman (1964, p. 89) puts it, "the daily lives of these families seem ordered by the exigencies of earning a living . . . rather than by the sole

and so on. It was only half-facetiously that we noted in our interview records that she had twenty-five cows and ten children.

For this woman, the news of the deformities did create an initial shock. She remembers crying and thinking that the child would never be able to do farm work or marry. But this was quickly followed by passive resignation. Her family, too, considered it a pity, but mentioned that others had worse troubles. She was neither sedated nor placed in a private room. There was no discussion of the child's intelligence, or questioning as to whether the child should be institutionalized. The doctor recommended keeping the baby in the hospital for examination and operations, and the mother's attitude was that "he knew best." The child was, in fact, kept in the hospital for seven months and subjected to five operations and twenty changes of plaster casts.

In view of the different patterns that underlay the overt manifestations of minimal reaction, it is not surprising that this is an unstable category that falls apart soon after the mothers' return from the hospital. And yet, in one important respect this category is a cohesive one. Whatever the factors that led each of these mothers to be able to assume a position of minimal reaction, for all of them the immediate birth crisis can be characterized as a low-dissonance, low-intensity situation. In contrast to the first group, none was overwhelmed by this crisis; on the other hand, like the mothers who experienced intense shock, none was conscious of much conflict.

Acute conflict. Eight women were told by their doctors that their children were severely deformed but neither hopeless nor dying. Two of these women were more hopeful than their doctors, and their reactions were classified in the minimal reaction category.

---

demands of the damaged child." Although we have only one case of this type in our sample, it should be noted, as Kelman points out, that families of this nature are grossly under-represented in clinic populations of handicapped children, and consequently are excluded from most studies which seek to measure the effects of a handicapped child on the family.

Thus six women of this original group accepted the potentially high-dissonance diagnosis and manifested neither complete hopefulness nor hopelessness, but a rapid oscillation between the two. In this form of reaction, they were joined by three other women. Two of the women, as we have noted, were originally given "hopeless" diagnoses; their movement into the acute conflict or "conflicted" group was based partially on the fact that another doctor had disputed the original physician's diagnosis. In the remaining case, the doctor's diagnosis was of "minor" handicap; the mother accepted the diagnosis, but was unable to accept the child.[10] These nine women constituted the conflicted group.

The nine women in the conflicted group differed markedly in terms of personality, quality of marital relationship, socioeconomic status, geographical area of residence, ordinal position of the handicapped child, sex of the child, number of other children, religious adherence, and in other ways. Their babies' handicaps varied too: six were cases of upper-limb phocomelia, two were cases of lower-limb phocomelia, and one was a minor deformity of one hand. Nevertheless, these nine mothers can be grouped into the same category because all manifested a high intensity of feelings accompanied by a rapid oscillation of hopes and fears concerning themselves and their babies.

As a group, it was these mothers who tended to be the most introspective in the total sample and who reported the most intense feelings of guilt and anger as they considered: "Why did this happen to me?" None was able to arrive at a definitive meaning of the event during the stay in the hospital, but all were acutely aware that it marked a potentially decisive turning point in their lives.

In their feelings toward their babies, it was these mothers who vacillated most between hoping that the babies would soon die and

[10] This is not the same mother who reacted with intense shock to a baby diagnosed as having only a minor handicap because of the mores of her particular cultural group. In this case the woman agreed intellectually with the diagnosis of minor handicap but was nevertheless revolted at the prospect of having to mother an imperfect child.

hoping for some miraculous cure. But in addition to these general feelings—and it is this that differentiates them most clearly from the other mothers—these were the mothers who were most concerned about concrete details of the diagnosis and its implications. One mother remembers pleading with her doctor, when he told her that the baby had no arms, and begging that maybe there was "just a little bit of arm." Concern about the potential intelligence of the child was also most intense for these mothers. And one mother remembers worrying whether her baby would ever be able to hold a doll.

The actual sight of the baby also made the greatest difference for these mothers. As we shall see, it was only within this group that the mothers attribute any role to the baby himself in influencing their perceptions of the event.

All these conflicted women achieved some measure of resolution by the time they had left the hospital. But not only the outcome differed (eight babies were brought home, one was institutionalized), but the manner of resolution varied. The two major modes of solution can be termed the "social" and the "personal."

For the four women who achieved a "social solution," theirs was a decision against institutionalization, rather than one for the baby. All four of these women hoped the babies would die and did consider institutionalization as an alternative, but for them it was not a workable solution. In two cases, the mothers were unable to institutionalize their children because they believed that their babies had normal intelligence. As one mother put it: "Where do you institutionalize an intelligent child?" To them, putting a child with normal intelligence in an institution for mentally retarded children was a more murderous act than simply wishing the baby would die. And so these children were taken home mainly because the mothers were unaware of any institutions that would fit their babies' unique combination of normality and abnormality.

In the third case, the mother had some awareness of the fact that she had taken thalidomide before the birth and was very anxious during the latter part of the pregnancy. When the baby was born, she found the handicap less severe than she had antici- pated. And yet, while she accepted intellectually the fact that the handicap was minor, emotionally she was revolted by this child, hoped he would die, and would have preferred to place him. But neither her husband nor the environment provided much support for her feeling that she didn't want this child. Instead, there was only the guilt at being an unnatural mother. She not only took the child home with her, but also canceled the plan she had made months previously of placing the child for two weeks in a nursery. Even this small act of separation now had the connotation of re- jection for her.

The social solution for the fourth mother in this subcategory was provided by her father-in-law. Hers was another of the babies diag- nosed as severely deformed but intelligent, and the mother's conflict was severe. At times she had the hope that arms might be grafted, while at other moments she hoped the baby would die. The hus- band, too, hoped the baby would die; in fact, at first he told his family that the baby was dead. But the father-in-law, with the reluc- tant consent of his wife, decided that he and his wife would keep the baby while the parents decided.[11]

By the end of their hospital stay, then, these four women had resolved their conflict to the degree that all had decided against institutionalization, but none had really come to terms with the baby himself as a living human being.

For four other mothers in this group, however, it was the baby himself who provided some resolution of the conflict. The handicap was similar in all four cases—bilateral upper-limb phocomelia— but apart from that the cases were quite different. Nevertheless, for all these women it was the fact that the babies were diagnosed as deformed, but healthy and intelligent, that led them to overcome

[11] At the time of the research interviews, it was this mother who offered the most specific suggestions of how one could help the new mother of a deformed baby. According to her, the essential aid necessary was for some woman to offer to care for this baby while the mother herself had a period of recuperation, preparation, and adjustment for this birth. Indeed, she of- fered to do this herself for other mothers of handicapped children.

their initial reluctance to see their children. And for all the confrontation was decisive. Since these cases are particularly important from a theoretical and clinical point of view, we shall discuss them in detail.

In one case, the nurse brought the baby, but the mother pushed him away. The baby started to cry, and the mother asked that he be brought back. This time she held the baby in her arms but didn't look at him. The same day she asked for the baby again and looked in his face. According to her, the baby looked back with "big black eyes." Following this, she unwrapped the baby's blanket and touched his deformed hands but didn't look at them. Nevertheless, it was this "perfect face" that led her to decide to keep and, as she put it, "cherish" the child.

In the second case, the mother was also initially reluctant to see her baby and was seriously considering institutionalization. The nurse brought the baby to her. She looked at this child warily and was afraid to touch him. But the baby's eyes caught her glance, and she had the impression that his eyes were talking to her. As she put it, the eyes pleaded with her, "Mother, don't abandon me." Following this, she took the baby in her arms, and later that day told her husband that she had decided to keep him.

In the third case, the mother is less explicit in describing what in the baby's appearance led to a resolution of the conflict. She simply states that, once she saw the baby's face, she had the impression that the handicap was much less severe than she had imagined it. The fourth mother also describes a similar experience; her initial reaction to the sight of the baby was a surprised "she's pretty." She, too, comments that the baby had expressive, intelligent eyes.

Robson (1967) has summarized much of the recent research on the importance of eye-to-eye contact in maternal-infant attachment. According to him, it may rank with the smile as one of the two critical releasers of maternal feelings. In attempting to apply this concept to these mothers, two cautions must be noted. For one thing, the chronological age of these infants was two to five days rather than four weeks; that is, the kind of visual fixation possible at this age may be very different from that discussed by Robson. One must recognize, too, that whatever the importance of eye-to-eye contact in the establishment of the mother-child relationship for these mothers, it did not occur in a vacuum. These mothers were already in a highly conflicted state that made them potentially receptive to any behavioral clue. In a sense, one can describe the social situation at this time as an evenly balanced scale. Instead of being at rest, however, this equilibrium was an extremely dynamic one; there were strong forces pulling both for and against the babies. Nevertheless, according to the mothers, it was the psychological factor of eye-to-eye contact that tipped the scales in favor of the babies.

For the ninth mother within this group, the conflict was resolved by the decision to institutionalize the child. This was a child with bilateral lower-limb phocomelia where the original diagnosis was "healthy, hopelessly deformed (that is, would never walk), but should be taken home." In order to understand the mother's decision in this case, one must examine both her personal background and the social situation.

The mother comes from a very deprived rural Quebec background; she summarizes her deprivation by stating, "I wore rags all the time, I never had a dress." At the time of the birth, she had two sons, but longed for a daughter so that she could dress her in the pretty clothes she herself had never had. She was told of the deformities soon after the birth. According to her, a nun then forced her to see the child; the baby was lying "blue, undressed and unwashed" on a table. She does not recall seeing the deformities at all; instead, her horror and revulsion were focused on the nakedness of the child. During the interview on the birth period, when she described her first sight of the child, she burst into tears.

In addition to this personal trauma, the social situation was poor. The doctor could offer no hope beyond the child's survival as a helpless invalid at home. The mother was aware, too, that the small community in which she lived was frightened of and hostile toward the prospect of integrating this "monster." Thus, according to the

the mother, the local social service agreed to arrange and pay for institutionalization, but refused to provide any financial help or professional guidance if she insisted on keeping the child. After three weeks the mother finally agreed to institutionalization but, according to her, kept insisting that she would find a way eventually to bring the child home.

If one compares the mothers' initial perceptions of the severity of the handicaps with the physicians' diagnoses, the pattern shown below emerges. More than two-thirds of the mothers tended to see their children the same way the doctors did, but in the remaining cases the mothers could be more or less hopeful.

Comparison of mothers' initial perceptions of handicap
with physicians' diagnoses

Mothers' perceptions of severity of handicap compared to physicians' diagnoses	*Number*
Same	14
More severe	2
Less severe	4

MOTHERS' PERCEPTIONS OF ENVIRONMENTAL REACTION

As a sociological study, environmental reaction to the birth of a deformed baby is worthy of detailed consideration. From the mothers' description of their perceptions of this reaction, there is considerable evidence to speculate that the birth of a living deformed baby may create a stress situation not only for the mothers, fathers, and professional people involved, but also for the general environment. Particularly in small communities, the birth of such a child was not only a personal and family problem, but also a source of community gossip, speculation, controversy, and horror. Thus in one small town the news of the birth made the headlines of the local newspaper. Two mothers recall that hordes of curious people came to the hospital asking to see the freak. The etiology of the deformities was also a source of community speculation. It could be attributed to the "loose morals of the women of today," to the practice of birth control, or to a mother's visit to the zoo during her pregnancy. Where the etiology was known—thalidomide—the doctors were besieged by phone calls from pregnant women asking if they, too, had been given the drug.

Inevitably, all the women were affected sooner or later by these environmental currents. But for the study of the period we have termed the birth crisis, we are simply concerned with mothers' perceptions of the environmental reaction as they themselves considered it a salient factor in their efforts to arrive at some preliminary adaptation to these children. In short, it is the mother's perceptions of the environmental reaction as a factor in the decision-making process concerning the fate of the baby that is most relevant. And here we are confronted by the fact that the mother's perceptions of environmental reaction is selectively influenced by the acuity of her own conflict. While all these mothers are able to offer some description of the environmental reaction to these births, it is only nine mothers—those whom we have termed the conflicted group—who emphasize minute details of who counseled for or against institutionalization, who sent the baby gifts, and so on. The other eleven mothers may have perceived the reaction as very intense or "normal"; it is these nine mothers who perceived it as both intense and ambivalent.

Retrospectively, it is impossible to trace the etiology of this process. Did these mothers perceive ambivalence in the environment because for personal reasons they were the ones in a state of high dissonance and therefore most receptive to small clues? Or was there something in the initial environmental reaction that led these women to become more conflicted and, consequently, to turn to the environment for help? In order to answer these questions, one would have to undertake a detailed study of the birth crisis as it occurred. If, however, our aim is simply to understand the mothers' perceptions of what happened, we can restrict our discussion mainly to a consideration of these nine women.

Perhaps the most surprising aspect of these women's perceptions of the environmental reaction, is how little importance they attribute to the husbands in the decision-making process concerning the fate of the baby. Chronologically, the husband was usually the first non-professional person told, and it was he who usually informed the family or even told his wife of the deformities. Moreover, unlike the other women in this sample, these nine women were neither too shocked nor too "unaffected" to be unaware of their husbands' reactions to this as a crisis situation; in contrast to the other women in the group, most of these mothers have at least some knowledge of when the husband was told, how he reacted, and what he told the family. And yet only one mother believes that her husband exercised a decisive influence in the decision to keep or institutionalize the baby.

Partially, this may be understood by the nature of the husbands' reactions. Seven of these nine women believe that their husbands were so affected that they were unable either to console their wives, or to make any decision concerning the children. Their shock, according to the mothers, was so great that some of the husbands were unable even to accept the fact that these deformed children were considered healthy. Though in none of these cases had the physician's diagnosis included a prognosis of imminent death, two of the husbands told the families that the children were dying, and one said that the baby was dead.

Even the two husbands who were perceived as less affected were unable to deal with both mother and child but split their concern, one to the wife and one to the child. Thus a husband who was unable to tell his family about the deformity, nevertheless did come to see his wife and tell her that "we must love each other more than ever now." In the other case, the husband was unable to deal with his wife's shock but did insist that the baby must be kept.

Whatever the husband's reaction, the fact remains that none of these women was able to discuss the baby's future with her husband during this time, and all but two believe that they alone decided to keep or place the baby. (In the two cases where the mother believes she did not make the decision, one attributes it to the father-in-law and one to the husband.) These women were seeking for environmental guidance, and yet did not consider their husbands' opinions as crucial. Indeed, one mother who did decide to keep her baby states that she would have left her husband had he opposed her wishes.

Here again one can only pose questions as to the underlying reasons for this perception. Is it because the husbands are perceived as so shaken that they cannot offer stable guidance? Or it is that the needs of husband, wife, and baby are so overwhelming and conflicting at this period that one can only adapt by splitting? Whatever the reason, it should be noted that this isolation of husband and wife concerning the baby is one that will be shown by most of the women in the months that followed the birth, and manifestations of it were still evident at the time of the interviews.

These nine mothers' perceptions of environmental reaction also manifest another interesting limitation. Although the mothers can give detailed tabulations of contradictory opinions, the sources of these opinions are found to be mainly professionals, or family and religious authorities. According to these mothers, friends and neighbors played a relatively small role in the days immediately following the birth. A few mothers do mention that friends came to visit, but the mothers placed much less emphasis on what friends said, compared to what relatives said. This may simply be a reflection of the general social functioning of this particular group (that is, relatives are viewed as much more important parts of the social environment than are friends), or it may be a reflection of the nature of the crisis itself. Certain events in our culture tend to emphasize family relationships (for example, birth, marriage, death), and this was a crisis linked to birth. In addition, the tragic and shameful elements perceived in this particular type of birth may have made friends wary of intruding.

In describing the immediate family reaction to the birth, one must make a clear separation between the mother's perceptions of the reactions to her as an individual, and her perceptions of the reactions toward the baby. Here again there seems to have occurred a "splitting" between mother and baby. With only a few exceptions, the mothers describe that they themselves received much expression of sympathy and were treated as afflicted women to be pitied. Even here there were undercurrents that contradicted this general policy; one woman was told that hers was "the first family tragedy," and a cousin wondered out loud whether the deformity might be a punishment for the mother's previous practice of birth control. These, however, were the exceptions rather than the rule.

It was toward the baby that the environmental ambivalence was mainly directed. In contrast to the experience of some of the other eleven women, none of these nine mothers report that the family refused to talk of the baby. In fact, most recall that there was a great deal of discussion about the baby. However, their perception of what people said and did reflects confusion and contradiction.

At times the ambivalence was reflected mainly in the form of omission. Thus one mother remembers that her in-laws were very warm and sympathetic but that they did not choose to see the baby until the mother brought him home. In another case, where the father-in-law decided to care for the baby, his wife formally consented to the plan, but did not see the baby until she brought the child home. Two of these mothers remarked that they did not receive any baby gifts during their hospital stay. Another remembers that her sister-in-law told her that she had bought her a gift but returned it when she discovered that the baby was deformed. In other cases negative wishes were more openly expressed. A number of these mothers were advised by members of their families to place the baby. In one case, a sister consoled the mother by offering the hope that the baby would soon become "a pretty angel."

Support for the baby was equally forthcoming. One mother remembers, for instance, that her own mother upon hearing the news, "though it nearly killed her," put on a bright red dress, came to the hospital, saw the child, and then assured her daughter that the child was beautiful. In another case, it was the husband's family who insisted that the child must be kept. And another mother remembers gratefully that her mother-in-law brought her a gift "as if it were a normal baby."

In view of the fact that many facets of the crisis were as much moral as medical, it was inevitable that religious authorities would also be implicated. Of the nine mothers who were in the conflicted state, eight received advice from one or more priests or nuns. The priests' advice could vary from urging that the mother keep the baby, to counseling placement, to suggesting that no special precautions need be taken to keep the baby alive. In one case a nun offered to exchange the deformed baby for a normal one. Zuk (1959) has suggested that the religious affiliation of the family may make a difference in the attitude toward a deviant baby and that Catholic mothers may accept retardation more easily than others. On the basis of our data it is difficult to make any generalizations concerning religious attitudes, since our sample is overwhelming Catholic, and one would have to measure such factors as strength of religious adherence, the sociological structure of the religious milieu (that is, to be Catholic in Quebec may be very different from being Catholic in urban U.S.), and so on. Nevertheless, two observations are relevant in that (1) all the mothers who consulted or received advice from religious authorities were Catholic, and (2) this advice manifested the same variation evident in the general milieu.

In summarizing the environmental reaction schematically, one may make it appear simpler than it actually was. A simple tabulation of the opinions received by one mother in a period of five days may indicate some of the conflict and confusion which these mothers perceived in the environment:

1. The doctor who delivered the baby told the husband that the child was a monster who should be placed immediately and not talked about. He never returned to see mother or child.

2. Another doctor in the hospital examined the child and told the mother that the baby was intelligent, in good health, and should be kept.

3. A nun in the hospital advised the father to place the child and tell his wife that the child was dead.

4. The hospital chaplain insisted that the mother see the baby.

5. The mother-in-law insisted that this was a shame for the family and the child should be placed.

6. Two brothers recommended placement.

7. A sister suggested that the baby would soon die.

8. The Monsignor offered a personal baptism.

9. The mother phoned a priest and asked him to place the child. He responded that he had found a place for the baby "in your home."

10. A woman working in the nursery offered to take the child if the parents didn't want her.

MOTHERS' ATTITUDES AT END OF HOSPITAL STAY

To classify the change in the mothers' perceptions of their children at the end of the period we have termed "the birth crisis" is not an easy task. For one thing, while some mothers' initial reactions did not change, others—particularly those in the conflicted group—underwent a complex process of development. And it should be noted that the behavioral indices (that is, the mother's decision for or against institutionalization) were not necessarily in accord with the mother's feelings about the child. If, however, one attempts a rough categorization of the mothers' reactions at the time of their departure from the hospital, the classification shown in Table 1 can be made.

Eleven mothers did not change their initial perceptions during the period of hospitalization. Of these, five mothers manifested only a minimal reaction to the news of the abnormality; all of these took their babies home. Six mothers, on the other hand, reacted with intense shock; two of these took their babies home, while four left them in the hospital expecting them to die, or institutionalized them.

Nine mothers experienced intense conflict that led to some form of resolution. In four cases, there was a personal acceptance of the baby, accompanied by the decision to take the baby home. In four other cases, the baby was taken home because of the mothers' "social" acceptance. And one mother decided for institutionalization.

Table 1. Classification of mothers' initial reactions, reactions at the time of their departure from the hospital, and decisions regarding the disposition of children

Initial reaction	Number of mothers	Reactions at time of departure from hospital	Number of mothers	Disposition of children	
				To be taken home	Not to be taken home
Intense shock	6	Intense shock	6	2	4*
Minimal reaction	5	Minimal reaction	5	5	0
Conflict	9	Personal acceptance	4	4	0
		Social acceptance	4	4	0
		Temporary abandonment	1	0	1

* After a month one of the mothers in this category did take her child home. According to her, she still remained hopeless about the child's future, but the child's continued survival and "mischievous eyes" made her decide that she wanted this child at home.

SUMMARY ON THE BIRTH CRISIS

There is much that could be said about the data we have presented on the birth crisis. Most of this discussion will be reserved for the general conclusion when an attempt will be made to integrate this partial aspect with the more general developmental view. Here we shall simply summarize some of the most salient points:

1. There is no single factor that explains the nature of the social reaction (maternal, professional, or environmental) to the birth of a visibly defective baby. The objective severity of the handicap, the physician's perceptions of its implications, the mother's personality and cultural background, and the immediate reaction of the general environment are all important, and there appears to be a complex interaction between the four aspects. But, depending on the individual case, each of these factors could be of greater or lesser significance.

2. Neither for professionals, mothers, nor families did the existing social structure provide a clear social framework through which to interpret the meaning of the event, or a ritual mode of procedure. The most consistent pattern was one of confusion, contradiction, and ambivalence.

3. In dealing with the ambiguous and contradictory nature of the situation, the phenomenon of "splitting" appeared to be an almost universal reaction. Neither physicians, mothers, nor families seemed able to deal with all aspects and implications of the situation. Instead, physicians tended to choose between the affective needs of the mother and the instrumental needs of the baby. The mothers, too, tended to focus on one aspect, such as their own mourning, or the needs of the baby. Environmental reaction also showed this splitting by a clear demarcation of attitudes toward the mother and reactions toward the baby.

4. Surprisingly enough, most mothers do not attribute a decisive role to the husbands at this time.

5. The decision to institutionalize or bring the baby home was not necessarily an accurate reflection of the mother's perceptions of and

feelings about the baby. At least one mother who opted for institutionalization claims that she maintained the desire and hope that some day this child would come home. On the other hand, two mothers took home babies perceived as hopeless or dying. And in another case, the mother took home the baby (who was diagnosed as having a minor handicap) very much against her own inclinations.

6. Most of the mothers experienced the wish or hope that the baby would soon die.[12] This wish was strongest for the mothers in the "intense shock" group, appeared only fleetingly for those in the "minimal reaction" group, and was intense, but ambivalent, for those in the "conflicted" group. In almost all cases, however, this wish was not connected with any murderous intentions toward the actual baby. Only one mother states that she asked the doctor to kill the baby, and none believes that she actually experienced the temptation to kill the baby herself. Rather, the wish that the baby might die appeared to reflect the magical hope that some external authority would provide a final solution for this painful situation.

7. Only nine of the twenty mothers experienced the birth crisis as a conflict linked to marginality. Thus, for at least this period, our original hypothesis holds true only for slightly less than half the sample. Once again, there is no single factor that will explain why these particular women experienced the birth crisis in this form. But, in spite of considerable diversity within this group, there were certain common characteristics in their behavior and feelings: (a)

---

[12] The fact that all of the mothers had at least fleeting wishes that their children would die may shock the reader. Certainly it is not in accord with the mythology of mother love prevalent in our culture. But those readers who have clinical experience will testify to the fact that death wishes are a very common way of expressing ambivalence. Much as we would prefer to deny this, there are few mothers who have raised children without experiencing such feelings at one moment or other if only to the extent of wondering: "What would have happened had I remained childless?" Given the type of conflict faced by these mothers, it is not particularly surprising that they wished for a magical solution of this kind. What is more remarkable, perhaps, is that no mother mentions being tempted to translate the wish into action.

the belief that the child was basically healthy and not likely to die soon, but that the deformities had serious social and personal consequences; (b) an interest in the details of the deformities—of particular importance as criteria of relative normality and abnormality appeared to be the factors of normal intelligence and undeformed faces; and (c) a sensitivity to environmental cues. These factors may have been causal in producing the conflict, or simply symptoms of it, but they are there.

The Mother Returns Home: Initial Social Adaptations

Although there was considerable variation both in the time elapsed between the mothers' return home from the hospital and the entry of their children into the formal habilitation program at the RIM, as well as in the amount of time the child spent at home during this period,[13] nevertheless there are certain common characteristics that permit us to categorize this period as a stage. The developmental crisis characteristic of this stage lay in the mothers' gradual realization that the handicapped child would neither die nor be cured, but would continue to live and be deformed. Depending on the mother's initial perceptions of the child, this realization could have very different consequences. Thus the mothers who had believed or wished that their children would die, were now confronted by the fact of their survival. On the other hand, the mothers who had initially considered the handicap as very minor, or curable by operations, now had to accept the fact that these children were deformed and that no medical treatment available could offer a complete cure. But for all the mothers there was a change in the time perspective; the immediate crisis of the birth period was replaced by the realization that this crisis was a long-term one. If the period of the birth can be described as one of intense drama, this

[13] The mothers' stay in hospital ranged from 3 to 14 days; most of the children began active treatment at the RIM somewhere between the ages of 11 to 18 months. During this time, 4 children were institutionalized and did not come home at all. The 16 "home" babies, on the other hand, came home anywhere from the same day the mother did to 7 months later, and almost half had subsequent periods of hospitalization before they entered the RIM.

period was one characterized by the process of working through. Perhaps the clearest manifestation of this changed time perspective lay in the mothers' frequent comment: "One day I sat down and realized that I couldn't go on this way, but I would have to live with this on a day-to-day basis."

For many mothers the crucial aspect of this task lay not in the social arena, but in their beginning personal relationships with their babies. But if the relationship with the environment constituted the background rather than the foreground of the mothers' concern, it nevertheless remained important. For the moment, the mothers were granted the benefits of a moratorium; they could afford to place less emphasis on the social verdict passed on their children. But their habitual environment still remained the main source of reference for their values. To the degree that mother and child were seen as having a potential place in this society, personal solutions would have to be tested against social realities.

In addition, the social horizons of these mothers inevitably changed; they were potential if not actual members of the community of mothers of handicapped and thalidomide-deformed children. Whether or not a mother had personal contact with this group, articles, radio programs, T.V. programs, and the crippled child down the street, all assumed a new relevance for her. And all began their initiation into one of the most characteristic activities of mothers of handicapped children, that is, the search for professional help. It is the delineation of their relationship to these three groups—the normal social environment, the community of the handicapped, and the arena of the professional in the field—that constituted the mothers' social task during this period.

MOTHERS' PERCEPTIONS OF THEIR RELATIONSHIP TO THE
NORMAL ENVIRONMENT

Not all the mothers experienced a sense of total estrangement from their habitual social environment during this period. Depending on the degree of the mother's own identification with the deviancy of her child, and her perception of the community's attitude toward this child, the social disruption caused by the event could vary from minimal to maximal. Nevertheless, there was a modal pattern of social adjustment, one characterized by elements of continuity and discontinuity. It is this modal pattern that we shall describe first, before undertaking a consideration of individual variations.

Initially, the element of continuity was the most striking one. Regardless of the mother's distress, the process of living was not suddenly arrested, but inevitably went on. In rereading the interview protocols, one is struck by the numerous references to other events taking place during this time, for example, a husband's change of employment, a grandmother's death, and so on. At first, one is almost annoyed at these extraneous events; they appear to be irrelevant intrusions upon the story we are attempting to trace. But eventually, as the mothers did, we are forced to accept and assimilate them as essential parts of the story. The period of the birth crisis might be one of intense drama, but for most mothers this drama was soon diluted by the requirements of daily living.

Nevertheless, in spite of this superficial participation in the external world, the most characteristic pattern manifested by the mothers was one of psychological and sometimes physical isolation. The term isolation is used in a very general sense and covers a wide variation in overt social behavior. At one extreme, five mothers describe a period of total withdrawal from social activities that lasted from six months to two years. At the other extreme, eight mothers report little observable difference in their social lives. But even these eight mothers manifested some indices of isolation; for instance, all report that it was difficult for them to share their feelings or discuss the babies even with their husbands.

In some respects this withdrawal was voluntary and related to the mother's own need to assess the meaning of this event for herself. Besides the depression and physical disturbances that can be considered residues of the shock experience, the mother was now confronted with resolving the problem of why she had been singled out for misfortune, and with evaluating the long-term effects of this event for herself and the baby. A mother might react with shame, anger, resignation, or revulsion. She might deny that this really affected her as a person, or feel that it had destroyed her life. But all were aware that there was at least a potential difference in their lives.

If one had to choose one feeling that was typical for this sample, it would be the experience of being alone. The most frequently repeated comment during the research interviews was: "You don't know what it's like if you haven't been through it." Others might be sympathetic or hostile, but the mother felt herself to be the sole victim of misfortune in a world that had not felt its impact. Thus a number of mothers mention that during this period the sight of a normal baby became an extremely painful one for them. Even the news of the death of a baby could be greeted by the reaction that "these parents are lucky."

The images used by the mothers to express this sense of being entirely alone are often extremely vivid. One mother, who was and has remained a devout Catholic, went to church to seek the consolation of the afflicted. For her, however, even the attempt to identify with the Virgin Mary's plight during the crucifixion only emphasized how different she was. She reports that, as she looked at the portrait of Jesus on the cross, all she could think of was, "Lord, You gave arms to Your Son, why did You not give them to my daughter?"

In some respects, however, this withdrawal was involuntary; in conformance with the rites of mourning, friends and neighbors might be reluctant to approach the mother or to discuss the baby. To cite only one example, a mother, who quickly "accepted" her child and refused to go through a period of open mourning, was shaken when she discovered on the following Christmas, two months after the birth of her baby, that relatives and friends did not send the usual Christmas cards but instead chose the type considered appropriate for those in mourning. The difference between "My thoughts are with you" and "Merry Christmas" confronted this mother with the knowledge that, despite her belief that little had changed, she was perceived as different (cf. Wright, 1960, pp. 242–44, for a discussion of the requirement of mourning).

In some cases, the mothers not only felt isolated from their communities, but perceived the environment as actively hostile. It is interesting to note, incidentally, that this hostility was not necessarily related to the actual presence of the child in the community; at least one of the mothers who had institutionalized the child nevertheless perceived her environment as very hostile. Usually, the cruder forms of hostility were restricted to small rural communities, but almost all the mothers can cite instances where the baby or the mother provoked anger and derision. It was as if this punishment indicated that some unknown sin had been committed. Thus one mother remembers being told that giving birth to a deformed child was due to the "loose morals" of modern women. Another claims to have been told by a priest that the malformations constituted a punishment for her failure to bear a large family. An incident reported by another mother is even more bizarre. This woman, whose child had been born with bilateral lower-limb phocomelia, won a raffle at a ladies' auxiliary meeting two months after her baby's birth. The prize was a pair of baby shoes. At this point, according to her, there were shouts of derision and laughter and the taunt, "Your baby will never need these."

In alleviating the mothers' sense of alienation, the husbands played a relatively small role. Three-quarters of the women report that they were unable to discuss their own feelings or talk about the babies with their husbands during this time. This isolation from the husband could have many causes. For a few mothers, it was only a specific manifestation of the general emotional and sexual separation they experienced from their husbands following the birth. In other cases, the mother perceived the husband as too shaken himself to play the role of comforter. And the fact that the husband and the wife were unable to "break down" with one another may be related to the type of wishes that each harbored toward the child. Both mother and father may have felt too guilty about or too frightened of the possible consequences of their own wishes to be able to express them. One mother remembers telling her husband one day that she wished the baby would die. Although she herself felt this to be a "normal" wish, the husband appeared so shocked and revolted at her disclosure that she never raised the subject again.

Since it was at this time that most women discovered that the etiology of the deformities lay in a pill—thalidomide—an additional dimension was added to the social adjustment of the period. Seventeen mothers report that they experienced an initial feeling of relief when they discovered or were told that the baby's deformities were due to thalidomide; the other three claim that this news made them feel worse or didn't really matter. The major reason for feeling relief was the removal of uncertainty, mainly as to the stigma of hereditary defect; the source of the deformity became something in the external world, rather than in the mother. Those who felt worse, on the other hand, dwelt on the aspect of preventability: the deformities of this baby were not inevitable but could easily have been prevented.

However, even this broad categorization constitutes a deformation of the reality perceived by these mothers. For most mothers, the fact that their babies could be labeled as thalidomide-deformed children did not evoke clear-cut feelings of guilt or anger; instead, there was an oscillation between the two. Like so many other aspects of this story, the known etiology solved some problems but created others. A mother could be relieved that the deformities were due to thalidomide, because her husband had been an adopted child, and this knowledge removed her uncertainty about his heredity; at the same time, the knowledge aroused conflict because it was her own mother who had given her the pill and was thus responsible for the child's deformities. Or, a mother might blame society or the doctor for the fact that this pill was allowed on the market but, when she considered her son's future reaction, be afraid that if he were to feel this same anger at society, he might be led to delinquency.

And so for most mothers there was no workable solution to the conflict. However guilty a mother might feel at taking the pill, the fact that she had to raise a child like this made her a victim as well as an aggressor. On the other hand, anger was equally dangerous as a solution; to the degree that these women continued to live in society, the mothers were confronted by the necessity of coming to terms with it. One could blame a husband for giving his wife the pill, but could one really hold a father responsible for deforming his child and continue to live with him? Even anger at the government, doctors, or drug companies, was futile in a world where the mothers were very dependent on a government-sponsored, medically directed habilitation program. For most mothers the process of questioning "why" petered out without resolution. The gains were too meager, and the price was too high.

This then was the modal pattern. There were some elements of continuity in the mothers' resumption of their habitual social roles, accompanied, nevertheless, by the feeling of isolation and difference. But not all women reacted similarly; the mothers' perceptions of this period could range from a feeling of total alienation from the community to one of very little difference.

In trying to understand the determinants of the mothers' social adjustment at this time, the social status ascribed to the handicapped child becomes an important factor. The problem here is a complex one. The issue was not simply one of home versus institution, or even the mother's perceptions of the severity of the handicap. Instead, the potential for conflict arose from the mother's difficulty in reconciling two social roles: (a) as a member of the community, and (b) as the mother of the child. As a member of the community, the mother was expected to recognize that her child was deviant and to accept the community norms concerning this deviance. As a mother, however, she was expected to love this child no matter how deviant he was. Balint and Lynd write as follows on this point:

For all of us it remains self-evident that the interests of mother and child are identical and it is the generally acknowledged measure of the goodness or badness of the mother how far she really feels this identity of interests (Balint, 1953, p. 116).

Shame for and with one's children . . . comes near to testing the limits of one's faith in the possibilities of life. The sensitivity of this area of awareness is suggested by the fact that many people would hesitate to speak of shame for their children. If the feeling of shame for one's children receives psychological recognition, it is quickly codified as a parental defect (Lynd, 1958, pp. 59–60).

It is on the basis of the mothers' perceptions and attempted resolutions of this conflict that three broad patterns of reaction can be distinguished.

The alienated. There were five mothers who report a period of intense depression and complete social alienation lasting from six months to two years. These five mothers claim that they didn't want to go out or see anybody, and all felt as if their personal lives had come to an abrupt end. In some, this sense of alienation was manifested by a loss of faith; others report an intense sense of revulsion toward the prospect of sexual relations. In three cases the women were so depressed that they were unable to perform even normal household chores. Thus, for all these women, the element of discontinuity was far more prominent than the element of continuity.

Originally these five women had all manifested a reaction of intense shock to the birth of their babies, and all had considered their babies as hopeless or dying.[14] Two of these mothers had institutionalized their babies, while three had brought them home. All, however, had hoped or expected that their babies would soon die, and their original reaction was analogous to the mourning situation. What complicated the mourning process, however, was the fact that none of these babies did die. And the mothers were unable to view these surviving babies either as psychologically dead (that is, separate completely from them) or as having any meaningful life. Thus the three "home babies" lived in a social limbo; they continued to exist in their families, but there was no contact between baby and

---

[14] It will be recalled (cf. p. 70) that originally there were six mothers in the "intense shock" group. The sixth mother, however, followed a very different developmental pattern and at this period fell into the "minimally affected" category. She will be discussed under this heading.

community (the communities were not even aware that these children were at home until they were six months old). The case of the institutionalized babies within this group was slightly different; the two mothers involved had never seen their babies during the hospital stay. Once the children survived till the age of three months, the mothers started to visit them and continued to maintain contact,[15] however irregular, with them. But still the babies were viewed as too deviant to be shown even to siblings or most relatives.

For these women, the termination of the mourning period did not occur suddenly or completely. In most cases it was not until the formation of the habilitation program that some reconciliation of mother, child, and community became possible. But to this day, these are the women who remain most affected personally. It is as if thalidomide not only deformed their babies, but also deformed their lives.

And yet one prominent feature of their reaction pattern should be noted. The trauma here was an intense one, but it was a personal rather than a social one. The influence of the social milieu operated indirectly through an internalized set of social values rather than directly; none of these mothers sought to test her personal perceptions of the child against the reality of her actual environment. There was conflict linked to the mother's inability to separate completely from or find social meaning for the child, but it was internal rather than external. The social alienation was merely a result of a personal sense of alienation.

The minimally affected. In contrast to these five women, there were eight women who report that the birth of the thalidomide child made little overt difference in their personal or social lives. Although all these mothers did manifest some physical symptoms or transitory

---

[15] In spite of the mothers' inability to come to terms with the social implications of the birth of these children, the efforts to maintain contact were sometimes heroic. Thus, one of these mothers used to travel 13 hours by bus to visit her child. She also sent $20 a month from her meager resources to the institution where he was kept so that the nuns would send her news of him. It was only when her child started to cry one day at the sight of this "stranger" that she stopped visiting.

feelings of depression, the general impression given is that life soon resumed its normal course. For these women it is the element of continuity that is most prominent.

The reasons that led these women to continue to function "almost normally" are quite different in each case. Nevertheless, this form of reaction can be subdivided into two broad categories: those mothers who did not perceive their babies as very deviant, and those who did see their babies as deviant, but who did not feel that their own social status was implicated.

For the three mothers in this first category, the integration of the baby within the normal social environment did not create difficulty because the baby was not perceived as sufficiently deviant to provoke conflict. Two of these mothers had originally been in the "minimal reaction" category, and for them the perception of a normal baby with minor deformities had never been viewed as a source of intense social conflict. In the third case, the mother had originally been in the conflicted group, but had arrived at a personal acceptance of the child and believed that the environment would also. She perceived the child as different, but believed that society could be educated to understand, accept, and even admire this difference. For her, the word thalidomide created the possibility of a third community, neither normal nor abnormal, but different and special. And so for none of these mothers was the mother's perception of the child and the environment of such a nature as to induce social conflict.

The success of this strategy—not perceiving their babies as very deviant—depended, in large measure, upon environmental compliance. For the two mothers who saw their children as "normal," any act that suggested that this child was being treated differently could be interpreted as threatening. One mother even became resentful when a sales clerk in the bakery store, where she habitually shopped, started to give candy to the handicapped child, but not to her siblings. As she put it, "X wasn't any cuter than any other child." But, on the whole, this tactic of ignoring the child's deformities proved to be a relatively workable one. In part, this may be because two of the children whose mothers used it do in fact have relatively minor handicaps, and the third comes from a community which has been unusually supportive toward mother and child.

The five mothers in the second category perceived their children's deviancy as a source of social conflict, but they were able to put a distance between themselves and their children. To these women, whatever the stigma attached to the child's deviancy, the mother did not consider that she herself was directly involved.

The most extreme example of this pattern was a mother whose initial reaction had been one of intense shock, and who had viewed the child as hopeless and dying. The child was institutionalized, and the mother soon resumed her normal mode of living. In spite of the fact that the child continued to survive, the mother was able to treat this child as dead. For over a year the mother didn't see her and was not even sure where she had been placed. Shortly after the birth, the mother moved to another city, and most people in the new community were unaware of the existence of this child.

In the other four cases, the reaction was less extreme. All four babies were living at home, and the mothers were involved—sometimes intensively—in their care. But in each case, the mother was able to perceive the child's handicap mainly as the child's problem, rather than as hers. One of these mothers initially perceived the child's handicap as very minor and took the baby out as usual. When her mother-in-law and the neighbors made comments about the child's ugliness, she stopped taking the baby out but continued to go out frequently herself. In another case, the mother was able to use the child's hospitalizations as a convenient opportunity for her own vacations.

Conflict and negotiation. In terms of overt social behavior, the seven mothers in this group can be considered in an intermediate category. None experienced the total alienation of the maximally affected mothers, but all experienced some sense of disruption in their lives. What distinguished these mothers, however, was their attitude toward their babies. All believed that the child was too deviant to be easily or completely acceptable to the community, but none was willing to relinquish her role, either as member of the community, or as mother of the child. The attempt to reconcile child and community could be undertaken through pleading, defiance, or negotiation, but all considered that the only resolution lay in some form of mutual accommodation.

In placing these mothers in an intermediate group, one is not describing their intensity of feeling. Many of these women suffered as acutely as any mother in the alienated group. What differentiated them from the alienated group, however, was that the conflict did not lead to withdrawal but to the mother's testing and retesting of the child's acceptability against the current social reality.

At the time of the birth crisis, all seven of these mothers had been classified in the conflicted group.[16] Six had brought their babies home, while one had decided for institutionalization. And yet, for all seven, the problem of the child's marginality continued to be a major issue.

This position contained the most possibility for overt social conflict, and, at times, the mother's relations with her community could be characterized by hostility. One of these mothers reports that when she came home with the child she expected the neighbors to be watching from their windows. She deliberately put a smile on her face and carried the child proudly: "I wanted a daughter and I was going to show them that this was the daughter I wanted." Two days after returning home, she started to sew clothes for the child to substitute for the baby gifts she had not received. Nevertheless— and this is very characteristic—she was gratified when, in the following weeks, she received 150 tardy baby gifts.

Even the mother of the institutionalized baby maintained a continuous dialogue with her community about the status of the child. She perceived her community as very hostile toward the child but, nevertheless, continued to argue that the child could and would

[16] The conflicted group had originally comprised nine women. Two, however, moved into the minimally affected group at this time. One was a mother who was able to view the child as sufficiently special as not to provoke social conflict, while the other was a mother who saw the child as abnormal but was able to put some distance between herself and the child.

come home as soon as she could find a way of caring for her at home. The communication here was an angry one, but it never stopped.

For most of the mothers in this group, however, the major stratagem was one of negotiation. The clearest example of this process lay in the mothers' attempts to delineate boundaries for the showing of the child at a given time or place. Because the child was viewed neither as completely alien, nor as completely acceptable, his contacts with the community were selective. Boundaries could be drawn with reference to the child (that is, the normal part would be shown, but not the deformed part), with reference to the geographical location (the child's deformities would be shown at home or in the neighborhood, but would be covered in public places), or with reference to the person involved (an uncle would see the deformities, but not an acquaintance). At times, these boundaries could become very complex. For instance, one mother would not take the child out with the handicap uncovered, but expected anyone who came into the house to accept the sight of the handicap. When the visitor was a pregnant woman, however, the mother would make an exception to the rule.

MOTHERS' PERCEPTIONS OF THEIR RELATIONSHIP TO THE
COMMUNITY OF HANDICAPPED AND THALIDOMIDE-DEFORMED
MEMBERS

If the mothers weren't quite sure about their babies' status in the normal environment, they were equally unsure about their status in the world of handicapped or thalidomide children. Entry into this world may have offered a feeling of belonging to compensate for the isolation following the birth of a deviant child, but most mothers were unwilling or unready to adopt this potential solution.

As usual, the reasons for this reluctance were both negative and positive ones. Most of the mothers at this time were dealing with their own depression and fatigue; they were still unsure about how the child's deviancy would affect his standing in the normal community, and many were still hopeful that another form of resolution was possible, that is, that the child would die or be miraculously cured. But, in addition to these factors, it was their perception of the nature of the world of the handicapped that, on the whole, made entry into it an unacceptable solution.

None of the mothers seriously considered her child "handicapped" in the more general sense of the term. Some of the mothers judged the deformities too minor, while the others found them too unusual to fit any of the usual categories of handicap. The experience of a blind, deaf, or retarded child, for instance, was considered too different to be applicable. The category that the environment was most likely to use for these children was precisely the one that the mothers themselves were most anxious to avoid: that of mental retardation. They constituted a minority group even within the world of the handicapped, and the mothers were anxious to preserve their separate status.

Neither did the new community of thalidomide children prove attractive. During this period all the mothers became aware of the fact that their children's deformities could be categorized by the term thalidomide. While only two had any personal contact with other thalidomide parents, almost all were exposed to articles, T.V. programs, and so on. Most, however, reacted very negatively to this form of publicity and were anxious not to be identified with such a group. Much of their distaste could be linked to the form of publicity then prevalent. According to the mothers, the pictures shown were of the most severe cases, and the label most commonly applied to the thalidomide child was that of "monster." Not unnaturally, the publicity stressed the most dramatic aspects of the tragedy. As a result, there was considerable attention given to isolated cases of abortion and euthanasia.

In spite of the general dislike of this publicity, the response to it reveals a new division in the sample: minor handicaps versus severe handicaps. As will be recalled, there were five children whose handicaps were originally classified as minor. The mothers' initial perceptions of these children, and the subsequent development of their perceptions, were very different. But in relation to the thalidomide population, they suddenly formed a cohesive group. Compared to the other thalidomide children, theirs were definitely different. In a sense, their dilemma was a double one. They were not only marginal in relation to the normal environment, but also in relation to the thalidomide population.

Essentially, there were fourteen mothers who recognized their children in the thalidomide publicity.[17] Most did not like what they read. A few acquiesced to the hopeless tone of the articles and the label "monster" (particularly the mothers of institutionalized children), but others reacted violently. As one mother put it, "My child is not a monster." In fact, one of these mothers was so incensed by an article of this type that she canceled her subscription to the newspaper. Only three of the mothers found any of the articles useful. It is these mothers who mention references to habilitation programs in Germany and England. Not surprisingly, it is only these three mothers who mention having had any desire for contact with other thalidomide parents.

One can say that thalidomide served mainly as a negative identity during this period. Most of the mothers were not anxious to be identified with this group of known thalidomide children and their parents because it conferred notoriety without any redeeming benefits. Since their own relationship with these children was extremely vulnerable, most mothers found the thalidomide affiliation an added threat. It is difficult to mother a baby and, at the same time, enroll this child in a population that is composed of monsters, a population, indeed, for whom the possibility of euthanasia is openly debated.

THE SEARCH FOR PROFESSIONAL HELP

The search for professional help prior to the inauguration of the formal habilitation program at the RIM can be summarized very briefly. In essence, it manifests the same pattern of search and un-

---

[17] The remaining mother is the farm woman previously described. She claimed that she never read any newspapers, listened to the radio, or even watched T.V., and so remained unaware of any publicity.

certainty that has already been described many times for other handicapped children (cf. Ehlers, 1966). In this case, however, there was an added complication: for limb-deficiencies the body of professional knowledge was much smaller than for more common handicaps.

Except for the four children who were institutionalized, and one child who remained in hospital for treatment, all the other mothers report that they themselves embarked on this search. Here, however, a clear distinction becomes evident. The "minor" handicaps and the more typical phocomelia syndrome were treated very differently.

Of the ten children with phocomelia living at home, only two were referred to medical specialists by their family doctors. The other mothers were told not to waste their money, or else the family doctor did not know where or to whom to send them. Once these parents— by whatever route—reached a specialist the situation was not improved. The usual advice was to wait and see. The parents might be told that the phocomelic digits would have to be amputated, were advised to "forget about the hands," or were offered the possibility of prostheses at some unknown date in the future. But for the present, few doctors had any specific treatment, or even advice, to offer. Only two children in this group received any active treatment prior to their arrival at the RIM. Both children underwent operations, but in neither case could the mother see any visible improvement.

For the five children with minor deformities, the medical situation was rather different. Here the original hope had been that the hand defects could be corrected or cured by operations. At the time of entry into the RIM, three of these children had already undergone surgery. But at least two of these mothers were very disappointed by the results of these operations; instead of making the children "normal," it made them, according to the mothers' perceptions, more abnormal. The difficulty here seemed to lie in a lack of consensus between doctor and mother on the aim of treatment. The doctors strove for functional normality; the mothers stressed visual normality. Thus one of the mothers remembers how shocked she was when she discovered that her child's thumb had been amputated; [18] regardless of the functional improvement, this procedure constituted a betrayal of the perfect hand she sought.

Eventually, all these children would reach the RIM. But, in spite of the general disappointment of the mothers with the existing medical treatment, there would remain a clear distinction between the expectations of the mothers of the severely handicapped children and those of children with minor handicaps. By the time the mothers of the severely handicapped children arrived at the RIM, this institution represented an island of hope in a sea of hopelessness. They could be frightened, angry, or grateful at the implications of what was offered, but they were all intensely involved because there was no clear alternative. Their children were neither dying nor curable, and habilitation, even to a less handicapped status, represented a significant gain.

The five mothers of children with minor handicaps, on the other hand, had a very different set of expectations. They were both less involved—because their needs were perceived as less—and at the same time expected more. The children were so close to normal that the slow process of habilitation was viewed as a threat as well as a help.

SUMMARY ON THE RETURN FROM THE HOSPITAL

1. The mother's return from hospital did not mark an end to either the crisis or the mourning process. On the contrary, all these mothers experienced some degree of isolation from their habitual

[18] For a number of complex reasons, the possibility of amputation has been raised for 6 of the 20 children in the sample, 4 with minor handicaps and 2 with lower-limb phocomelia. In general, the mothers of the two groups reacted very differently to this possibility. For the children with lower-limb phocomelia, amputation was seen as a means of enhancing their normality; the phocomelic feet were perceived as functionally and visually abnormal, and their removal was desired. On the contrary, the parents of the children with minor handicaps treated the prospect of amputation as a threat; the digits might be functionally useless, but in terms of visual appearance five digits were more normal than four.

environments, and at least seventeen faced an actual or potential conflict in their roles as mother of the child and member of the community.

2. While many mothers did perceive their husbands as experiencing a severe personal trauma, few were able to discuss their own feelings or the future of the child with their spouses. In relation to the child's ambiguous status in the social environment, most mothers perceived their husbands as being less involved and less affected.

3. Three mothers did not experience much conflict because they perceived their children as sufficiently normal or "special" so as not to induce any social difficulties.

4. For the remaining seventeen mothers the type and intensity of the conflict varied considerably. For five mothers it was mainly an internal conflict that led to withdrawal and a period of alienation. Five other mothers, however, continued to function as members of the community, but at the price of experiencing a partial or complete estrangement from the child. Only for seven mothers did this conflict lead to an active attempt to reconcile mother, child, and community by pleading, defiance, and negotiation.

5. What appeared to distinguish the mothers in the conflict-negotiation group was an emphasis on details, rather than on global perceptions. These mothers underwent a continuous process of testing their own perceptions of the children against environmental reaction.

6. There is some relationship between the mother's reactions during the birth period and her reactions at this point in time, but this relationship is neither simple nor perfect. All five mothers in the original minimal-reaction group continued to avoid acute conflict and intense social disruption, either because they considered the child as not sufficiently deviant to produce conflict, or else because they were able to preserve some distance from the child. Of the six mothers who were originally in the intense-shock group, five remained severely traumatized, but one was able to separate completely from her child and recovered very quickly. Of the nine

mothers who were in the conflicted group originally, seven continued in the conflict-negotiation group, but two moved into the minimally affected group.

7. Even more significant than the shift from one category to another, however, is the fact that the nature of the categories themselves changed with the course of events during this period. Thus a mother who manifested little reaction during the birth period, because she saw the child as essentially normal, and continued to show little overt reaction, because she was able to separate herself from the stigma attached to the child, had not "changed categories" but had undergone a considerable change in perception. Even the mothers who remained in the intense-reaction group were now mourning a living, hopeless child rather than a dying, hopeless one.

8. The patterns of maternal reaction were not identical for the normal environment, the community of handicapped, or the body of professional helpers. While the delineation of the handicap as minor or severe was not a crucial factor in explaining the mother's relation to her habitual environment, the mothers of children with minor handicaps did constitute a distinct group in their perceptions of their relationship to other thalidomide children and with respect to their experiences with professional treatment.

9. It would appear then that the mothers' social behavior during this period was a complex synthesis of a number of factors. These would have to include (a) the mother's initial perceptions of the child, (b) her present perceptions, (c) her evaluation of the social reaction to herself and the child, (d) her degree of identification with the child, and (e) the nature of the environment—whether normal, handicapped, or professional—under consideration. But regardless of the complexity of the determinants, the developmental process constituted the basic substructure. One can say that it was impossible for a mother to remain fixed in one position; either she herself changed, or else the quickly changing nature of the reality she encountered led to the same attitudes acquiring a different significance.

The Formal Habilitation Program

The relationship of the patient and his family to the hospital, as a field for research, is not virgin terrain. On the contrary, the subject has aroused considerable interest among sociologists (Parsons and Fox, 1958) and, in the case of young children, among pediatricians and psychiatrists (Robertson, 1958). Nevertheless, the issues are far from settled. Opinions about the optimal nature of this relationship range from those who consider the hospital and the family two completely separate subsystems performing different functions to those who would prefer to make the hospital more homelike (cf. Davis, 1963, for a discussion of both points of view).

However, the major difficulty in applying the concepts used in these studies to the Rehabilitation Institute of Montreal lies more in the nature of the RIM than in the unresolved issues in the literature. The RIM as an institution is very different from the acute treatment hospitals described in most studies. It is not a hospital in the conventional sense of the term but a habilitation center.[19] Unlike a hospital, a habilitation center cannot be conceptualized as a temporary interruption in the course of normal development. Instead, the treatment center becomes an integral part of the normal development of its patients, in this case the children and their parents.[20] Its basic function is bound neither by time (that is, there is no determinable end to this form of program; it may continue as long as the patient lives), nor space (that is, the values it seeks to inculcate are not restricted to its own geographical boundaries; on the contrary,

[19] The general institution is, of course, a rehabilitation center. However, when treatment of congenital anomalies is undertaken, rehabilitation becomes habilitation. Although the two functions may coexist under one roof, each has very different psychological and sociological features.

[20] It would appear that the mothers themselves are very conscious of this difference. The interviewer was present when one of these mothers was having her child admitted for surgery in a general hospital. The admitting clerk asked about previous hospitalizations. The mother mentioned two previous admissions at different hospitals but did not include the child's lengthy stays at the RIM. When questioned about this omission, she replied, "But that wasn't because she was sick; that's part of her hands."

the aim is to make them transferable to the patient's habitual environment).

Indeed, the function of a habilitation center is a paradoxical one. The aim of the treatment is to make the child more "normal," but the social values it embodies can be summarized as "acceptance of abnormality." The Institute itself is a constant reminder of the child's inherent abnormality and serves as a model for a way of life that is very different from anything the parent has previously encountered. Thus Brooks (1966, p. 99) describes the first visit to the prosthetic center as one of the "predictable periods of major stress in the life of the limb-deficient child and his parents."

A full understanding of the unique and pervasive influence that the RIM has exerted on the lives of these children and their mothers would have to include the RIM's multiple facets as agent of the government-sponsored thalidomide program, as the institutional embodiment of a set of social values concerning physical handicaps, as a complex social bureaucracy, and as a treatment center. Moreover, it would also have to consider the varying needs and expectations of the parents who used its services, for the RIM was not about to interact with a *tabula rasa* child or mother. By the time these mothers brought their children to the habilitation program, they not only brought with them a set of expectations linked to socioeconomic status, previous experience with hospitals, and so on, but, in addition, had begun to develop different and unique modes of interpreting for themselves the meaning of the child and his handicap—a meaning that might or might not be concordant with the values embodied in the Institute. Furthermore, the complexity of the relationship between mother and Institute was greatly increased by the process of maturation and development itself, for the beginning phases of this relationship did not take place in a context of stability, but instead occurred during a time period when mothers, children, and Institute were all changing rapidly, often in an unpredictable fashion.

Here we shall not attempt to treat the mothers' perceptions of the RIM as a single topic, but shall instead deal with their ramifications as they impinge upon the story we are attempting to trace. When we turn to a consideration of the process of normification (cf. note 1, Chapter 5 for explanation), the policies of the RIM will obviously be crucial. We shall also have to consider the influence of the RIM when we discuss the child in the family (cf. Chapter 4); the repeated separations of the child from the family, often at crucial points in the developmental process, will constitute an integral part of the child-rearing experience of these mothers. But in this chapter the aim is to focus on the social normalization of abnormality; consequently, the emphasis will be on the role of the RIM as the embodiment of a set of values and as a social environment.

In order to do this, however, it is necessary to depart from our usual procedure of simply describing the mothers' perceptions of events. The initial encounter of mother and habilitation center marked the intersection of developmental paths that previously each had been pursuing separately. In earlier sections we traced the development of the mothers' perceptions. Now it becomes important to understand the expectations and purposes that the RIM as an institution brought to the encounter. The review given here is not comprehensive; instead, it is a problem-oriented account of those aspects of the RIM which were to prove most salient and most difficult for the mothers.

THE REHABILITATION INSTITUTE OF MONTREAL AS A SOCIAL INSTITUTION

Geographical location. The RIM is located in Montreal. Although the hospital staff is officially a bilingual one, the building is located in a largely English-speaking section of the city. Thus, for many of the rural French-speaking mothers, the strangeness of the Institute itself was compounded by the bewilderment aroused by a large city and an unfamiliar language.[21]

---

[21] It is interesting to note that the language used at the RIM served as an unintentional projective stimulus. For the French-speaking mothers, it was described as "English," while for the English-speaking mothers the reverse was true.

The fact that, for some of the mothers, the RIM was geographically and socially remote from their habitual environment also created difficulties in transposing the social values of the RIM to the home communities. Some mothers were able to use the RIM as a powerful, if distant, authority and tell neighbors, "You shouldn't pity X; the RIM says it's not right." But for others, the values propounded by the RIM remained geographically bound. As one mother put it:

Here in Montreal it's normal you know a child like X. There's a lot, there are hospitals here. But in —— there's nothing like this, you can say there's no handicapped children. You don't see them; they're placed or hidden. You could say that there it's a shame. You understand?

Habilitation within a rehabilitation center. The RIM is designed to treat the sequelae of a number of disabilities, for example, of strokes, traumatic amputations, and others. The thalidomide program constitutes but one small aspect of its total program. There the mothers were confronted not only with the sight of children "like theirs," but also with patients of varying ages and many different types of disabilities.

For many mothers entry into the RIM marked their initial entry into the world of the disabled. This encounter proved difficult for a number of reasons. Whatever a mother's feelings about her thalidomide child, the sight of a large number of such children could be very disturbing. The general milieu, too, was a difficult one to assimilate. Here physical disabilities were not discreetly hidden but were instead openly displayed. For some mothers the sight of amputees with no limbs or with uncovered artificial limbs proved extremely traumatic.[22]

And since this revulsion was neither easily verbalized, nor acceptable, the conflict would emerge in a disguised form. Some mothers visited very little. Others did visit, but they were extremely resentful, for instance, of the hospital rule that required them, if they wished

[22] In order to facilitate treatment, ambulatory patients at the RIM usually wear shorts and short-sleeved blouses.

to be reimbursed, to eat lunch in the cafeteria used by the patients.

Government sponsorship. The RIM acted as the government-sponsored habilitation center. In order to receive financial compensation for treatment, it was necessary for the child to be evaluated by the staff of the RIM and either be treated there, or by an alternative facility that was approved by the RIM. For some parents this rule removed freedom of choice; they perceived themselves as captive consumers of the services offered by the RIM. However, on the whole, this factor was relatively unimportant. As we shall see, most parents did not wish this freedom of choice because there was little else to choose. In fact, the greatest virtue of the government program, according to the mothers, was that it offered a centralized, comprehensive, and continuing service.

Instead, the difficulty of government sponsorship lay in another factor. Because the program was sponsored and paid for by the government, the physician-patient relationship was quite different from the model derived from private practice. There was no contract between an individual mother and a given doctor, in which she paid the bill, and his primary responsibility was to satisfy her. Instead, the model used was much closer to that of the typical clinic. Depending on the mother's socioeconomic status and previous experience with medical care, this could be a source of serious friction. The mothers whose previous medical experience had been mainly on a private basis complained bitterly about such factors as waiting time, and resented that "the doctors never tell you anything." They, too, were the ones who were most resistant to the social worker, because they perceived her work as an invasion of their privacy.

Financial intermediary. The government program for thalidomide children involved an unusual attempt to help families bear the costs of rearing a handicapped child. Among parents of handicapped children, thalidomide parents definitely constituted a privileged group financially. For most mothers, however, this extensive financial aid was perceived as a realistic necessity, rather than as a cause for gratitude. For one thing, the costs were so high in relation to the families' income (some children had already accumulated bills of

$40,000 to $50,000 by the age of four), that no family within the sample felt capable of trying to pay them alone. Even more important was the mothers' feeling that this was the least that society could do in reparation for the harm it had inflicted.[23]

The financial aspects of the program, therefore, did not make the mothers feel particularly grateful toward the RIM. On the contrary, the role of the RIM as intermediary between government and parent in administering the financial program tended to increase the mothers' hostility toward the Institute. The situation arose from a particular combination of circumstances. The government program, according to the mothers, had never spelled out what financial aid they were entitled to, nor for how long. Consequently, although the RIM itself was ultimately responsible to the government, most mothers perceived it as the final authority that could decide whether to pay a given bill or not.

This difficulty was further intensified by an administrative decision made within the RIM. In order not to complicate the social worker's relationship with the mother, responsibility for the financial aspects of the program was given solely to the Medical Director of the RIM. This certainly had the effect of splitting the good and bad objects. The mothers could revile the Medical Director, but had little personal contact with him. At the same time, this policy had the result of curtailing much of the effectiveness of the social worker. The latter was left the job of handling the mother's "feelings," but the mother herself might be feeling most intensely about money. In this area, the social worker was often uninformed and had little authority. To cite only one interview that illustrates this point, the mother's major concern here was her resentment of the fact that trips to the RIM by public transportation were reimbursed, while trips by pri-

[23] In spite of the fact that all mothers considered some form of financial assistance necessary, attitudes varied widely. Some parents simply regarded the RIM as a bountiful and benevolent fairy godmother and proceeded to send it all their medical bills, even those antedating the birth of the baby. Others, on the other hand, were anxious to participate in the financial care of their children. Thus one mother, during the period that her child was hospitalized, regularly sent the Family Allowance check to the hospital.

vate auto were not. To this the social worker could only offer the recommendation of more casework.

Attitudes toward parents. The philosophy underlying the treatment policy at the RIM was that thalidomide children could be habilitated to lead almost-normal lives in their families and in society. The basic value here was that early and effective treatment of child and family could and should lead to a successful mutual adaptation. Although the alternatives were not stated, it was evident that the criterion of success, initially anyhow, lay in the achievement of this aim.

In view of the emphasis on the integration of the child within the family, it is not surprising that the cooperation of the parents was considered essential for the treatment of the child. At times the role of the parents could be viewed as that of partners in the rehabilitation team (Mongeau, 1967). At other times, however, the parents themselves were perceived as patients. In fact, the parents became the patients who were considered to be most in need of help and the most difficult to treat.

The roots of this attitude are complex. During the first few years of life, of course, the abnormality is much more traumatic for the parents than for the child. As we have seen, the basic philosophy underlying habilitation is that this trauma must be resolved by helping the parent to "accept" the child. Actually, the parent becomes the patient. If one has the additional conviction that the mothers who ingested thalidomide were a selected group manifesting neurotic symptoms (Lazure, 1963, p. 963), then the transition of the parent to patient status is further facilitated. With these premises, it was not surprising that it was expected that the mothers would require intensive psychiatric therapy (Moreault *et al.*, 1963).

The habilitation program itself further intensified this tendency. As enthusiasm mounted with the possibilities for habilitation, any difficulties that arose could be seen to lie not in the presenting condition, nor in the mode of treatment, but in the parents' inability to "accept" the situation. In many ways the parents' status as patients provided a rationale for using them as scapegoats. Statements such as those quoted below became frequent.

Canada's thalidomide babies are likely to find that their biggest handicap are not their stunted limbs, but their distraught mothers (*Vancouver Sun,* August 24, 1963, p. 8).

There is little doubt today that these children will become useful adults. The sole barrier is the mental effect on their parents (*Canadian Doctor,* 1965, p. 31).

This attitude did not originate with the RIM, nor was it limited to this institution. But it did have serious consequences for the type of treatment offered to the mothers at the RIM. Some of the case records of parental interviews are indistinguishable from those of patients in psychotherapy or psychoanalysis. There are numerous references to "therapist" and "patient" and considerable speculation about "psychodynamics."

More important, in these records, the RIM, instead of being seen as a complex, changing institution, was used as the equivalent of the psychoanalytic couch. If parents complained of the lack of highchairs, they were "disguising" their guilt. If a mother was told that her child would be kept for one week and the ensuing hospitalization lasted six months, the mother's rising anxiety was interpreted as separation anxiety. An attempt to form a parents' group was seen as a "reflection of guilt." [24]

This does not mean that the RIM was impervious to the parents'

---

[24] The theme of guilt is one that constantly reappears on the pages of these records. Some parents are simply overtly guilty, while others manifest "false guilt," and some are characterized by "disguised guilt." But the basic conviction is that all inevitably feel guilty. One of the senior psychologists, who was present during the initial phases of the program, was recently asked why so much attention was paid to the mothers' guilt and so little to their anger. He replied that no one had ever thought that the mothers might feel angry and consider their anger legitimate. This, too, may be a significant aspect of the social values embodied in a habilitation system and of the parents' patient status within it.

complaints. On the contrary, the hospital changed a great deal during this time, and part of this change was in response to parental pressure. Highchairs were purchased, lengthy hospitalizations were curtailed, and the RIM itself is currently considering the formation of a parents' group. But the diagnosis and treatment of the parents were never related to these ongoing changes.[25]

The essential point here is not that the professional staff was using a particular value system. All treatment is based on value systems, and the application of a psychiatric model of sickness and treatment to these parents had many benefits. By defining the parents as the patients and nonacceptance as the illness, the staff, instead of being divided in its loyalties, could now focus on habilitating the child. In a simplification of utilitarian philosophy, the "good" of the child became equated with "the greatest good of the greatest number."

What did create difficulty was the fact that the professional staff appeared largely unaware of the values that it was using. In a sense, the RIM can be viewed as a class system in the Marxian sense in which the professionals did not perceive themselves as operating within the system. They could see how the mothers were affecting the children; they tended to be oblivious to the manner in which they, as a social class within the social system, were affecting the mothers.

But whatever the philosophical basis for this mode of treatment, its implication was clear. The good parent was one who was willing to accept the status of patient. This status in itself was not necessarily an unwelcome one. Depending on the mother, the situation, and the professional involved, it could even be perceived as a mode of help and support. Rather, it was the guilt-inducing dogma underlying the

[25] Thus, to cite one example, a mother spent most of her first interview with a new social worker complaining about the parking regulations at the RIM. The social worker concluded the interview summary by stating that this confirmed the previous social worker's hypothesis that the mother did not accept the child or the handicap. The same week the social worker exerted considerable energy to have the parking regulations changed. The diagnosis of the mother, however, remained unchanged.

treatment process that came to be viewed by the mothers as a threat to their psychological survival.

The problem of integration. The RIM attempted to offer a comprehensive habilitation program that would treat the whole child and his family. With this purpose in view, the hospital staff was keenly aware of the fact that treatment could not be limited to medical care within the hospital, nor should it be restricted to the child. If the child were to be habilitated, the family and the community in which the child lived became appropriate concerns of the Institute. In fact, many of the paramedical services that exist within the Institute (for example, the social worker, teacher, or psychologist) are designed to facilitate the integration of child, family, and community.

Unfortunately, the professional staff was far less aware of the fact that the RIM itself constituted a complex bureaucracy; for many mothers, the task of integrating the various services within the hospital was far more difficult than the effort to integrate the hospital with the environment. In the process of habilitation, it is impossible for any one person to undertake the whole task; inevitably, there will be many services and many individuals involved. And the route by which these various services would be integrated into a total program for a whole child remained unclear.

The task of integration of services within the Institute was not assigned *de jure* to any one person. Instead, it oscillated *de facto* between two people: the social worker and the physiatrist (the medical specialist in rehabilitation who heads the treatment team). Because of the particular status that each of these occupied with the Institute, and in relation to the mother, neither was able to fulfill it satisfactorily.

The role of the social worker was made more difficult by a particular set of historical circumstances. Originally, the treatment staff working specifically wtih the parents consisted of a consulting psychiatrist (a medical specialist in mental disorders), a social worker, and a psychologist. There seems to have been no precise definition of the role of each of these professionals, and from the records it would appear that many of the mothers underwent three almost identical evaluations in one day. Gradually the psychiatrist and psychologist withdrew, and the social worker was given the main responsibility for work with the parents. Unfortunately, the social-work staff has been one of the most unstable departments in the hospital, and, in the five years of the program, the average mother has been exposed to four social workers. Usually, because of the timing of the control examinations on a twice-yearly basis, a mother would have only one or two contacts with a particular social worker before she, too, left.

But the deficiencies of the social worker as an integrator were not derived simply from the changes in personnel. Rather, the problem lay in the paradoxical connotations of her role. In relation to the outside world, the social worker was the main channel of communication between hospital and environment. However, the hospital she sought to interpret to the parents was one in which she herself functioned with a limited status and a limited perspective; her knowledge of long-range goals and policy was restricted.

This paradox was manifest in many areas. For instance, the social worker had little knowledge of financial policy, even though this was one of the mothers' major concerns. Again, she might know the child's current medical status, but not the long-range program. Thus, although the physiatrist in charge of the child's program might be planning a major change in treatment policy (for example, an operation), the social worker might be unaware of this and continue to work with treatment goals that were no longer relevant. Or, to cite another example, the social worker could be very sensitive to the fact that a given mother had five children and needed time to find a baby sitter, but she had little influence on the hospital practice that gave the mother but two days' notice for a coming hospitalization (even though the admissions clerk might know months earlier that this hospitalization was scheduled). In short, the social worker was in the position of interpreting a hospital structure of which she had only partial knowledge and in which her authority was restricted. Where she did intervene, it was usually on an individual *ad hoc* basis rather than on the policy level.

The social worker's role as intermediary between hospital and parent was complicated by yet another factor. The emphasis in the habilitation center was on treatment of limb-deficiency, but because of the complex nature of the thalidomide syndrome, some parents were far more concerned about other medical problems. This difference in orientation could result in considerable confusion in the identification of the "problem." Thus, to cite one example, a social worker saw the parents of a child a few weeks before the youngster was due to be admitted to another hospital for surgical repair of a congenital cardiac anomaly. According to the social worker, the parents were too concerned about the coming operation to be able to discuss the child's "handicap." The problem, of course, lay in who was to define the handicap.

In contrast to the social worker, the physiatrist was stable during the five years of the program and had the most knowledge of and authority within the hospital. But the knowledge he had of the mother was limited, and, in general, the mothers perceived the physiatrist as too busy and too medically oriented to deal with the petty problems of their personal lives. Even in the realm of strictly medical problems, he was perceived more as a specialist than as a family physician. Except for a few isolated instances, whenever the mother was concerned about any other medical problem besides the limb-deficiency, she felt reluctant to bother the physiatrist.

Apart from the difficulty in integrating all the services at any one time, the question of time itself was unclear. All the mothers were aware that they were involved in a long-term program, but few had any conception of the sequence of steps. In part, this may be due to the fact that the doctors themselves were often unable to predict events in advance; the program was too new, and there were too many unknown variables. Nevertheless, this uncertainty tended to increase the mothers' dependency on the RIM as the omniscient authority which would reveal its plans as it chose.

In this context of lack of integration, some of the confusion manifested by the mothers became more understandable. Indeed, a mother might be very unclear about what problems in general the

RIM was prepared to handle, and whether a given problem was the province of the physiatrist, the social worker, or the nurse. Some parents simply brought all their problems to the hospital; for example, a member of the staff would be expected to handle marital difficulties, a sibling's poor school performance, the mother's personal medical problem, and so on. Other parents, though, would not discuss certain very relevant problems with the staff because they perceived these as lying outside the scope of the program.

In finding their way through the social maze that characterized the RIM, the mothers used a number of solutions. A few were able to choose one person, regardless of official rank, as the preferred contact. But for most, it was the presence of the RIM as a personified institution that served as the integrating force. As one mother put it: "It's no special person; it's the whole place."

The problem of change over time. The RIM opened its doors in its present building in February, 1962. In October, 1963, "Operation Thalidomide" formally began, and the hospital received the first of what appeared to be an avalanche of thalidomide children. Given the relative newness of the Institute, its inexperience with such young patients, and the "crisis" nature of the treatment program, it is not surprising that there were many rapid changes in policy and staff.

These fluctuations had two important implications for the mothers' perceptions. First of all, what kind of a hospital the mother found, depended on the time of her arrival at the RIM. Thus differences in the mothers' initial perceptions of the hospital are related not only to differences among the mothers, but also to the fact that some of these mothers encountered a very different reality from others.

Even more important than this initial difference, was the changing structure and personnel of the Institute. To cite only one example, originally there was no distinct pediatric nursing team. Subsequently, a team was formed and constituted a cohesive unit. Currently the team has been disbanded, and most of these nurses are no longer there. Under such circumstances, then, one can say that the mothers kept returning to the same Institute, but the Institute itself kept changing. At times, the element of continuity was provided by a few stable key staff members (in general, the physiatrists and the occupational therapists have been the most stable). But, as mentioned above, for most mothers it was the Institute itself that was perceived as the symbol of continuity.

In presenting this capsule review of the characteristics of the RIM, two important distortions of reality have been made. For one thing, the emphasis here has been on the features that were to prove barriers to treatment. If this were the whole story, the program should have proved a disastrous failure.

The second problem with this account is that it is not only retrospective, but also summarizes the mothers' perceptions of their continuing experience with the RIM, and in this type of summary it is particularly easy to confuse past and present. Indeed, a mother who currently very much resents her patient status may forget that initially she welcomed it.

And finally, whatever the shortcomings of staff and policy, it should be remembered that the luxury of detached observation is reserved for the historian and the researcher. For those who are called upon to act immediately, inadequate policies may be better than none.

MOTHERS' PERCEPTIONS OF THE RIM AS A TREATMENT MILIEU

For almost all the mothers in this sample, the initial prospect of a government-sponsored habilitation program was greeted with enthusiasm. This enthusiasm could vary in intensity and might be accompanied by some feelings of apprehension about the unknown nature of the treatment center. Few parents had heard of the RIM previously, and the whole concept of a habilitation center was new. Nevertheless, all the parents were sufficiently interested at least to investigate its possibilities.

In the intervening years, little has changed in the mothers' formal affiliation with the Institute. Only one family has refused to participate after its initial contact with the RIM. The other mothers, whatever their complaints, still prefer it to any existing alternative.

Though almost all the mothers have continued in active treatment, their attitudes toward and involvement with the RIM have varied considerably. To understand this variation fully, one would have to present each of the twenty case histories in great detail. If, however, our interest is in modal patterns, the mothers' relations with the RIM can be classified in four broad categories.

The battleground. For two mothers the RIM was perceived mainly as an antagonist that threatened their previously formulated solutions. For them, the encounter with the treatment center became a battleground where each encounter was accompanied by mutual distrust and recrimination. However, in spite of their common opposition to the RIM, each of these mothers was very different in her relationship to her child and her environment. One of these women perceived the battle as an attempt by the Institute to foist an unmotherable child on her. The child had been institutionalized since birth, and, although the staff at the RIM felt that many of the difficulties manifested by the child were due to the lack of a proper home environment, the mother, in turn, considered the child "strange" and unacceptable in any family environment. The other case was diametrically different. The mother, for a number of complex reasons, was so opposed both to the separation caused by hospitalization and to the proposal of prostheses that she withdrew from the program. Thus, in neither case did the habilitation program change the mothers' perceptions of their children. On the contrary, it was the fact that their previous attitudes were incongruent with the values of the RIM that led to this conflict.

The savior. For three mothers, on the contrary, the dominant perception of the RIM was that it offered a solution to an impasse. All three had children who were hopeless but refused to die. The mothers were unable to find a meaningful social existence for the children, but they were equally unable to separate completely from them. When the RIM entered the scene, the situation was at a stalemate. The offer of a treatment program, in these circumstances, had the impact of a miracle; it constituted a virtual resurrection of these children.

These three children had spent the first year of their lives in hospitals and custodial institutions. Two were the most severely handicapped in the total sample (all four limbs were involved, and there were other anomalies as well); they had originally been diagnosed as dying monsters. The mothers agreed with this diagnosis, and even though they had begun some contact with the children after a few months, they still considered the children as socially hopeless. The mothers, in their relation to their habitual environments, had each undergone a period of severe depression and total estrangement.

The third case was slightly different. At birth, the child himself was considered healthy, but the handicap (bilateral lower-limb phocomelia) was judged hopeless. The mother had institutionalized the child but, according to her, had maintained, in the face of considerable hostility in her community, that this child would come home. In fact, the mother did bring the child home as soon as she was aware that the RIM would treat the child, even before the process of habilitation had begun.

As can be seen, these three mothers differed somewhat in their perceptions of the children and in their past modes of resolution. As it happened, one child came home before the prostheses were fitted, one after, and one has never lived at home.[26] But for all three mothers the existence of a habilitation program for children like theirs became the first concrete hope offered them. If the children were to exist, the habilitation program constituted their only chance at any form of meaningful life. In short, the RIM was a savior that had undertaken to salvage hitherto unsalvageable children. In these circumstances, one does not criticize.

The minimally involved. A third group of six mothers were less intense in their feelings about the RIM but more ambivalent. All were enrolled in the program, none had any serious intentions of

[26] It should be noted that in this case the understanding between the mother and the RIM was based on the fact that the RIM was willing to modify its value system and accept the idea that a "good" mother might be unwilling or unable to care for her child at home. Whether this shift was due to the RIM's perception of the child as more deformed than others, or the mother as unusually fragile, or both, is difficult to determine.

dropping out, but all had serious reservations. However, because of their perceptions of the nature of their children's handicaps and the type of care offered by the RIM, they tended to have a common attitude toward the Institute. They accepted the proffered help but were able to maintain their distance. These became the minimally involved.

Five of these mothers had children whose handicaps have been categorized as minor. As will be recalled, the mothers' initial perceptions of the children were very different, and the modes of adjustment to the habitual environment varied. In addition, some of these mothers were very involved in the social fate of their children, while others were quite detached. It was only in their reaction to other thalidomide children that these mothers had recognized themselves as a separate group.

This separateness continued in their relationship to the RIM. The initial impact of the hospital milieu was a depressing one. Whatever their own feelings about their children's handicaps, the mothers did not feel that their children were like the other thalidomide ones. At the same time, they began to realize that others did perceive their children as part of the category of the handicapped. As one mother put it: "It was only when I came here that I realized for the first time that I was the mother of a handicapped child."

The process of treatment, too, appeared irrelevant for their needs. The focus of the RIM was on the use of prostheses. For these parents, however, the major hope was that the anomalies could be corrected surgically. Since the RIM itself had no surgical facilities, it was not perceived as the institution which could provide the help they sought.

A further difficulty was provoked by the difference in perspective between professional staff and mothers. For professionals involved in the long-term care of the severely disabled, these mothers were, comparatively, the lucky ones. Their anguish at the handicap and impatience at the treatment were "unrealistic." For the mothers, however, the frame of reference remained the world of the normals.

Regardless of their own feelings about the child, abnormality was not yet a way of life for them.

In general, these mothers had much more limited contact with the hospital than any other group. Because the children did not require the lengthy prosthetic training or constant readjustment of prostheses, hospitalizations were less frequent and shorter. But their general reaction to the hospital was one of disappointment. The lengthy process of habilitation only emphasized their children's abnormality without conferring any visible benefits.

Despite their disapproval or impatience, none of these five women was ready to withdraw from the program. For some, it was the financial help that was most desired. For others, it was the Institute as an integrated, comprehensive service that proved most attractive. In a sense, the RIM was perceived as an insurance program. The children might not need it or benefit very much at this point, but the government program provided the assurance that they would receive whatever help they might eventually need.

The sixth mother continued in the habilitation program because the government wanted it and was willing to pay for it. But neither the medical nor paramedical services of the RIM really had much impact on her. It was too remote from her major concerns to have much meaning.

The maximally involved. The remaining nine mothers constituted a group who were both maximally involved and maximally ambivalent about the RIM. In these circumstances, it is not surprising that they provided the most complex judgments about the advantages and disadvantages of the habilitation program.

The previous developmental paths followed by these mothers had been quite different. Two had undergone a lengthy process of mourning and estrangement; it was only very gradually that they became able to accept that their children would live. One mother had passed from initial conflict to "acceptance" of the baby and the belief that the environment would accept him, too. Four had begun in the conflicted group and continued the conflict negotiation with their habitual environments. In short, these nine women represented almost all possible combinations of our previous classifications of perceptions.

But in spite of many individual differences, all had two features in common at the moment of their entry into the RIM. All these children manifested some form of phocomelia, and the mothers perceived these disabilities as severe and requiring professional help. At the same time, none of these children had been institutionalized; consequently, all the mothers had had some experience in rearing them in a normal environment. It was these two factors that were to lead to both the maximal involvement and the maximal ambivalence.

Initially, these were the mothers who were most eager to enter the habilitation program. Indeed, during the time the program was in the process of preparation, they were the ones who bombarded the RIM with letters asking when the children could come. In part, this was due to the mothers' previous decision that these children would not be institutionalized, accompanied by their own belief that the future would be bleak. Previous attempts to find professional help and guidance had been largely fruitless. Now the RIM offered the prospect of a government-financed, comprehensive treatment program that would provide the most advanced medical care. Glowing articles about the benefits to be derived from early fitting of prostheses added to the allure.

In spite of this anticipatory enthusiasm, the initial encounter with the RIM was a painful one that appeared only to increase their sense of loss, bewilderment, and disorganization. The general milieu was frightening, the procedures and rules were unfamiliar, and the parents became aware that help meant prolonged separation from their children, and their own involvement with psychiatrist, social worker, and psychologist.

The adaptation required here was that of accepting dependence. The good mother now became the good patient and, in some respects, the good child. All the mothers were keenly aware of their initiation into this status. It occurred in relation to the head nurse who now had the authority not only to care for the handicap, but also to forbid the pacifier or to reject the mother's usual medicine for a cold. It occurred in relation to the doctors who, as one mother put it, "measured arms and talked among themselves." And it occurred in relationship to the psychiatrist and social worker who now had the authority to probe into every detail of the mother's history and feelings.

In regard to the children, the most difficult adaptation required was acceptance of the length and ambiguity of the treatment plan. The usual procedure, for example, for the initial evaluation was to ask the parent to bring the child to the hospital. The mother might believe that this evaluation would last a day, since no time period was given. In fact, it usually stretched for weeks and months. The mother would be continually reassured that the child was well, but no one could or would tell her why, and for how long, the child would be there. The same process occurred for scheduled operations, prosthetic fittings, and so on.

But to the degree that the mothers accepted their new status, the benefits became apparent. Here was a comprehensive program and a stable Institute that offered instrumental and affective help in the bewilderment aroused by their maternity. Thus, a favorite social worker was perceived by many of these women as "a mother to us"; the physiatrist was seen as an expert who would handle the medical aspects of the problem; the occupational therapist was seen as a source of concrete advice, for example, on how to teach the child to walk; the psychologist was perceived as able and ready to help with problems in child-rearing. Even more important, the RIM as an institution now provided an alleviation of the mother's former sense of isolation; here, at least, her child was understood and accepted.

Gradually the mothers achieved some sort of balance in dealing with the impact of the RIM. A few accepted the dependence and help completely and were largely grateful. A few, by accentuating the distance between themselves and their children, could accept the child-centered aspects but largely reject the parental treatment plan. Others were overtly rebellious. But much of this defiance reminded one of the bravado of a small child. For like the child who threatens to run away from home, these women had no other home to run to.

In relation to the social normalization of the children, however, the effect was generally positive. The child, instead of being an isolated deviant in relation to the world, was now perceived as a member of a very special program. The RIM, as the embodiment of society's concern for and positive evaluation of these children, provided a powerful counterforce to the pity and stigma attached to physical deviancy.

MOTHERS' PERCEPTIONS OF THE RIM AS A COMMUNITY OF THALIDOMIDE MEMBERS

For most of the mothers, entry into the RIM provided their first personal contact with other mothers of thalidomide children. Nevertheless, in spite of the fact that all these mothers shared the common experience of bearing thalidomide children and participating in a unique habilitation program, they never formed a cohesive group.

In some respects, this contact with other thalidomide children was a welcome one. For one thing, it provided a norm against which each mother could measure her own baby's development. In addition, it also served as a consolation, since every mother felt that at least one other baby was more handicapped than her own. In a few cases, too, a personal relationship would be built between two mothers, as when a Montreal mother would send an out-of-town mother news of her baby. But beyond this point, there was no further process of group formation.

In some respects, this lack of cohesiveness can be attributed to the differences among the mothers, as in the case of the mothers of children with minor handicaps who tended to feel pity but little kinship toward the mothers of more severely handicapped children. Differences in language, socioeconomic status, cultural background, and geographical area of residence also created barriers to communication.

In addition to these pre-existent factors, the presence of the habilitation program itself was a negative force because it removed much of the necessity for group formation. Most groups of parents of disabled children unite not only for educational and mutual-help purposes, but also to fulfill the function of a pressure group; by extensive publicity and lobbying, the government and community can be persuaded to provide needed services. In this case, however, the government had already agreed to provide in one "package deal" the required facilities.

And finally, the patriarchal attitude of the RIM itself must be included as one of the factors that tended to discourage group formation. Indeed, if the files at the RIM are correct, the one attempt by a father to form a parents' group in Quebec, similar to those in England, was actively discouraged by hospital staff. The reason given for this reluctance was that the father's activities constituted a form of acting-out.

Thus, although the public tended to view parents of thalidomide children as a distinct group, the mothers never really felt this affiliation. The RIM constituted another common bond in their lives, but the identification here was with the leader (cf. Redl, 1942) rather than with each other.

SUMMARY ON THE FORMAL HABILITATION PROGRAM

1. There is no simple relationship between the mothers' perception of and reaction to the new environment of the RIM and their past perceptions and patterns of behavior. In a few cases, the RIM produced a radical change in a mother's behavior that could not be anticipated on the basis of past behavior; for example, a mother who had initially considered her child as a hopeless, dying monster to be institutionalized, and herself had undergone a lengthy period of severe depression, was able, after the child had been fitted with prostheses, to take him home, integrate him in the community, and function very adequately as his mother. Another mother, however, whose previous history was superficially similar to this, showed little apparent change. On the basis of our data, anyhow, there is no reliable way of predicting from previous history how an individual mother might respond to the RIM.

2. In spite of this complexity and inability to predict, one general

rule appears to offer a broad *post hoc* explanation of how the mothers reacted. Most mothers perceived the adaptation to the RIM as a stress situation that included certain benefits. To the degree that these benefits were judged to be necessary and relevant in alleviating other stresses resulting from the birth of a limb-deficient child, the mothers were willing and able to adjust to and tolerate the stresses inherent in the RIM; to the degree that these benefits were viewed as minor and irrelevant, the mothers became indifferent or antagonistic. In concrete terms, this meant that adaptation to this milieu was most likely to occur when the mother (a) perceived the child's condition as seriously disabling, (b) was strongly identified with the child and willing to rear him at home, and (c) previously had been unsuccessful in finding a mode of social normalization of the child.

3. While these three factors were the most crucial ones in determining the mothers' willingness to engage actively in the habilitation program, they do not explain fully the mothers' feelings about the RIM. For the mothers who committed themselves to the habilitation program, the RIM was judged not only as a global entity, but also as a multifaceted agency that served many functions. In particular, there were three major aspects that helped to shape the mothers' feelings about the Institute: (a) the RIM as an embodiment of a social philosophy concerning physical handicaps, (b) the RIM as a social system, and (c) the RIM as a treatment milieu.

Social philosophy. In contrast to the ambiguity and confusion that characterized professional and environmental reaction to the birth of a limb-deficient child, the RIM offered a clear social philosophy about the meaning of a handicapped child. This philosophy emphasized that the child's abnormalities required special help and consideration but that, apart from this, the disabled child needed and deserved the same family care and social opportunities that all children do.

As it referred to the child, most mothers welcomed this philosophy. It not only conferred dignity and stature on a child who could arouse pity and ridicule in the general environment, but also enhanced the previously devalued maternity of the mother. While most mothers faced some difficulties in transposing these values to their communities, the RIM served as an important authority and countervailing force in the social normalization of the children.

As it was interpreted in relation to the mothers, however, this philosophy engendered considerable resistance. The optimism manifested about the children could lead to a policy in which any difficulty in the child's adjustment would be attributed to the mother's failure to "accept" the child. Most mothers viewed this guilt-inducing doctrine as adding another stress to an already heavy burden.

Social system. Although "acceptance" of the child was the major criterion used to judge the goodness of the mother theoretically, in practice the good mother was also, usually anyway, the one who was able to adjust to the existing social system at the RIM. Thus, in terms of the system, the ideal mother became the one who (a) had a child whose major anomaly was limb-deficiency; (b) perceived the child as sufficiently abnormal to require habilitation, but at the same time as sufficiently normal to be integrated into the family and the community; (c) was involved enough with the child to participate fully in the program, but detached enough to permit lengthy separations; (d) was sufficiently passive to accept a dependent status in relation to the RIM, but sufficiently active to function independently as the mother of the child in the home and the community (that is, able to encourage the use of prostheses and to exert pressure to have the child admitted to school); and (e) was disturbed enough to welcome her patient role at the RIM, but not sufficiently disturbed to make short-term and sporadic therapeutic intervention ineffective.

Because of the many paradoxes inherent in the requirements of the RIM's social structure, none of the mothers was able to adjust to the habilitation program without considerable stress. Nevertheless, though the mothers would often be very emotional and quite vocal about this stress, it in itself did not lead any mother to abandon the program.

Treatment milieu. The effect of the RIM on the mothers' perceptions of their children was paradoxical. For while the habilitation program offered a process of social normalization of deviant children, and a treatment plan of normification, it also increased the mothers' awareness of the serious consequences and multiple implications of physical abnormality.

In general, mothers who had previously perceived their children as seriously abnormal judged that the habilitation program increased their normality, while those who had previously considered their children to be relatively normal found that the process of habilitation emphasized their abnormality.

The Present

The timing of the research interviews coincided with a period of social moratorium. Most of the children were between three and four years old, and the early struggles—the birth crisis, the initiation of the child into the community and the RIM—were safely in the past. The new crises, such as entrance into school, remained in the future. Thus for most mothers this was a period of relatively low tension; the conflicts and adaptations required were subtle rather than gross ones.

Nevertheless, in spite of the relative quiescence of this period, it did include an important developmental step. For the first time, the mothers' perceptions included the children as active participators, rather than merely as passive pawns, in the social process of normalizing the abnormalities. Now it was not only the mother's relationship to her community, but also the child's own reactions to the deviancy and to the community of the deviant that were gradually becoming increasingly salient.

In one other respect this period differed markedly from previous ones. In contrast to the diversity of perceptions and reactions that characterized the mothers at other phases of the developmental process, at this time we find only two general patterns. And, for the first time, the relevant criterion for distinguishing these patterns is the absence or presence of the child at home.

In part, this new division within the sample can be understood as a result of the influence of the RIM. Before the intervention of the habilitation program, the mothers' decisions for or against institutionalization could result from any one of a number of chance factors that characterized the social limbo in which they lived. But the habilitation program offered a possible, if difficult, manner of reconciling mother, child, and community. Those mothers who could accept this reinterpretation of values manifested it by the decision to rear the child in the family. Those who could not, on the other hand, left their children in institutions. Thus the crucial decision became one for or against social normalization of the deviant child within the normal community.

Our discussion in this section will be focused on the social progress of those children living with the family, since it is their development that is most complex and relevant. Nevertheless, it is necessary to summarize briefly the status of the two institutionalized children. Both children had spent their entire lives in various hospitals and institutions and, at the time of the research interviews, were residing at the RIM. Neither had ever been taken home, even for a day's visit, by their parents, and they had never met their siblings. The nursing staff at the RIM tried to remedy this deficiency of normal experience by a variety of techniques; for example, the children were taken to the nearby shopping center, or a nurse would take a child home for the weekend. In one case, too, a member of the psychological research team spent a year working with the child individually (cf. Hill, 1966). But, in general, these children's contacts with the normal community remained sporadic and limited.

Thus, in a sense, both of the mothers of the institutionalized children were still dealing with the global issues of the birth crisis. They accepted the knowledge that their children would continue to exist physically, but they had no clear convictions about the social or psychological meaning of this existence. One major dimension, however, had been added to their conflict. At the time of the research interviews, the RIM felt that these children no longer required hospital care and, if the mothers could not or would not take them, proposed to place the children in foster care. It was extremely difficult for these women to face the possibility that another woman could mother the child that they found unmotherable. Indeed, one of these mothers refused to believe that all the other thalidomide children had indeed returned to their homes.

In establishing this new classification of the sample solely on the basis of the child's presence in or absence from the home, we are ignoring a form of difference among the family children that at previous periods exerted considerable influence on the mothers' perceptions: the relative severity of the handicap. At this point, however, there was remarkably little difference between the children with "minor" and "major" handicaps in the area of social integration; for all practical purposes, they can be treated as a single group. Thus the story concerns the social history of the family children, regardless of the type or severity of limb-deficiency.

MOTHERS' PERCEPTIONS OF RELATIONSHIP WITH THE
NORMAL COMMUNITY

At the time of the research interviews, most of the mothers had recovered, superficially at least, from the period of social isolation that followed the births and had resumed more or less normal lives in their communities. Considering the extent and intensity of the trauma experienced by most of the women, overt signs of permanent social disruption or change were surprisingly few. Except in a few isolated cases(for example, a mother who left the church, a few women who became less active in community organizations), the permanent scars were not easily visible.[27]

[27] If the scars were not easily visible, however, they were not necessarily absent. The study of the continuing effects of bearing—and in most cases rearing—a deformed child on the personal lives of these women is worthy of detailed consideration; unfortunately, the problem is outside the scope of this project.

The most common reaction is one of physical illness. Almost all the mothers report transitory or relatively permanent disturbance with digestion, sleep, etc. A number report more serious physical problems. To take the most extreme example, one mother who claims that her physical health prior to the pregnancy was good, except for some fatigue, has subsequently had two miscarriages, a kidney operation, elevated blood pressure, eczema on her hands, headaches, and irregular menstruation. In other cases, gall-bladder

In part, this reintegration into the community was aided by the fact that, with time, the communities proved far more able to accept these mothers and children than the mothers had originally expected. It would appear that at least some of the initial environmental horror of the child, and ambivalence about his social status, were linked to both shock, and fear of the unknown. Once the shock wore off, and the community gradually realized that the mother could and would raise the child at home, relatives, friends, and neighbors could accept this *fait accompli* and respond with sympathy.

In this process, the mothers attibute the greatest role to the RIM; the habilitation program embodied a moral authority and a capacity for concrete help that made it the most potent single force in the process of social normalization. But the children's unexpected capacity for personal and social development, and the more positive publicity later given thalidomide children, also greatly facilitated this process.

One aspect of this process of reintegration and habituation was that mothers and children now moved about freely in their com-

---

attacks, ulcers, eczema, and extreme loss of weight (40 lbs.) have been reported.

Difficulties with menstruation and child-bearing are particularly common. Eight mothers mention dysmenorrhoea and amenorrhoea following the births, and two currently desire hysterectomies. Of the ten women who have subsequently become pregnant, five have borne one or more living children; the other five miscarried.

It is possible that these physical problems can be understood as the result of a severe and prolonged stress experience. Similar reactions have been reported for concentration camp victims and for prisoners of war (Chodoff, 1963; Kral, 1951; Kral *et al.*, 1967; Niederland, 1961). All these diverse experiences have the common characteristic of being traumatic without being fully understandable or resolvable.

In the case of these mothers, however, there is a unique element in the fact that the etiology of the trauma lay in a remedy; the illness was iatrogenic. One of the common therapies for illness is the prescription of drugs, but at least five of these mothers are currently afraid to take pills. The most common method of contraception has become the pill, but for a number of mothers this pill is too reminiscent of the other pill.

munities; the initial conflict about how one exposed the child to the stares and questions of others had largely been resolved, at least in the neighborhood and in the immediate social circle of the parents. For one thing, by now most friends and neighbors knew the child, and the sight of the anomalies was an accustomed one. Most of the mothers had, as well, become habituated to the occasional comment or question. Thus, whatever taboos still remained about the child's social exposure were partial and relatively minor ones (for instance, one mother would not take her daughter to the public beach; two others refused to take the children out without prostheses).

Far more difficult was the process of coping with the curiosity of strangers or new acquaintances. At least four mothers still felt uneasy about taking their children to new places.[28] Another mother would respond to questions with the conventional explanation, but then quickly add, "but I have four other normal children at home." For her, exposure of the child's handicap still called into question her own normality.

Nevertheless, the mothers had developed stable, if varied, patterns of coping with this form of environmental curiosity. A few mothers, whose children's anomalies were relatively minor, opted for a policy of oblivion; they expected strangers neither to look, nor to question. Actually, one of these mothers even enrolled the child in nursery school without mentioning the handicap. It was the mothers with seriously disabled children who were most exposed to casual curiosity. They too, however, had developed defensive patterns. Approximately half encouraged questions and preferred to talk about the child rather than have people simply stare and turn away; the other half accepted stares but were annoyed at questions.

Regardless of these variations, almost all the mothers felt very ambivalent about discussing the thalidomide etiology of the anom-

[28] The complexity of the developmental paths followed by these mothers is illustrated once again by this finding. For neither the objective severity of the handicaps, nor the mothers' initial perceptions, nor their current modes of adjustment explain why it is these particular mothers who are most uncomfortable in taking their children to new places. Only in this single reaction do these mothers form a group; in all other respects their reactions differ.

alies. On the one hand, to say that thalidomide was the cause of the deformities lessened the need for lengthy explanations since, by 1966, most people had heard or read about the thalidomide tragedy. On the other hand, the mothers still suffered from the notoriety that thalidomide had conferred on them, and a few still felt very guilty about this etiology. Thus, in general, the mothers felt uncomfortable in introducing this factor but would respond to direct questions. This is just another example of the complexity of the mothers' feelings about the thalidomide aspect of their situation.

In spite of this general atmosphere of good social adaptation, however, there was an undercurrent of tension as the mothers discussed the present situation. In a few cases, the tension could be explained by the idiosyncratic problems that these particular women were facing. One mother, whose child was older than the others, had to face the prospect of school entrance in a few months. Another mother was in the process of coming to grips with her daughter's retardation, and two others knew that their children would undergo serious operations in the next few months. But for the remaining mothers, the tension was not limited to specific, immediate problems; rather, it resulted from three general factors: the residue of their past experiences, their present sense of vulnerability, and their fears of the future.

As we have noted, there were few clear changes in the mothers' social behavior that would indicate the extent of the trauma these women had experienced. And yet, the trauma had left a residue of mistrust and reserve in their relations with other people. As one mother explained it: "Before this I used to meet people with friendliness and I thought everybody was nice; now I am wary and distrustful of people."

The sense of vulnerability was based on the fact that the mothers' present social adaptation depended largely on environmental compliance; a chance remark by a stranger, or the action of a neighbor, could easily upset the delicate balance they had established. All the mothers could recount "unfortunate incidents" resulting from someone's refusal to respect the conventions surrounding the children. In some cases these incidents were relatively banal, as for example, when a man jerked away as a thalidomide child approached him or when a child on a train stared too long. In some cases their potential consequences were more serious, as in the case of a teacher who told a class, which included the brother of the child, that all thalidomide children were monsters who should be put away. But in all cases, the possibility that a traumatic incident could occur anywhere, anytime, and without warning, heightened the mothers' sense of vulnerability and made for a constant atmosphere of tension.

But the potent factor in maintaining the mothers' sense of tension was their fear of the future. For the moment, mothers and children were socially accepted. But would this tolerance endure during the tests of school entry, adolescence, vocational adjustment, and marriage? A community could sympathize with a three-year-old deviant child. But would this community be able to make the special adjustments required for school attendance? Even more important was the question of how the community would react to the deviance when it was embodied not in a "cute" child, but in an adult.

For the children, too, the present was a period of relative normality; most of the children living at home appeared to have been easily integrated by their peers. The wide variation in the children's range of social activities was linked far more to idiosyncratic factors, such as the presence or absence of children their age in the neighborhood, or the closeness of a park, than to the disabilities themselves. In part, this can be explained by the fact that the restrictions on play activities resulting from the handicap, like inability to dress dolls, to throw a heavy ball, or to ride a scooter, were surprisingly few and, at this age, easily tolerated. The neighborhood children would comment freely on the handicap but could assimilate it relatively quickly. For a three-year-old child a playmate's "funny" arms are no more puzzling than many other aspects of his bewildering world, and for him the disability does not have the serious social connotations that it has for the adult. Indeed, none of the mothers found it necessary to use any special inducements to win friends for their children, nor had they encountered any incidents of rejection linked to the handicap.

The precautions and taboos that governed the social activities of the children were subtle ones. For instance, almost all the mothers exerted special care that their children should be attractively dressed; for a thalidomide child, the habitual casual play clothes of children could be interpreted as a sign of neglect.[29] Most mothers chose the children's clothes with special care (such as full skirts for a child with lower-limb prostheses), and a few devoted considerable time to creating special patterns and sewing (for example, capes for children with upper-limb deformities).

A few of the mothers were more cautious than usual in allowing the children the freedom of the street or park and restricted them largely to the yard or balcony. In part, this caution resulted from the children's impaired balance which made them more likely to fall. But at least one mother also worried: "If an accident happened to X, the neighbors would say it's because I didn't care about him."

The prostheses, too, could pose some social problems. Only one mother reported that the neighborhood children were frightened of the hooks; in other cases, children responded with curiosity or indifference. But a number of mothers were concerned that the unexpected strength of the prostheses could transform a childish fight into a potentially dangerous battle.

Surprisingly enough, the most serious restriction of the children's social activities was linked to the seasons. In summer most children managed very well, but in winter the snow could decrease their already shaky balance and, consequently, increase the tendency to

---

[29] In fact, the appearance of these children at the time of the research interviews was striking in that this was by far the most carefully dressed group of children the interviewer has yet encountered. While most of the children were dressed with taste and ingenuity, in a few cases the emphasis on clothes definitely hampered the child's freedom of action. Thus, for one little girl, the researcher working with the children was unable to carry out the usual painting session, because each day the child appeared in a frillier and more elaborate party dress.

fall. As a result, most of the children could play freely with other children during the summer but in winter could only go out when accompanied by an adult.

If the children lagged behind their peers in some respects, in other ways the mothers considered them precocious. The rural mothers emphasized the fact that, by virtue of their participation in the habilitation program, the children had traveled more and been more widely exposed to different social situations than had their siblings or friends. Not all this social experience was considered beneficial, but in some cases the children did display a superficial social maturity beyond their chronological age.

As perceived by the mothers, the social normalization of the family children had progressed extremely well, at least for the time being. But even for the family children there was an undercurrent of tension linked to the children's gradual awareness that they were different. According to the mothers, all the children were aware of the handicaps, but in most cases this realization had been a gradual one rather than a sudden discovery. Few mothers could pinpoint the exact moment at which the child first noticed the handicaps, but all the mothers could cite verbal and nonverbal examples of the children's awareness. In a few cases, the children simply showed it in the course of daily behavior; for example, one little girl, when counting herself and her friends, would always use her little finger to represent herself. In other cases, this awareness was more dramatic, as for example when the little girl who, with her mother, was following a series of exercises on T.V., suddenly burst into tears because her arms were too short to reach her head.

According to the mothers, most of the children were unaware of the social implications of the handicap. But a few used the disability as a manipulatory technique; one boy, for instance, would ask his younger sister to perform disliked tasks because "my arms are too short." And some children manifested their knowledge in ways that were extremely anxiety-provoking for the mothers. Thus, one mother remembers that, as she was bathing her child one night, the child suddenly held out her phocomelic arms and asked: "Do you still love me even though my arms are short?" Another child watched the marriage of her favorite actress on T.V. and then told her mother sadly that she would never be able to marry, "like Helen, because my arms are too short."

In spite of this awareness, most children were relatively indifferent to the cause of the handicap. Most accepted the explanation that they were "born that way" without further questions. A few verbalized the phantasy that their arms would grow as they themselves grew. For the mothers this was a particularly difficult phantasy to deal with, because it was one that many of them had themselves held for a long period of time.

In general, the mothers were made extremely uncomfortable by their children's questions. A few tried to avoid the issue completely. Thus one mother responded to her daughter's question as to why she could not wear gloves with the answer that her hands were too pretty to cover with gloves. This mother was made doubly uneasy by her awareness that habilitation philosophy disapproved of this approach. But, as she put it, "If you had an ugly daughter, would you tell her of her ugliness?" The others tried to respond as best they could, but all were grateful if questions were not forthcoming.

The major source of the mothers' uneasiness was their knowledge that soon they would have to expose the thalidomide etiology. At the time of the research interviews, only one mother had told her child. The others knew they would have to do it in the future. Some planned to do it before school entry, a few expected to postpone it for a few more years, and one or two hoped that maybe it could be hidden forever, even though they realized the incompatibility of this wish with their children's participation in a thalidomide habilitation program. Regardless of the mother's own reaction to the thalidomide etiology—guilt or anger—all were afraid that the children might blame them.

In a few cases, too, the mothers were afraid that the children's awareness of their handicaps could lead to secondary social difficulties. While most mothers were afraid of depression and social isolation, a few mothers expressed the fear that the children might react with aggression. For instance, one mother had the phantasy that her son might be so angry at society that he would become a delinquent.

MOTHERS' PERCEPTIONS OF RELATIONSHIP WITH COMMUNITY
OF HANDICAPPED AND THALIDOMIDE-DEFORMED MEMBERS

Most mothers had changed very little in their attitude toward affiliation with other parents of handicapped children. Only one mother had joined an association of parents of handicapped children. The others preferred to emphasize their children's normality, or else found that their specific experiences were too unique to be aided by membership in this community.

In particular, the mothers were still extremely anxious to avoid identification of their children with the community of mentally retarded children. For instance, at the time of the research interviews, one of the mothers was angry because of a recent incident in which her child had been grouped with retarded children. The mother in question had heard of the swimming program for thalidomide children at the RIM and called the local YMCA to arrange for swimming lessons for her child. The woman in charge of the program was cordial. There was a special swimming group for mentally retarded children, and she was sure that this child would fit beautifully into the group. For the mother, this was extremely threatening because it represented the denial of her child's major claim to normality.[30]

No mother, it would appear, made an effort to initiate her child into the community of the handicapped. Although no mother, upon direct questioning, claimed that she would discourage her child from meeting or playing with other handicapped children, none found it necessary to make any special effort. In general, the impression given

[30] Although this incident reflects the experience of only one mother, the underlying attitude was found among all the mothers. One clear example of their feelings was in their choice of language. The French-speaking mothers, particularly, tended to use the term "normal" for their children, as contrasted with other handicapped children. At first, one might be startled to hear a mother of an obviously deformed child refer to him as "normal," but gradually one realized that the antonym of this term was reserved for the mentally retarded or mentally ill.

was that the mothers greatly preferred to foster their children's integration into the normal community. Affiliation with other handicapped people might prove useful as the child grew older and encountered rebuffs from the normal community, but for the time being it was both threatening and unnecessary to emphasize this aspect of their children's identity.

Relations with other parents of thalidomide children were equally casual. In particular, the mothers of children with relatively minor anomalies felt uncomfortable in this group. Not only did they tend to emphasize their children's normality, but they felt that other mothers might resent them because of their relative "luck." The mothers of more seriously disabled children were, in general, more favorable to the possibility of a parents' group or newsletter, but none was prepared to take the initiative in starting one. The affiliation with the RIM remained a sufficiently strong source of support so that no further group formation was necessary.

In the case of the children the situation was different. In spite of the fact that all these children had been exposed to many adult handicapped people, at the RIM if not in their communities, few children, according to the mothers, made the link between these adults and themselves. A child might comment on the missing limbs of a patient she saw at the RIM, but, according to the mothers, the children manifested no curiosity or anxiety greater than that shown by the average child.

In contrast to this, identification with other handicapped children, particularly other thalidomide children, was far stronger. For instance, one mother recalls that her son watched the picture of an unknown thalidomide child on T.V. and then commented that "he's like me." In another case, a little girl used to carry on long, imaginary telephone conversations with a thalidomide child she had casually met. According to the mother, her daughter liked this child specifically because "she's the only one like me." [31] And a few children had formed friendships with other thalidomide children during

[31] This was the one child who did not participate in the habilitation program and consequently was the only one who had not frequently encountered other thalidomide children.

their common sojourn in the hospital. The mothers reported that sometimes the children would talk about these friends at home. Sometimes, too, they would be disappointed to find during subsequent hospitalizations that their friends were no longer there.

But in general these identifications were limited to the similarity in visual appearance and were only reinforced by sporadic encounters. Only one child in the sample was aware of why these children were similar; the others were still ignorant of their common thalidomide heritage. Moreover, according to the mothers, the children had not yet posed questions about the differences in extent and type of disability.

MOTHERS' PERCEPTIONS OF RELATIONSHIP WITH PROFESSIONAL HELPERS

For most of the mothers, many of the stresses inherent in the habilitation program had been resolved. Some of the most acute problems had been helped by a change in policy. To cite only one example of a "stressful" policy that had been modified, the children were no longer subjected to lengthy hospitalizations unless absolutely necessary. At the time of the research interviews, most of the routine control examinations were carried out on an outpatient basis, with both mother and child staying at a nearby hotel. In other cases the mothers had become habituated to these stresses. Familiarity with hospital staff and routine also greatly facilitated this process of normalization. Thus most of the mothers accepted their visits to the RIM, and a few even welcomed them.

However, close association with the mothers during the week they visited the hospital brought to the fore many less dramatic problems. The need for the out-of-town mothers to leave their families was a frequently repeated event but still a source of anxiety. The mothers' loneliness in Montreal (many of these women did not speak to a single person from the time they left the RIM each day until their return the next morning), the long waits for appointments, and the children's reactions to this disruption in routine were additional stresses. The need to lay out the money for fares, hotel bills, and meals (the parents were not reimbursed until they had returned home and submitted receipts), and to remember to ask for receipts, often in an unfamiliar language, was another problem.

In addition to these difficulties, there were many anxieties connected with their children's progress. Were the arms growing in proportion to the body? Would the child need a change in prostheses? Was another operation to be scheduled? Would the physiatrist, social worker, occupational therapist, and psychological consultant be satisfied with the mother's efforts?

The mothers spoke relatively little of these problems. They mentioned them but, on the whole, considered them of secondary importance compared to the dilemmas that they had faced and would face. Nevertheless, these issues served as a constant reminder that, in spite of the process of normalization, they were still living with abnormality. The difference now was that for many abnormality had become a way of life.

As far as the children were concerned, most of the mothers reported that they reacted with little resistance to a return to the RIM. Once they were reassured that they would not be separated from the mothers, the major source of anxiety had been alleviated. A few even welcomed the prospect of seeing a favorite staff member or meeting old friends.

In a number of cases, however, the children did verbalize their disillusionment with habilitation. For example, one young lad told his mother that he had already come a few times for new arms and hadn't received them; why bother to return? A few children, too, manifested residual effects of their previous hospitalizations; they refused to be separated from their mothers at all while at the RIM and categorically declined to visit the floor where inpatients were housed.

SUMMARY

1. In contrast to the severe problems and conflicts that had characterized previous periods, the period of the research interviews was one of relatively low tension. For the mothers, it was one

where the normal aspects of living received more emphasis than the difficulties associated with abnormality.

2. Mainly, this adjustment was facilitated by the fact that mothers and children were experiencing normalization within their communities in a fashion that had not been anticipated.

3. As a consequence of this normalization, most mothers had little interest in or need for affiliation with the community of the handicapped.

4. In spite of this social adaptation, the mothers still manifested considerable tension. In part, this tension was linked to the many recurrent stresses produced by the handicaps, including visits to the RIM. More important, though, was the mothers' fear that the present social equilibrium was vulnerable and, perhaps, temporary. In addition, the children's growing awareness of their handicaps, and the need for further explanations, were sources of considerable anxiety.

The Future

Next to the interviews on the birth period, discussion of the mothers' future plans and expectations for their children proved the most anxiety-provoking topic introduced. When questioned in detail about the future, the mothers were visibly reluctant to answer, and most indicated that it was an issue they preferred to avoid, even in their own thoughts. A few justified this avoidance on the grounds of the child's youth. Thus, as one mother put it, "I've just finished toilet training X; how can I even begin to think of her marriage?" Many mothers, on the other hand, explained that concern about the future had been one of their major preoccupations in the days following the birth, but gradually they had learned to live on a day-to-day basis. Whatever the reason given, few mothers could easily expose their hopes and wishes.

To some extent there was a realistic factor that explained the mothers' reluctance to formulate detailed plans for the future. The three to four years following these births had been filled with so many complex and unanticipated changes that realistic planning for an equally complex and unknown future became *ipso facto* unrealistic. More than anything else, the rapidly changing nature of reality in the past few years had emphasized for these women that neither the past nor the present provided a reliable guide to the future. Thus, to attempt to predict the future ten or twenty years hence was a waste of energy that might better be conserved for dealing with present problems.

However, the emotional intensity that accompanied this avoidance clearly indicated that the future was not only a complex issue for these women, but also a "loaded" one. Regardless of the mother's past or present perceptions, there was not a single woman in this sample who was able to face the prospect of the future with complete equanimity. On the contrary, the anxiety and tension aroused by any discussion of the future were striking in that this appeared to be a universal reaction within the sample.

In spite of the universality of this tension, the factors underlying it could vary considerably. For one group of mothers, the dilemma of the future consisted of anticipating a normal future for children who were almost, but not completely, normal. For another group of mothers, the tension was linked to the necessity of envisioning an unknown, but obviously abnormal, future for children who were perceived as globally deviant. And for the third group of mothers, the problem became one of assuring an essentially normal future for children who were perceived as seriously deviant in one, but not all, respects. In essence, the key to understanding the mothers' future expectations lay in their present perceptions of the normality–abnormality ratio inherent in their children.

The group of mothers who considered their children as "essentially normal" consisted of five women, all of whom had children classified in the category of minor handicaps. As we have seen, these mothers varied greatly in their initial reactions to their children and, at the time of the research interviews, still manifested considerable heterogeneity in their personal feelings about both the children and the handicaps. But all these children had relatively minor handicaps, and the mothers' experience with the RIM, and their exposure to other thalidomide children, had convinced them that these children did not really belong in the group of the handicapped. Whatever the mothers' past and present tribulations, they hoped that their children could have essentially normal futures. As one mother put it, "I hope that I'll end up by forgetting this whole story."

Because their expectations were so high, even a relatively slight setback could be expected to have serious connotations. Thus, for a mother in this group, the prospect of a child being unable to learn to play the piano, or not being asked to a dance, could pose a serious threat to her wish for normality. But on the whole, the anxiety manifested by these mothers was linked to the child's success or failure in "passing" within the normal community rather than to the problem of open deviance.

At the other extreme, there were three women who considered their children as sufficiently deviant to be excluded from most of the social expectations attached to normal children. Two of these mothers had children who had spent their entire lives in institutions, and the mothers were largely unable to envision what kind of future awaited children who, to them, were grossly abnormal. In the third case, the mother's emphasis on her child's abnormality marked a relatively new development in the mother's perceptions. This mother had taken her child home, but during the intervening years she had become increasingly aware of the many demands that the child's deviancy would make on the family's limited resources. At the time of the research interviews, she was beginning to raise the possibility of institutionalization for this deviant and difficult child. Thus, for all three of these children, the mothers' anticipations of the future tended to emphasize the gulf between their children and normal ones.

The mothers' pessimism concerning their children's potentialities made the prospect of the future a difficult one. And yet, in one respect, this attitude did remove some of the potential for conflict. Because these mothers perceived their children as very deviant, they could hope that the major responsibility for coping with the future lay not with themselves but with governmental and institutional authorities. In a sense, their emphasis on their children's abnormality shifted the onus of the burden from the mother to society. Whatever the future held in store for their children, they would not have to cope with it alone, and possibly not even on a day-to-day basis.

It was for the remaining women in the sample—the twelve who perceived their children as seriously handicapped, but who sought to rear them at home—that the prospect of the future aroused intense ambivalence and conflict. Moreover, it was in this group that the expectations for the future played a key role in the mothers' present adjustment. In order to arrive at their present perceptions these women had undergone a process of radical adaptation in the past; it was the future, however, that would determine whether this adaptation had been successful or worthwhile.

Perhaps the easiest manner of understanding their position is to review the possible solutions they had already abandoned. By the time of the research interviews, three of the solutions that had figured most prominently during the birth crisis had been categorically rejected or reluctantly given up. Thus all these women no longer viewed institutionalization, early death, or total cure as realistic solutions for the problems posed by these children.

Inevitably, there was some variation in the ease with which each of these solutions had been given up. Institutionalization and death were possibilities that appear to have been rejected most conclusively; all these women were insistent that they would continue to rear their children at home, and only one mother mentioned that she still sometimes had the phantasy that her child might soon die. Not surprisingly, the hope for a total cure was the desire that was most reluctantly given up. The revolutionary advances in scientific knowledge in general, and medical treatment in particular, still fed the hope that eventually there might be some revolutionary medical treatment available for these children. But even this hope was no longer a focal point in the mothers' expectations for the future.

If these initial solutions had been gradually abandoned, however, another one had slowly developed in the intervening years. This was the expectation that thalidomide children could escape the usual fate of the stigmatized; the children might continue to be handicapped, but, unlike other types of deviant children (for example, the mentally retarded or the blind), perhaps they could be expected to function eventually as fully integrated members of normal society rather than as second-class citizens.

In large part, this hope resulted from the mothers' participation in the habilitation program with its emphasis on normalization. It had been fostered, as well, by their unexpected success to date in integrating the children in their communities. But whatever the reason, by the time of the research interviews these mothers were committed to rearing handicapped children who would grow up and live, in all essential respects, with the benefits and privileges that society confers on normal people. This was the implicit contract that underlay the mothers' acceptance of living deformed children. In a sense, it can be viewed as the bargain that these mothers had made with fate.

This contract could only be fulfilled in the future. It was the child's adult status that would provide the ultimate criterion for judging whether the goal of social normalization for visibly and seriously deviant children was a viable one. But when the mothers attempted to test these hopes against the existing situation of the adult handicapped people they knew, or their knowledge of the norms of the normal community, multiple difficulties loomed. In addition, of course, the children's own reactions to the stresses of the handicap remained an unknown factor. Thus the future was viewed both as a promised happy ending and as a serious threat. For these mothers the dilemma of marginality, with its inherent conflicts, was a very salient one.

In describing these three modes of perceiving the future, the emphasis has been on the mothers' global perceptions and general expectations. For the three mothers who considered their children to be essentially abnormal, this is a valid mode of procedure, because their perceptions were global ones. The anticipations of the mothers of "normal" children were more complex, but they, too, tended to view the future as a relatively smooth developmental process. For the mothers of the marginal children, however, the future was viewed as a series of individual crises; the unifying link might be the goal of social normalization, but there were many separate steps in this process. Consequently, it is for these mothers that we shall attempt to trace the perceptions of the various phases of the future.

FORMAL EDUCATION

In view of its chronological imminence, it is not surprising that school entry was the aspect of the future that had received the most detailed consideration. At the time of the research interviews, one child was already enrolled in first grade for the coming year, a few were attending nursery school, and the mothers of the rest of the children were being strongly encouraged by the professional staff at the RIM to plan for schooling. This was an issue of considerable concern to all. For the mothers of the marginal children, however, education assumed a unique importance both because they considered it as one of the crucial tests in determining the child's relative normality, and because they viewed extensive education as one of the major modes of compensating for a serious deviance. Whatever its inherent benefits, formal education was perceived as one of the major steps in the difficult battle for social normalization.[32]

Thus, in spite of the heterogeneity among these mothers and children, plans for schooling did manifest a common pattern. None of these mothers was willing to anticipate that her child would receive either no schooling or a type of schooling that she considered

[32] The mothers' emphasis on extensive schooling for their children is particularly interesting, because it illustrates one of the ways in which a change of values in the normal community may influence the mode of dealing with handicaps. Most of these mothers did not have extensive formal education themselves, and education had not been one of their personal life goals. But at the time these interviews were conducted—in the winter and spring of 1966—the Province of Quebec was in the throes of the "quiet revolution," and emphasis on greater educational opportunities was a prominent feature of the social reforms undertaken. Thus, education had become a major goal of the normal community. One wonders whether some of these mothers would have placed the same emphasis on education as a mode of compensating for the handicaps had the situation arisen 25 years earlier.

socially inferior. Consequently, special schools that housed mentally retarded, deaf, or blind children were categorically rejected. Whatever variation existed in the mothers' plans for schooling, the schools they had in mind were to be as good as or better than those attended by the normal child.

This insistence on equality did not necessarily mean identical schooling. Half of these mothers did plan to enroll their children initially in regular schools on the grounds that the children would have to become accustomed to normal society, and school entry constituted the initial step. But the other half planned to send their children to private schools or convents, some for the first year only and others permanently. The reasons given for this choice varied from those who wished the child to learn a second language, to those who believed that the child might receive more individual attention in the smaller classes of a private school. But the basic motivation here was that this type of schooling was believed to be better than average for the needs of this child.

A few of the mothers were willing to consider special schools as a second choice, if their children's integration in regular schools proved impossible. But they made the proviso that these schools must not have the connotation of inferior schools but, instead, must be truly "special," and designed specifically for their children's unique needs. In view of the fact that no mother knew of any existing school that fulfilled these conditions, this option played a very small role in their planning. Rather, the mothers' insistence on the government's responsibility to establish such schools if necessary was utilized mainly as a form of insurance; if, and only if, other schools proved completely unfeasible, then a special school would be another mode of dealing with the difference while escaping the stigma of inferiority.

In considering their children's integration within the school system, the mothers anticipated a number of serious problems. None perceived her child as being sufficiently independent to function within the school without extra help. Toileting, dressing, putting on and removing prostheses, were areas in which all the children would require special attention. In addition, the children with upper-limb deficiencies were expected to have serious difficulty with writing,[33] while the children with lower-limb deficiencies were expected to find stairs a major problem.

But instead of these deficiencies serving as a barrier to regular school attendance, the mothers hoped and expected that the schools would make the necessary adjustments and concessions. Some mothers expected the teacher to provide special help; a few suggested that another child could be assigned as a "companion" for the handicapped one, and one mother was willing to come to the school herself as an aide. The general feeling was that all children this age require some help, and the extra burden of these children was a relatively minor one.

Very few mothers considered intellectual ability as a potential problem in their children's school adjustment. At first sight, this attitude is a surprising one in view of the psychological consultant's finding that a number of these children scored in the borderline or retarded range on formal intelligence tests, and many manifested serious retardation in language. Upon closer examination, however, this attitude becomes more understandable. For one thing, the developmental timetable of these children had been so different in general (for instance, many of the children with upper-limb deformities had initially been seriously retarded in walking, and then had learned to walk well) that present functioning was not considered to be a reliable predictor of future ability. Furthermore, many mothers were unable to assess the relevance of a low I.Q. for school success. But perhaps most important was the fact that intellectual ability, according to the mothers, constituted these children's major claim to normality and their major difference from the stigmatized. To question the child's intelligence posed a major threat to the mother's present adjustment.

Social integration within the classroom was seen mainly as the re-

[33] The process of learning to write is currently being studied in these children by another member of the research team, Mme Francine Bonnier-Tremblay.

sponsibility of the teacher, who was expected neither to neglect the child, nor to single him out, but "to treat him like the others." As one mother put it, "I don't want the school to undo what I've done the last few years." But once again, the premise underlying the concept of equality was not that of identical treatment. The teacher was expected to provide unobtrusively any necessary extra help and to insure that the child was not "picked on" by the other children. She was not expected, however, to permit the child any leeway in escaping academic responsibilities or school rules that were within his competence. Here, too, the ideal policy was viewed as one that would manifest tolerance for the child's deviance, while respecting his basic social normality.

Eventually all these children were expected to go "as far as possible" in school. Depending on the individual mother, this could be interpreted as university education, professional training, or comparable specialized training. But the general wish was that these children would have as much or more formal education than the norm. For a number of mothers this type of education was beyond the family's financial resources, but they expected the government to provide financial assistance, since they considered this goal to be one of the basic components of a successful habilitation program.

In spite of the mothers' emphasis on education as a means of compensating for the handicap, few placed any stress on one type of education that has traditionally been viewed as a consolation for affliction. Most mothers did not consider religious education any more important for these children than for their siblings. In fact, a number of mothers mentioned that they were anxious to avoid the use of religion as a "crutch." As one mother put it, "It's not God who did this, it's the pills." A few, too, were openly hostile toward religious authorities as a result of their own experiences following the birth. But whatever the mother's personal views on religion, it did not appear to provide a viable alternative to secular integration. The ability to endure the stresses of the handicap would have to come from success in this world rather than from the consolation of a future one.

Thus, in the area of formal education, these mothers' tolerance for abnormality was limited. This tolerance was expressed in the choice of "better schools," the hope for special consideration in regular schools, and the desire to provide more extensive schooling than usual. It did not include the prospect of rejection by the school system, nor the possibility that these children might be handicapped intellectually as well as physically. Education was especially important for these children because they were seriously handicapped, but its net result was viewed as an enhancement of normality.

EXTRACURRICULAR ACTIVITIES

In contrast to their relatively precise expectations for formal education, most mothers had given little thought to the children's ability to participate in extracurricular activities. This was not because the mothers considered the issue to be completely unimportant. As one mother put it, "X, too, needs to laugh sometimes." But compared to formal education, this area of activity was considered less crucial for social normalization. Consequently, much less attention was placed on potential difficulties and possible modes of resolution.

To the degree that they did consider the problem, the mothers saw two distinct types of barriers to be confronted: the physical incapacity of the child in performing certain activities, and the social exclusion that might result from this limitation. To the first type of barrier they reacted with uneasy passivity; to the second, with active resistance.

All the mothers in this group anticipated that their children would be physically incapable of participating in some of the recreational and athletic activities undertaken by their peers. The ambiguous consequences of phocomelia, even physically, made it difficult for them to predict precisely what activities would prove impossible for their children. As one mother put it: "What I thought would be impossible she has already done." Moreover, it was still difficult to know in detail how effective the prostheses would eventually prove in circumventing the physical limitations imposed by the handicap. But if the mothers were still very uncertain about what specific problems might occur, all were conscious of the fact that there would be some activities in which their children would be unable to participate.

In spite of this common expectation of difficulty, few mothers had any detailed plans for coping with a child who was excluded from the neighborhood baseball team, for instance. The general policy appeared to be one of "waiting and seeing"; problems would be dealt with as they arose. In part, this passivity in the face of anticipated problems could be ascribed to the mothers' greater tolerance for deviance in this area; play was not perceived to be as crucial as school. A few mothers, for example, were willing to consider special summer camps for handicapped children, in spite of their insistence on "normal" schools.

An additional factor that fostered the mothers' tendency not to plan for this eventuality of exclusion from some play activities was their ignorance concerning alternative techniques. Few mothers had any precise ideas on how to foster substitute activities for a child excluded from "normal" ones. It appeared that once the child failed to meet normal expectations, the mother had no active modes for coping with this deviation beyond hoping that it would not be too extensive or apparent. Only one mother mentioned that she expected to turn to the RIM for help; the others had not even considered this possibility.

If the mothers were prepared to accept the idea that their children might not be able to perform all the activities indulged in by their peers, they were not prepared to accept that their children would not have friends. Once again, the ability to have friends became an important distinction between their children and the stigmatized. As one mother expressed it, "X is better off than retarded children; they have no friends."

In this area, however, the mothers perceived the major responsibility for fostering normalization as belonging not to them but to the children. While all the mothers expected that there would be some incidents of rejection, all were very insistent that the children should not accept second-class citizenship in their peer group.[34] Thus, one mother hoped her child would respond to taunts about the handicap with the retort, "My arms are crippled, but my head's O.K." Other mothers were less specific, but almost all used the same phrase, "It's up to X." It appeared that their children's confidence in their own sense of worth, and their ability to press for equal status, became, for these mothers, one of the basic tests of the socialization techniques they had used.

In general, one can state that the mothers were prepared to tolerate more difference in the area of extracurricular activities than in the area of formal education. But the mothers had few techniques for coping with this difference. And while they were willing to accept that their children would not be physically identical to their peers, they were extremely vehement in asserting their children's basic social equality.

ADOLESCENCE

For almost all the mothers, adolescence was perceived as one of the most difficult periods in their children's growth to adulthood. Not all the possible difficulties were seen as linked directly to the handicap; in accordance with the norms of the general culture, adolescence was believed to mark a difficult transition for all children, normal as well as deviant. But the mothers did feel that adolescence would pose many specific problems for their children, because it was at this period that they expected the pressure for conformity to be greatest and the tolerance for deviation smallest. A number of

---

[34] Some idea of the importance attached to this concept of avoiding second-class citizenship can be gained from an incident reported by one of the mothers. This mother had enrolled her daughter in a ballet class; when she later attended one of the classes, she discovered that the teacher had placed her daughter in the back row and had made no effort to integrate her in the class. According to the mother, her immediate reaction was to "bawl out" the teacher and complain to the directress. Then, however, she took her child home and, "for the first time in her life, I spanked her as hard as I could for accepting a back seat." The child still attends the ballet class but now dances in the front row.

mothers expressed the conviction that, while the birth crisis had been most traumatic for them personally, adolescence would constitute their children's severest trial.

With respect to this time period, the differences between the anticipations of mothers who perceived their children as normal, abnormal, or marginal became relatively slight. The mothers of the almost-normal children could anticipate that there might be fewer or less severe problems, but they, too, believed that, at least for the period of adolescence, the deviance might become significant. The mothers of the abnormal children were, as usual, more pessimistic, but even within their general picture of an abnormal future the prospect of adolescence aroused a special pain.

In spite of their general dread of this period, the mothers tended to be vague in specifying the problems involved. Most mothers simply mentioned factors such as "inability to date" or "feel she doesn't fit in." It would appear, however, that for many mothers the anxiety was augmented by their fear that it was at this time that the children would at last realize fully the social meaning of the difference. And, because of the etiology of the deformities, it was thought that this might be the time when the children would turn upon their mothers for what they had done. A few mothers were able to hope that the mother-child relationship would remain close even during this period, but, for most, the feeling was that adolescence would not only mark their children's estrangement from society, but also from them. The mothers, therefore, would not only have to watch their children's suffering, but would also have to bear the burden of knowing that the children blamed them for their plight.

In addition, the mothers' dilemma was intensified by the belief that, as their children reached sexual and social maturity, they themselves would become relatively powerless to help and protect them. A few mothers hoped that the RIM might be able to step into the breach; what the mother could no longer do, professionals might be able to accomplish by psychological advice or formal psychotherapy. Others were resigned to the fact that adolescence would constitute a severe stress period.

It may be the mothers' expectations of powerlessness during adolescence that led some of them to consider a technique that was radically different from their present attitudes. When talking about the problems of adolescence, a number of mothers suggested that, at this time, the child might derive help from affiliation with other handicapped children, particularly the other thalidomide children. Not only would the child see that "others were worse off than him," but he would also derive support and encouragement from others who were facing the same problems.

In describing this potential solution one must emphasize that consideration of this compensatory technique was limited mainly to the mothers of the severely handicapped children, and not all the mothers of even these children thought they might adopt it. Since for none of the mothers of family children did permanent integration within the community of the handicapped appear as a viable way of life, this would constitute a betrayal of their hope for normalization. But it was hoped that affiliation with other physically handicapped adolescents would serve mainly as a temporary prosthesis to counteract some of the effects of social isolation during adolescence.

In spite of the fact that the mothers were apprehensive about the trials of adolescence, they did not consider it as a permanent threat to the process of social normalization. In common with most parents of adolescent children, they could hope that this, too, would pass. Adolescence, because of its specific social stresses, would highlight their children's difference, but once adulthood was reached, it was felt, the pressure for conformity would decrease. Thus, if the children could be helped to avoid secondary scars (for example, retreat into withdrawal, or the converse, rebellion), they would be able eventually to find a niche in normal society.

VOCATIONAL ADJUSTMENT

As would be expected, the mothers' anticipations of their children's eventual occupational possibilities were still very vague. A few mothers responded that they hadn't given much thought to this problem. Others were concerned, but the choice of a specific career would depend on the child's interests and abilities. Only a few mothers expressed definite preferences, and even these goals were quite broad.

In some respects, the mothers' uncertainty about eventual occupational choice was similar to the plight of any mother of a preschool child who attempts to predict his future ten or fifteen years hence. For to the degree that vocational selection was viewed as an adult choice, it was one that might not depend solely, or even mainly, on the mother's preferences. A mother had the right and responsibility to choose an elementary school for her child, but, if she was prepared to accord him adult status eventually, her role was much more limited in the area of vocational choice. And secondly, many mothers mentioned that it was difficult for them to discuss vocational opportunities in detail, because they had not yet reached this developmental crisis with any of their children. When they considered the problems of latency and adolescence, many mothers could use their experience with older siblings as a guide. In the area of vocational choice, however, their personal experience was too different and remote to help them direct the children in what they perceived as a rapidly changing world.

In addition to the general problems having to do with occupational choice, there were specific difficulties linked to the handicaps. Thus, a very salient factor in the mothers' uncertainty was the inability to predict the children's physical capacities as they grew older. Would the handicap become better or worse as the child grew? How much would surgical intervention or the prostheses ameliorate functioning? How much time would the child have to spend in the hospital for treatment?

The mothers' vocational expectations, of course, were heavily dependent on the children's success or failure in meeting earlier crises. For most of the mothers, the successes of the preschool period had led them to expect integration within the regular school system. Now the anticipations of vocational choice would depend on how well the children met the academic and social challenges of schooling.

Thus the subject of vocational aspiration was surrounded by an aura of indecision and uncertainty. Nevertheless, this area was a fundamental one. Even more than formal education, the mothers judged the ability to compete successfully in the world of work as a crucial test of their children's social normality. According to their perceptions, an interesting profession or a responsible job was a fundamental prerequisite for ensuring social status. Moreover, intense and successful involvement in work would constitute one of the major modes of compensation for missed social and personal opportunities, such as failure to marry. Thus, both for its social and therapeutic implications, these mothers emphasized successful vocational adjustment as one of their major aspirations for their children.

It was the mothers' attempts to define what they meant by vocational success that revealed the many contradictions and ambiguities underlying this concept. Perhaps the most common feeling was the belief that a successful job implied a high-status one; ideally, the child's occupational achievement should arouse the respect and admiration of the normal community. Moreover, while the mothers were willing to accept that the children's physical capacities might impose some limits on choice, none was willing to anticipate that the child's appearance might close some doors to him. Even a mother whose child manifested severe deformities of all four limbs, as well as absence of the tongue, did not consider this a barrier to occupations that would require continuous contact with the public. In this respect, the mothers' expectations emphasized their children's normality.

But if the mothers anticipated that their children would benefit from the status conferred by prestige occupations, they did not necessarily expect that their children would fulfill all the demands usually imposed by this type of job. A number of mothers emphasized that their children could not be expected to work hard, either mentally or physically; the ideal job would be "light, but interesting." And while a few mothers did think of specific skills that these children would bring to the job market, such as facility in languages, others were far more interested in the appearance of social normality rather than in any real productivity.

An interesting example of this tendency is the mother who hoped that her child would find a job cheering up physically handicapped people in a rehabilitation center; by the example of his successful existence, this boy would serve as an inspiration to others. According to the mother, this type of work would have the prestige of social work without the demands of this profession. The fact that this appearance of normality would imply a professionalization of the abnormality did not appear to be an important consideration for the mother.

In one respect the mothers' aspirations for vocational normality differed markedly from normal expectations. Most of these mothers did not consider financial independence an important criterion of their children's vocational success. Many hoped that their children might eventually be able to support themselves completely, but if this proved impossible, either because of the child's limitations or the additional costs associated with the handicap, the parents were prepared to consider financial subsidies, by either the parents or government pensions. It is interesting to note, however, that in referring to government pensions the mothers used the analogy of veterans' pensions rather than the type of allowance made to the blind. Once again, the implication appeared to be that these children were to be treated as those who had suffered in the service of society rather than as recipients of charity.

Like the wish for formal education for their children, successful vocational adjustment constituted another of these mothers' major aspirations. In this area, tolerance for abnormality appeared limited to ruling out certain types of occupations because of their physical unsuitability. But in stressing vocational normality, the mothers appeared concerned more with the social appearance of normality than with the child's productivity.

MARRIAGE AND PARENTHOOD

In contrast to their general aspirations for social normalization, in the area of marriage and parenthood the mothers of the marginal children anticipated that their children would deviate from the norm. Only one mother in this group emphasized marriage as one of her basic aspirations for her daughter; the other mothers were uncertain or doubtful.

Even if these children did eventually marry, most of the mothers were resigned to the fact that their spouses would probably be handicapped, too. Only three of these mothers maintained that the only acceptable marriage would be with a normal person. The other nine saw marriage with another handicapped person either as the most desirable option ("They'll have nothing on each other"), or else as the only realistic possibility ("He's too handicapped to marry a normal person").

A number of mothers expressed the hope that perhaps the child need not marry either a "normal" person or a "handicapped" one; the conflict might be resolved by choosing a partner from the thalidomide population. Once again, affiliation with the thalidomide population appeared to be a way of escaping the dilemma of normality–abnormality. If the child could not fit into the normal community, then this alternative would permit him to be classified as "special," rather than as socially inferior.

As can be seen, the mothers of the marginal children were unsure of whether, or what type of person, their children would marry, and yet, in one respect, their expectations were clear. If their children were to marry, it must be the type of marriage in which they would be cared for, protected, and cherished. This emphasis on marriage as a relationship in which the child would find a new form of dependency may be linked to the sex of the children (most of the children were girls), or it may be associated with the mothers' belief that the children's handicaps would create a state of perpetual dependency. But it is significant that only one mother—and this was a mother of one of the boys—insisted that her child must achieve physical, social, and financial independence as a condition for marriage.

In their expectations of parenthood for their children, we find one of the rare instances where the attitudes of the mothers of boys differ sharply from those of girls. Since there are only two boys to ten girls within the group of children perceived as marginal, these data must be approached with caution, but, nevertheless, the difference is interesting. The mothers of the boys are emphatic that, if their children are able to marry, then there are no further barriers to parenthood. In fact, one mother hoped that once her son fathered a child then "maybe he'll be equal at last." The mothers of the girls, on the other hand, were much less certain of their daughters' capacity for maternity. Two mothers raised the possibility that their daughters might be physically incapable of bearing children. Another mother was worried whether her daughter might not bear handicapped children. And one mother posed the question, "How will she hold a child in her arms?"

Even when the mothers did consider that their daughters might bear children, most suggested that one or two would be ample. For some mothers within this group, the devaluation of large families may have been one of the by-products of their own disillusionment with maternity. But for others it expressed the desire to give these children the appearance of normality without imposing all the demands inherent in this state. Thus one child would be sufficient to give the daughter the personal fulfillment and social status of maternity, without subjecting her to the burdens of a larger family.

The area of marriage and parenthood appeared to constitute an exception to the mothers' usual demand for social equality. More than in any other respect, in their expectations for marriage the mothers of the marginal children were prepared to accept that their children would remain deviant. Perhaps the difference in the mothers' expectations can be explained by the fact that they viewed marriage not only as a social relationship, but also as a personal one. One can demand respect and equal opportunity far more easily from society at large than one can demand love from an individual person. Moreover, to the degree that the mothers tended to identify with the prospective spouses, the difficulties loomed large. As one mother expressed it, "How can I expect someone to marry X, when I couldn't marry someone like him?" A mother could learn to love a child with missing arms or legs, but it appeared difficult for her to imagine that a prospective husband or wife could do this, too.

SUMMARY

1. For all the mothers in this sample, the anticipation of the future aroused some conflict and anxiety, but the nature of the conflict appeared to vary with the mother's present perceptions of her child's normality and abnormality.

2. The three mothers who perceived their children as essentially abnormal had the least-detailed expectations for their children's future. They assumed that it would be very different from the developmental path of normal children, but they didn't really know what form this difference would take. Moreover, they expected "professionals" to assume most or all of the burden of coping with this future.

3. The five mothers who perceived their children as essentially normal envisioned a future in which their children would function largely as normal, even though they still manifested minor handicaps. The social significance of the deviance was expected to be strongest during adolescence, but, apart from this, the mothers anticipated an almost-normal developmental process.

4. The twelve mothers who perceived their children as marginal placed the highest stakes on the future and manifested the greatest ambivalence toward it. The basic causes for their conflict appeared to be (a) that they recognized the handicap to be sufficiently severe to have serious social repercussions, and (b) that they considered the goal of social normalization not only as a necessary ideal for their children, but also as a justification for their past and present struggles.

5. Because of their particular orientation toward the future, these mothers tended to perceive it as a series of successive crises rather than as a global whole. In general, formal education and vocational adjustment were viewed as areas where social equality could be achieved, in spite of the differences linked to the handicap.

Social activities during latency and the time period of adolescence were anticipated as problem areas, but the mothers viewed their children's difficulties here neither as permanent, nor fundamental. Marriage and parenthood, on the other hand, were the areas where the greatest permanent deviance was expected.

6. The complexity and inherent conflicts linked to living with this form of marginality were manifested not only by these mothers' segmented view of the future, but also by the multiple meanings attached to the term "normality." As used by the mothers of the marginal children, the concept of normality could mean the attainment of a social facade, or the appearance of normality, rather than the ability to fulfill the full range of responsibilities and achievements usually implied by this term. To cite only one example, the mothers of marginal children were insistent on the need for vocational "normality." To them, however, the basic criterion of success appeared to lie neither in the child's real productivity, nor in his financial independence, but mainly in the appearance of normality.

Conclusions

Our concern here has been with one aspect of the bearing and rearing of a congenitally limb-deficient thalidomide child, that is, the mothers' perceptions of the social implications of such a birth. Thus the basic questions that now confront us are the following: Were there any characteristic social problems that faced these mothers of deviant children? How important were these social repercussions in the mothers' total experience of maternity? Were there any common elements in the mothers' modes of perceiving and responding to these challenges? If so, how can these patterns be described and interpreted?

Perhaps the clearest finding to emerge from the mass of data presented in this chapter is that the social aspect constituted an essential element of these women's maternity. For none of these mothers did the deviance of the child lead to the formation of a mother-child relationship existing in a vacuum, without reference to a larger social environment. On the contrary, at every point in the developmental process, the mother's perceptions of her ability or inability, success or failure, in rearing this child were greatly influenced by social criteria.

Examples of this are numerous. Even at the moment of the mother's initial awareness of the fact that she had borne a deformed baby, her attitudes toward this crisis were based not only on her own feelings, or on the physical diagnosis of the child, but also on the social prognosis. It was the social implications of normal intelligence, rather than its medical relevance, that made this factor play such a primary role in the birth crisis. Moreover, the importance of the social consequences of the handicap increased, rather than decreased, with time. The mothers who sought to rear their children at home were able to abandon their early desires for death or total cure, but the hope that was substituted was that of a meaningful social existence for this deviant child. At the time of the research interviews, when the mothers expressed the conviction that "things had become easier" since the shock of the birth, they were not simply manifesting a passive resignation acquired by habituation, nor even referring primarily to the improvement in their children's physical capacities. Rather, the basis for their optimism lay mainly in the fact that the children had achieved a degree of social integration within the normal community that, in most cases, was far greater than the mothers had originally believed possible. The importance of the social factor was also projected into the future. When the mothers discussed their hopes and fears for the future, they spoke mainly in terms of social potentialities and problems. The phenomenon of mother love is too complex to be fully explained by the social factor, or any other single factor, but the social environment cast a large shadow on the past, present, and future lives of these mothers and children.

It is their common attempt to come to grips with the social aspects of the deformities that permits us to delineate a modal developmental pattern for the varied experiences of a group of dissimilar women. The birth of a deviant baby called into question not only personal values, but also social ones; the attempt to resolve the resulting problems was heavily influenced not only by the specific personality of each mother, but also by the existing social forces. Thus, these women's experiences of maternity can be described in terms of the social crises they faced, and the social forces they responded to. Obviously, the mothers' individual interpretations of the crises varied, as did the modes of resolution, but the common element in their diverse experiences lay in the fact that all were confronted by a fairly similar series of social challenges and possible modes of resolution.

The conflict of social values aroused by the birth of a deviant baby is a dual one. The first aspect involves the social status of the deviant child himself. If a child is different, how do the social norms interpret this difference? (Should this difference lead to the destruction of the child, his segregation from normal society, or is he still a member of the normal social community, and if so, on what terms?) According to the mothers' perceptions, the existing social norms provided no clear guidelines for this problem; by the accident that caused these women to bear different children, they had tumbled into a social void. On the one hand, they did not perceive their culture as officially sanctioning the physical destruction of a deviant baby. This alternative did emerge in a *sub rosa* fashion, but it was one that was neither publicly discussed, nor approved. On the other hand, the mothers perceived the culture as manifesting very clearly that the physically handicapped baby was viewed as different socially, as well as physically; he could not expect an automatic integration within the social group. The mothers' perceptions of the manner in which they were told about and shown their babies, their experience of initial environmental anxiety, ambivalence, and confusion, underlined the fact that this baby could not be perceived or treated in the fashion of a normal baby. There was a relatively clear social prohibition against killing the baby, but few guidelines on how, or even where, he was to live.

The social ambiguity of the baby raised another basic conflict concerning the social status of his mother. The experience of maternity is not only a source of personal gratification, but also fulfills a vital social need. Society requires some manner of caring for its dependent children until they can eventually become contributing members of the social group. In the usual circumstances, the mother functions as the representative of society in assuming the task of primary caretaker of the child. Because this activity is viewed as a socially valuable one, the mother-child relationship is accorded unusual social approval and protection, and the social status ascribed to motherhood is an elevated one. The job of caring for a baby may require some sacrifice of personal goals, but the social recompense for devoting one's efforts to helping someone else grow is obtained by the mother's participation in the successes of her child. In this fashion, the interests of mother and child are rendered harmonious.

In the case of the deviant child, however, the social norms are far less clear. According to the mothers' perceptions, their children's deviance did not permit the mothers automatically or fully to disown them. The defensiveness and anxiety manifested by the mothers who institutionalized their children reflects the guilt they felt at having violated what was to them, too, a basic social norm, that is, the mother's responsibility for the child. But if the mothers did not feel that society permitted them to escape the task of maternity, they also did not feel that for them this activity was granted the habitual aura of social approval. A mother whose maternity aroused horror and shame, rather than pride, was deprived of one of the major benefits of maternity. Moreover, she could not bask in the reflected glory of her child's social success but must accept the fact that, in many respects, the fruit of her maternity was judged to be a social failure. And to the degree that mother and child were viewed as a social unit, the child's social failure could lead to a devaluation of the mother's social status. Thus, instead of the social interests of mother and child being identical, they could in this case become antagonistic and even irreconcilable.

These two conflicts involve sufficiently general values that they are probably encountered by most mothers of deviant children within the general context of Western culture. In the case of the particular sample used in this study, however, there were a number of specific social circumstances that not only influenced the form in which the conflicts were perceived, but also helped to provide a modal pattern of resolution. In particular, there were three factors that served as important social forces in shaping the pattern of the mothers' perceptions: the visibility of the deformities at birth, the thalidomide etiology that led to the formation of an unusual habilitation program, and the nature of the deformities, that is, limb-deficiency. The first factor, the immediate visibility of the deformities, was a negative one in that it tended to increase the initial anguish and conflict. The second factor, the habilitation program, was, on the other hand, the most important single force in the social normalization of abnormality. The third factor, the social meaning of limb-deficiency, was more ambiguous and could operate in both directions; compared to other deformities, limb-deficiency could be interpreted both as a sign of relative social normality or abnormality. Thus the mothers' experience of the social aspects of this type of maternity was shaped by one force that initially lowered their expectations, one that subsequently raised them, and one that could reinforce either tendency.

Not all the mothers in the sample perceived or reacted to these social influences similarly. Essentially, our sample can be divided into three main subgroups. The major pattern—both because it involved the largest number of women, and because the children of the mothers in this category manifested the most typical form of thalidomide limb-deficiency—appears to depend on whether the child's limb-deficiency was classified as major rather than minor, and whether the mother would rear the child at home. It was the mothers fitting this major pattern who faced the social dilemma of thalidomide limb-deficiency in its most acute form and who became most receptive to the mode of reparation offered by society, that is, to the values of the habilitation program. It is to the women in this group, then, that the title of this chapter, the social normalization of abnormality, is most applicable. In addition to this modal pattern, however, there were two alternative patterns. The women in these two subgroups followed different courses, either because their children were medically and socially different from the rest (that is, their handicaps were classified as minor), or because they themselves decided to diverge from the general stream at a given point (that is, even after the habilitation program, they decided against bringing their children home). We shall examine the modal pattern first, and then consider the two alternative patterns.

The social conflict aroused by the deviant child was perceived by the mothers in the modal group at an unusually early stage and in an intensified form because their children's handicaps were not only congenital, but also clearly visible at birth. Because the mother had no prior knowledge of this child and had made no specific commitment to him as an individual, she was more clearly exposed to the conflict between her interests and those of the child. On the one hand, her lack of knowledge of the child left her freer to imagine him as a "hopeless monster," and to focus instead on her own tragedy as a deprived mother. On the other hand, the lack of specific commitment left her more open to consider the various alternatives to assuming the responsibility for rearing him, whether it be institutionalization or death. A mother who wished for the child's death in this situation could view these murderous wishes as directed toward an unknown, unwelcome stranger rather than as toward *her* child.

But conflicting with these wishes of ridding oneself of an unwanted child were the mothers' feelings about the concept of a child in general and the possible libidinal investment in the child made during pregnancy (cf. Solint and Stark, 1961). In a sense, the mothers were faced with the conflict between their commitment to a child, and their lack of desire for this particular child. And it was the fact that the conflict was apparent at the moment in which active maternity began that made it emerge in such an acute form.

For the environment, too, the visible nature of the deformities at birth appeared to have created a unique conflict situation. When a doctor is called upon to treat an older deviant child, the mother and child already form a social unit. In such circumstances the doctor can view the child as a primary patient and ignore the conflict between the interests of the mother and those of the child. But the doctor who delivered a visibly deviant child was immediately drawn into the social crisis, because, instead of treating one patient, he was confronted by the conflicting needs of two: the mother and the child. Moreover, as we have seen, medical ethics provide no simple answer for the moral and social issues posed by such a crisis. Thus, instead of being able to help the mother through the ordeal, the professionals involved appear to have reacted largely in terms of their own anxiety and ambivalence. Not only was the mother deprived of the help she needed, but the anxiety manifested by the environment reinforced the acuity of her own conflict.[35]

As we have seen, not all the women in this group perceived the birth crisis as a conflict situation aroused by a living deviant child. Some mothers were able to escape the conflict initially by hoping that this situation would soon be resolved by the death of the baby. Other mothers could find some initial relief in minimizing the extent or the implications of the deviancy. But while all the mothers may not have been confronted by the conflict in its acute form, all began their maternity on a note of pessimism. At best, the mothers could feel that the situation left some loopholes for hope; none was able to feel that this was the ideal form of maternity.

The mother's return home from hospital, with or without her baby, did not mark a final resolution of the social dilemma, but it did lead to a form of "privatization." The locus of the conflict shifted from hospital to home, and from the official representatives of society (for example, the doctors and religious authorities) to the mother. In a sense, society could now treat the social problem mainly as a personal tragedy. Until the children reached school age there was no need for society as an institutionalized force to intervene; instead, the ambiguity of the social norms concerning physical deviancy could be ignored by everybody except the families directly concerned. Thus, as the mothers sought to test their own and their

[35] It is this factor that may help to explain why mothers are often not told of congenital handicaps that are evident to professionals at birth (cf. Prechtl, 1963). In this case, postponement not only delays the problem, but may change the nature of the problem.

babies' acceptability within the community, they were not confronted by any clear social forces, either positive or negative, but only by the varied reactions of individuals. More than at any other point in the developmental history, the record here becomes one of a group of different women with different babies in different communities.

It is difficult to judge how development would have proceeded had not a new social factor intervened at this time: awareness of the consequences of thalidomide usage. As we have seen, as individuals the mothers reacted to the thalidomide etiology of the deformities in very different ways. But thalidomide did introduce a common social mode of resolution in that it led to the formation of a unique government habilitation program founded on a particular set of social values. Thus, once again, the women were confronted by a common social force.

In a sense, the habilitation program can be viewed as a form of response to the two basic social conflicts aroused by the maternity of a deviant child. The social ambiguity of the child was confronted by reinterpreting the meaning of his difference. In the first place, the different child, instead of being devalued by society, was now entitled to its special consideration. In response to this attitude, an elaborate and expensive program was developed to reduce the area of disability. But even more important, this difference was not interpreted as constituting a permanent barrier to the child's eventual social normality. On the contrary, the basic premise underlying the program was the conviction that the thalidomide child could assume his birthright as a member of normal society.

For the mothers, too, the implications of these values were considerable. Now the mothering of a deviant child could be undertaken in the context of social approval; the truly successful mother became the one who sought to rear a deviant child not with shame, but with pride. Moreover, the RIM, as the institutional embodiment of these values, was ready to participate actively in the task of rearing the child.

This potential solution was not without its own inherent conflicts.

For one, the social values embodied in the habilitation program reflected the consensus of only a part of society rather than the whole. The RIM might advise the mother to exhibit her child with pride; it could not prevent a stranger from regarding the child with horror and the mother with disapproval. In this sense, the RIM introduced a potential conflict between the mothers' perception of its values, and their judgment of the mores of the communities in which they lived.

Secondly, the RIM was an institutionalized embodiment of society's recognition that the child's deviancy should be viewed and treated as a social problem rather than as a purely personal one. But the treatment of physical handicaps as a social problem was largely limited to the children; this perspective did not extend to the mother-child relationship. When the mother encountered problems in rearing the child, a retreat was made to the safer and older clinical model. The mother's difficulties, in contrast to the child's problems, were viewed almost completely as personal conflicts (conflicts having to do, that is, with acceptance, guilt), rather than as at least partly determined by the social stresses she was experiencing. And so the very institution that sought to make the maternity of a deviant child a source of pride inadvertently added to the burden of guilt and anxiety that these mothers were already carrying.

The conflicts aroused by the RIM help to explain why almost all the mothers—even those who rated it most successful—viewed their integration into the habilitation program as a stress experience. But regardless of its defects, the RIM was, on the whole, successful in changing the mothers' perceptions of the social implications of the handicap. By virtue of their affiliation with the habilitation program, these mothers were given a new basis for normalizing the abnormalities. In spite of the fact that the RIM was a treatment center for the disabled, affiliation with it did not lead to the formation of a new society of handicapped or thalidomide individuals. Rather, the RIM became the symbol of normal society's concern for these children, and its values were used as a wedge for demanding from society that deviant children need not become stigmatized ones. If society as represented by the Minister of Health set up an expensive and extensive habilitation program for these children, then society as represented by the Minister of Education could not refuse these children school admission. In short, if society was prepared to make this form of investment in the habilitation of these children, it could not then deny them the logical consequences of the habilitation program.

The most radical result of the mothers' participation in the habilitation program lay in the change in their social expectations.[36] A thalidomide child need not follow the identical course of a normal child; he might even meet incidents of individual or general rejection (for example, failure to marry). But he did have the right to expect the respect and consideration of society as different but equal.

While the visibility of the handicaps at birth, on the one hand, intensified the initial social conflict and distress of the mothers, the habilitation program, on the other hand, led these mothers to expect and demand from society more than many mothers of handicapped children can hope for (cf. Barsch, 1968; Ehlers, 1966, for a comparison). These mothers began their maternity with a relatively low level of expectation, but four years later they had reached a relatively high level of expectation.

This process of change was faciliated by the fact that the major deformity manifested by the children (that is, limb-deficiency) was itself very socially ambiguous and open to different interpretations. All physical handicaps have some social repercussions, but not all handicaps will have necessarily the same ones. Limb-deficiency of

36 As will be recalled, there was one mother who met the two criteria for inclusion in the modal group—a child manifesting a severe deformity and the decision to rear him at home—who did not join the habilitation program. This appeared to make little difference in the mother's perceptions of the social implications of the handicap. It seems that the social values propagated by the RIM exerted as strong an influence on her expectations as they did on the mothers who became formal members of the program.

the thalidomide type was a sufficiently rare and unknown condition that the social meaning attached to it was even more ambiguous than that ascribed to other handicaps.[37]

At the outset, the major interpretation of limb-deficiency was a negative one. Not only was this form of deformity clearly visible, but the horror and anxiety elicited by missing limbs appears to have been unusually strong. An example of this is the frequent use of the label "monster" in referring to these children. But even at the beginning, there were some indications that this form of deformity could be interpreted in a more hopeful light. Thus, limb-deficiency did not destroy the hope that the fundamental human qualities of intelligence and feeling were unaffected, and, consequently, these children fulfilled at least one essential claim to normality. As the mothers' success in social integration increased, and the effects of the habilitation program became apparent, this tendency to favorable interpretation of the handicap increased. Limb-deficiency was perceived as the "most normal" of all abnormalities, and the mothers were insistent in emphasizing the social gulf between their children and other handicapped ones.

The ability to differentiate limb-deficiency from other handicaps was facilitated by two other factors: the rarity of the condition, and the small number of children involved. Because the known cases of limb-deficiency prior to the thalidomide tragedy were few, no specific institutional structures had developed to accommodate this type of condition. And so, even at the moment of birth, one of the factors mitigating against institutionalization was that most of the existing institutions were designed mainly for the mentally retarded and not for the physically handicapped with normal intelligence. It was the lack of appropriate institutions, rather than any optimism

[37] Barsch (1968) has recently undertaken some research into the degree of social stigma attributed to various types of handicap. In his list of ten common handicapping conditions of childhood, however, there is no mention of congenital limb-deficiency. Even among "exceptional" children, limb-deficiency is an exception.

about their status, that led some of these babies to be taken home initially. At other crisis points the same phenomenon reoccurred. The mothers' ability to press for "normal" schooling was reinforced by the fact that in most localities the available special classes are largely meant for retarded children. If the choices available to a school board are limited to placing a physically handicapped child with normal intelligence either in a regular class or in a class with retarded children, the chances are good that the physical difference will be given less weight than the intellectual similarity.

In addition, even the dramatic thalidomide tragedy provided no more than two dozen limb-deficient children scattered throughout the Province of Quebec. Because their number was so small, it was possible to view these children as "exceptions" rather than as a cohesive group. For most communities, there was only one such child to be assimilated. A school board considering placement had to think only of the effect of one child in a class rather than of ten or twenty.[38]

It is these factors that help to explain why—in spite of the fact that thalidomide limb-deficiency was the most heavily publicized and intensively discussed form of physical handicap in recent history—the mothers never really perceived their children as belonging to the general community of the handicapped. At the beginning, their experiences were too different to permit easy assimilation. Subsequently, this initial isolation was transformed into a desire for affiliation with the normal community. Some mothers could use the potentiality for affiliation with the thalidomide population, or with the general population of the handicapped, as a refuge for certain time periods or in certain areas. But to have affiliated completely with the community of the handicapped was antagonistic to their basic premise of social normalization.

This history also helps to explain the particular type of tension

[38] The importance of this factor is illustrated by the fact that in Germany, where the numbers involved have been much larger, the social aspects of the problem have been treated very differently.

experienced by the mothers at the time of the research interviews. Whatever their initial despair or depression at the tragedy that had confronted them, four years later these women no longer regarded themselves solely as miserable victims of a tragic fate. Through the circulation of a dangerous drug, society had severely afflicted them. But by virtue of a unique habilitation program, society had issued them a pledge that reparation would be made. To engage in the maternity of thalidomide children was not a socially futile act. These mothers were not excluded from the hope that their children would eventually live meaningful lives in normal society. And yet, the mothers were still unsure how, or to what degree, this promissory note would be fulfilled in the future. In a sense, these women were extremely anxious about the future, not because they were hopeless, but because their hopes were so high.

In describing this modal pattern, we have been synthesizing the experiences of mothers whose histories differed at many points. Not only did the mothers' initial reactions and expectations vary, but the moment at which the decision was made to rear the child at home varied also—from one day to sixteen months following birth. And yet, by the time the research interviews took place, it was apparent that these individual variations exerted remarkably little influence on the nature of the mothers' social expectations. Regardless of the mother's point of departure, or the particular route she had traveled, all these women arrived at fairly similar destinations. By their decision to rear physically deviant children with the expectation of social normality, they had undertaken to live with a very complex form of marginality. What distinguished them from the other women in the sample was that, by the accident of circumstances and by their own decision, they continued to live in a situation embodying the tension of partial normality and partial abnormality in its most acute form.

In contrast to this group, there were five women whose children differed from the others in that their handicaps were classified as relatively minor compared to the rest of the thalidomide sample. Four of these women followed a similar course in their perceptions of the social repercussions of this form of birth.[39] Perhaps the major difference in the situation of the mothers of children with minor handicaps lay in the fact that they were not confronted with clearly deviant children, but with children who were judged essentially normal and yet different. These children were marginal not only to the normal community, but also to the thalidomide one. Thus the conflicts of these women tended to be far more subtle, if not less acute, than those of the other mothers.

Some indices of the different situation of these particular mothers were already apparent at the time of the birth crisis. As we have seen, these women could experience as great a personal shock at the news of their children's deformities as did the mothers of the more severely deformed ones; nor was the professional and environmental reaction to them and their children completely devoid of anxiety and confusion. And yet the mothers were given far less permission to express their distress, and the choices open to them were more restricted. As we have seen, professionals, family, and friends tended to treat their plight much more casually; the emphasis was more on the instrumental needs of the baby than on the affective crisis of the mother. Moreover, when a baby is judged to manifest minor deviations, the approbation for institutionalizing him or wishing him to die is lessened. It is significant that all these women took their children home, though in some cases this was contrary to their personal inclinations.

The same problem of slight difference continued once these mothers and children returned home. Whatever the upheaval in their lives, it was not as clearly visible. The mothers were not completely alienated from their communities; the children were neither institutionalized nor hidden from view. Moreover, the hope was strong that surgical intervention might produce a total cure. On the

---

[39] The fifth woman was the mother who came from a culture in which even a minor physical handicap was perceived as a major disaster. She reacted differently from the other women in this group, because for her the most salient factor, in terms of social implications, was not the extent of the handicap, but the mores of her particular cultural group.

social plane, then, these mothers were still living in the culture of normality; they had not been faced yet by the radical reorientation provoked by a grossly deviant child. And yet, apart from their personal anguish, there were constant subtle reminders that if their children were almost normal, they were not completely so.

In their relationship with the habilitation program, these women again constituted a marginal group. On the one hand, they were deprived of the major social benefit of the RIM—the reinterpretation of the meaning of social deviance—because they had never fully recognized their children as deviant. On the other hand, they could not separate from the habilitation program completely, because neither conventional medical treatment, nor the normal community, could promise them that their children would achieve full physical and social normality.

By the time of the research interviews, these mothers still expressed a high level of social expectations for their children. Time had brought disillusionment and disappointment in some of their initial expectations, but it had not destroyed their basic premise that these children were almost normal. And yet, whatever these mothers' aspirations for the future, they were characterized by a different quality from those of the mothers in the modal group. For one thing, their hopes for the future did not mark as radical a departure from their past expectations. Consequently, there was not this feeling of a leap into the great unknown.

Thus, while the story of the mothers of children with minor handicaps resembles the experience of the other mothers, it is a far less dramatic and clear-cut development. These women were also confronted by the social ambiguity surrounding physical handicaps, but for them this ambiguity was never exposed as clearly. Consequently, neither the initial pessimism, nor the change to optimism, was as pronounced for them. In a sense, the history of these women is characterized not so much by the process of normalization of abnormality, as by the experience of constantly living at the edge of normality.

The second of these two alternative subpatterns is manifested by the two mothers who continued to perceive their children as too abnormal to be reared at home. In spite of the fact that this group is composed of only two women, their pattern is the most difficult to describe in the total sample. Firstly, our data do not permit us to distinguish whether these mothers manifested a subtle difference from the mothers in the modal group right from the beginning, or whether this difference appeared only at the moment of their critical decision not to take the children home following the habilitation program. Secondly, it is difficult to judge how much the difference in these women's perceptions is attributable to the women themselves, and how much to the fact that the two children involved were indeed more abnormal than the others in the sample.[40] And thirdly, in terms of the effect of these births on their personal lives and their relations with the RIM, these two women constituted a very heterogeneous group.

And yet, whatever the factors producing this situation, the results, in terms of the mothers' social expectations, were clear. Both these women were very unsure about their children's social future, but both expected that their children would remain grossly deviant, socially as well as physically. These two mothers had undergone some change in their initial perceptions. If nothing else, they now recognized that they were the mothers of living children rather than dying ones. And both were struggling to assimilate the fact that their children were not universally perceived as monsters; another woman might be able to mother the child they found unmotherable. But for both of these women, the developmental history is character-

[40] Because of the complexity and multiplicity of the anomalies produced by thalidomide, it has been impossible to achieve any hierarchic ranking of the children in the sample in terms of severity of impairment, either by the use of objective criteria, or through a consensus of subjective impressions. One of these two children is the only case of tetraphocomelia in the sample, but there exists at least one "family" child who also manifests severe anomalies of all four limbs as well as absence of tongue. For the second of these children, the major limb-deficiency is bilateral upper-limb phocomelia, but this child has also manifested severe affective and intellectual problems. In insisting on her child's abnormality, the mother of this child placed considerable stress on her child's emotional "strangeness."

ized by the global tragedy of abnormality rather than by any process of normalization of the abnormality.

In describing the various social dilemmas and forces produced by the thalidomide tragedy, we have, of course, been dealing with the situation as it developed in the Province of Quebec. At this point, it would be interesting to compare the experiences of thalidomide mothers in other countries. Certainly, there is no basis for assuming that this type of development is either inevitable or universal. Even our limited acquaintance with the situation elsewhere has alerted us to the possible differences. In England there appears to be a strong, active organization of thalidomide parents. In Germany, too, the social aspects have been treated rather differently, in that thalidomide children have been viewed more as a cohesive group, and less emphasis has been placed on their integration into the normal community.[41] Unfortunately, however, there is little published literature on the basis of which to make detailed comparisons. To the best of our knowledge, there exists only one other systematic investigation of thalidomide mothers (Strasser, 1965). And this investigation has chosen to focus almost completely on the psychological and clinical problems of the mothers as individuals. Thus, here again, we are confronted with a lacuna.

But some indication of the influence exerted by different cultures can be gained by the experiences of two mothers within our sample. These mothers' patterns differed from those of the rest of the sample, because their social reality was derived not from the norms of the general culture, but from the mores of the specific subcultures in which they lived. One came from a cultural milieu in which physical handicaps are viewed rather differently and one woman did not share the middle-class orientation of the rest of the sample. On the basis of two cases one does not draw very general conclusions. And yet the existence of these cases within our sample does raise some difficult problems. One can but wonder whether the usual study of handicapped children tends to ignore these subcultural groups simply

[41] The information on the situation in Germany was gathered by Dr. Dé-carie through personal visits to habilitation centers in Munich and Heidelberg.

because they do not make use of traditional clinical services and thus are not there to be counted. But perhaps more consideration should be given to the importance of these subcultural influences in determining a mother's reactions to a deviant child—more at least than has been given so far.

Throughout this discussion of the social implications of a physical handicap, we have necessarily stressed social factors to the exclusion of all else. But if the social aspect constituted an essential part of these women's maternity, it does not explain the whole.

Chapter 4

Abnormality within Normality: The Child in the Family Environment

The range of this chapter can be summarized in a question: According to the mothers' perceptions, in what ways did the deviance of the child change the usual process of child-rearing within the family, and in what ways did it not? In attempting to answer this question, we shall retrace the same developmental history presented previously, but from a different perspective. In the earlier chapters the portrayal of the social repercussions of the deformities inevitably focused on the dramatic and unusual problems posed by the abnormality; here, on the contrary, the emphasis will be on the impact of abnormality on the multiple details of daily living.

This particular perspective—the description of abnormality within the context of normality—creates two serious problems for the selection and interpretation of relevant data. For one, the attempt to separate the unusual from the usual immediately plunges us into the problem of the many possible variants of "normal" child-rearing practices. Our sample of eighteen [1] mothers is heterogeneous in precisely those characteristics that have been found most likely to produce variations in child-rearing practices, that is, in socioeconomic status, cultural background, ordinal position of the child, and so on (cf. Bronfenbrenner, 1958; Davis and Havighurst, 1948; Sears,

[1] For this aspect of the developmental history, our sample is reduced to 18 mothers, because, at the time of the research interviews, 2 mothers had not taken their children home. Consequently, it is meaningless to speak of these mothers' perceptions of their children in the family environment.

Maccoby and Levin, 1957; Wolff, 1963). The difficulty is to isolate the specific differences elicited by the deviance of the child from the general background of grossly varying child-rearing attitudes and practices.

In dealing with this problem, two basic stratagems will be used. The first of these is the search for unusually uniform patterns of perception and behavior among these diverse mothers and children. In a sense, our expectation is that child-rearing practices in this sample will vary widely; where there appears an unusual consensus, either in the total sample or in relation to certain categories of children or mothers, this may be a clue to a common problem produced by the deviance of the child.

More important, however, will be the use of the mothers' *subjective* feelings of sameness and difference as a guide for the selection and classification of data. Did the mother herself perceive any modifications of her habitual or expected child-rearing practices toward this child? [2] If so, to what did she attribute this difference? If there was no difference, was it because the mother perceived the child as no different from any other child, or did she perceive herself as acting similarly toward a dissimilar child?

The second major problem in attempting to describe mothers' perceptions of the deviant child in the family environment lies in the definition of the term "child-rearing practices." Barsch (1968) defines the term in this manner:

A technique devised by a parent and employed actively in relationship to the child, in order to accomplish a specific change in the child which the parent deems desirable (p. 32).

For our purposes, however, this term will be used in a much broader sense. Depending on the issues that appear most salient during each

---

[2] Not all the mothers in this group could be said to have "habitual" child-rearing practices, because not all had reared another child. For six of these mothers, the thalidomide child was their first one and, at the time of the research interviews, three had not borne another one. But all the mothers could be said to have "expected" child-rearing practices based on memories of their own upbringing, their observation of other mothers and children, and their reading.

period, the emphasis will shift from consideration of the mothers' child-rearing techniques and actions, to attitudes, feelings, and values. In addition, considerable stress will be placed on the mothers' perceptions of the stimuli, that is, the children with whom they were interacting.

In summary, the structure of this chapter will be developmental in orientation with the major subdivisions provided by critical time periods. Within each time period, however, the emphasis will be on the mother's perceptions of the child's development, and her perceptions of her feelings and actions toward him. The basic question underlying the data will be that of sameness versus difference.

It should be noted as well that the presentation of data in this chapter will differ somewhat from the inductive methodology used in the previous one. Our account here will be much more schematic and condensed; it will focus almost entirely on the most typical pattern rather than on trying to classify the experiences of all the mothers. This difference is motivated by the fact that the subject matter of this chapter does not lend itself as easily to the use of categories. To fully account for the differences among mothers and families in this area would necessitate the study of individual case histories, an aim that is outside the scope of this work. Consequently, here we shall attempt to describe that which is most typical and common to the mothers, without even trying to do justice to all the variations encountered.

The Beginnings of the Mother-Child Relationship

For all the mothers in this sample, there was a time-lag between the birth of the baby and the mother's assumption of the physical and psychological aspects of maternity. Before the mother was able to build a personal relationship with this child as an individual, she had first to adjust to the general concept of mothering a deformed child. It was as if the usual preparation for motherhood experienced during pregnancy was undone by the unexpected nature of this child; now the mother had to undergo a new type of pregnancy before she could be ready for this birth.

The time required, the determining factors, and the sequence of steps in this preparation for maternity varied. One mother was able to complete the process in two days; most reached this goal in the first weeks or months of the child's life, but for a few this interlude could last for a year or more. Some mothers believe that their ability to love this child was accomplished mainly by a personal change in themselves, while others place great importance on some change in the baby. A few women had done most of the work of psychological preparation even before they assumed the physical care of the child, but for others a period of physically caring for the baby antedated the onset of psychological maternity.

Underlying this diversity, however, is a modal pattern that characterizes the beginning phases of the mother-child relationship. For most mothers, there were three distinct, if overlapping, stages in their growth to maternity. The first stage constitutes a prelude to maternity, both physically and psychologically. In this stage the mother had little contact with the child and was mainly concerned with her own internal mourning and attempts to adapt to the concept of the child. In the second stage, the physical assumption of maternity, the mother began caring for the child, although there were many unresolved doubts and anxieties. And the third stage, the psychological assumption of maternity, is characterized by the realization that this relationship would be an enduring and satisfying one, even if it still remained far from the ideal.

PRELUDE TO MATERNITY

The period immediately following delivery, the global birth crisis, marked the initial phase of this developmental process. But, except in one case, the development of this maternity-to-be remained embryonic. During the acute crisis period following birth, the emphasis was on the "abnormal" aspects of the birth, rather than on the building of the "normal" mother-child relationship. Consequently, few mothers were able to form any strong bonds to their children as individual human beings during this time. On the contrary, there are two clear indices of the wariness and uncertainty dominating this phase of the mother-child relationship. The first of these is the lack of physical contact; most mothers' contacts with their children were extremely restricted in the days following birth. One of the mothers didn't see her child at all during the period of the hospital stay. A few caught only fleeting glimpses of their babies behind the glass walls of the nursery. Even the mothers who saw and held their infants usually did so only once or twice. In fact, there were only two mothers within this sample who saw their children regularly and who participated actively in their care and feeding during this time.

Moreover, the mother's return home from hospital did not, in most cases, mark the end of the physical separation of mother and child. Only seven of these eighteen children came home on the same day their mothers did, and two of these seven returned to the hospital during the next few weeks because of illness and infection. Of the remaining eleven, eight returned home during the next six weeks, but one spent seven months in hospital, and two were initially institutionalized for more than a year.

There were good reasons to account for this separation of mother and child. In some cases, the babies were ill or undersized (due to prematurity or other factors), and it was necessary to isolate them in incubators or prolong their stay in hospital. But in most cases this separation was used as a technique to help the mother recover, physically and psychologically, from the shock of the birth. By and large, the doctors could do little to improve the children's condition, but they hoped that the prolongation of their hospitalization would give the mother a breathing space in which to recover before assuming the care of the child.

The mothers' reaction to this procedure varied. A few found that it added to their distress. Thus one mother describes her arrival home without the baby as "terrible; I felt as if I hadn't given birth to a child at all." Most mothers, however, openly welcomed this separation as a necessary reprieve. They were not ready, either physically or psychologically, to assume this charge.

In addition to the physical distance, there was an emotional distance as well between mother and child. For most of the mothers in this sample, even their sporadic contacts with the babies were largely dominated by distress and uncertainty about the future. In some cases the mothers were seeing babies that they hoped would soon die, or expected to abandon. In other cases the mothers were looking at babies the mothering of whom aroused resentment or pessimism. But whatever the cause, few mothers were able to view these initial contacts as the beginning of a permanent and satisfying relationship. Thus, even the mothers who were most stirred by their babies, report that they were wary of investing too much in this uncertain relationship.[3]

In terms of the mothers' internal adaptation, this period may have constituted a necessary preparation for maternity, but in terms of building a relationship with the actual baby, few mothers went beyond the tentative beginnings at this time. Thus the period of the global birth crisis can be considered a prelude to maternity.

THE ASSUMPTION OF PHYSICAL CARE OF THE BABY

Depending on the chronological age of the child at the time of his arrival home, there were two main patterns in the manner in which the transition from the first stage to the second was accomplished. These can be termed "delayed" and "early" motherhood.

Delayed motherhood. There were three children within this sample of eighteen who did not come home for some time after birth. In one case, the child was hospitalized for seven months and underwent a lengthy series of operations. The other two children were initially institutionalized and came home when they were one year and two years old respectively.

In many ways this postponement of motherhood helped to stabi-

---

[3] It will be recalled (see "The Birth Crisis" in Chapter 3) that four mothers believed that their first contacts with their babies permitted them to pass from a state of conflict to a "personal acceptance" of the child. But two of these mothers reported that they continued to be afraid to love their children "too much," because they might soon die. A third was happy to leave her child in hospital for a month. It would appear that even for these mothers the "acceptance" of their infants was far from complete or perfect at this stage.

lize the situation. By the time these children did come home, the mothers had largely recovered from the shock of the birth and had had time to reorganize their lives. Moreover, they had a much better idea of their children's physical status and of the possibilities for habilitation. All three of these children had already demonstrated their capacity for physical survival; in addition, one child had been fitted with prostheses by the time he came home, and another had been enrolled in the habilitation program though not yet fitted with prostheses.

In one instance the baby's delayed homecoming appeared to have made little difference in the mother-child relationship. This is the case of the farm woman whose unusual pattern has been described before. Throughout the baby's hospitalization, the child was geographically close to home, and the mother visited the baby every few weeks. When the doctors decided that the baby was ready to come home, the mother was satisfied: "It was time; she was my child and I wanted her at home." But the mother herself played a relatively small role in the child's upbringing. Because of her work on the farm, the care of the household and of the child were largely delegated to the older daughters in the family. Thus, at first, the mother was reasonably satisfied with the child's presence at home, but it didn't really mark much of a turning point in her life.

For the two mothers of the institutionalized children, however, this delayed assumption of maternity posed a number of severe problems. For one, there was a new process of mourning linked not to the deformities of the baby, but to the maternal deprivation they had suffered. If they were to be helped to mother these children now, why hadn't they been able to obtain this aid right from the beginning? In addition, their previous abortive contacts with their children had left a host of painful memories to resolve.

The second major problem resulted from the fact that during these babies' lives they had already had one or more "mothers." In trying to establish a relationship with their babies, these mothers had to compete with the previous caretakers and had, indeed, to woo children who regarded them as strangers. Thus one mother remembers vividly her initial visit to the RIM to see the child she would soon take home. As she entered the room, she could hear him laughing; when he saw her, however, he started to cry. As she put it, "I was a stranger to him; I wasn't his mother."

This emotional distance between mother and child was not overcome either easily or quickly. One of the mothers remembers that it took a long time before the child would respond to her overtures; according to her, at the beginning he much preferred his father and siblings. To this day these women manifest some insecurity in their maternity. They do not feel that the children are as close to their mothers as they would have been had the mothers started to care for them right from the beginning. Thus, in spite of their overwhelming gratitude toward the RIM, these women dread their children's hospitalization there. The mothers' perceptions of emotional distance between themselves and their children may be a realistic assessment of the situation or largely a product of their own guilt. Whatever the cause, it has cast a shadow on their maternity.

The third major problem in this delayed assumption of maternity lay in the very atypical developmental picture presented by the children. One mother, in describing her daughter when she brought her home at the age of a year, commented:

X was pale and quiet. She lay in the crib as if the only thing she had ever done was to lie on her back. She couldn't sit, couldn't feed herself. She was unused to solid food; the first time she saw me chew, she looked surprised. You could do anything you wanted with X; she was like a rag doll.

Eventually, the children passed from the initial state of passivity to one of considerable activity and even aggression. But in most cases the mothers had difficulty in adjusting to behavior that was unexpected—particularly, as here, where the developmental history remained unknown.

Early motherhood. The fifteen mothers who began the physical care of the child at an early age did so anywhere from one to six weeks following the birth of the baby. Since this pattern of maternity is much closer to the usual one, the delineation of sameness and difference here requires much more attention to detail.

Superficially, the physical setting was the same as for a normal child. In all but one case the mother was the primary caretaker of the child in the period following the baby's arrival home. The exception was a mother who employed a full-time baby nurse for a few months following birth. The other mothers might have a niece to help them for a week, or a baby sitter for a few hours daily, but were largely responsible for the care of the babies themselves. By and large, the type and extent of extra help used bore no obvious relation to the deviance of the child. Most mothers had made their arrangements for extra help prior to the birth, and the deformities of the child did not alter them.

If the data are examined closely, however, a difference does appear, in that the mother seems to have been more intensively involved in the care of the child than she would have been ordinarily. For example, two mothers had originally planned to place their children in nurseries for a few weeks following birth. Instead, they took the babies home with them from the hospital, one because she was afraid of "rejecting" her child, and one because "a handicapped child needs more care." Two other mothers usually employed maids to help care for the children in the family. For this child, however, the mothers preferred to assume sole charge. And a number of mothers mention that during the first few months they were leery of using baby sitters, because they feared that a baby sitter might not like the child.

It would appear then that the deformities of the child could have a bi-modal effect: initially a period of separation, but, once the mother did assume charge, a more exclusive contact with the baby than was usual. There are many possible explanations for this pattern. The most plausible is that the mother's own ambivalence toward the child made it difficult for her to believe that others would care for him adequately.

Whatever the cause, one effect of this pattern should be noted. Because of the almost total physical separation of mother and child during the prelude to maternity stage, most mothers went from a state of "no care of the child" to "total care of the child," without the gradual initiation into feeding, holding the baby, and so on, that usually takes place during the period of the mother's stay in hospital. Some mothers, particularly the more experienced ones, managed this transition well, but for others it was the complete strangeness of the child, as well as his deformities, that produced anxiety. As one mother put it, "I was afraid to hold X, because I didn't know how she was put together." For two other mothers, it was the feeding of this stranger that engendered problems. Both mothers had been assured by the nurses in the hospital that the children ate well, but neither had ever fed the child before she assumed total charge. When they discovered that the babies drank very little and vomited many of their feedings, the mothers didn't know whether they were responsible for a change in the babies, or whether they had been "tricked" about their babies' condition.

Husbands or other relatives might be expected to provide some relief during this difficult transition, and indeed some did. Particularly where the deformed child was the first-born one, a number of husbands or mothers-in-law attempted to help. But this aid could be a mixed blessing in that it could make the mother feel even more insecure in her maternity. For instance, one mother describes her husband constantly checking the temperature of the milk, and her mother-in-law sending a daughter daily to check on the baby's welfare. She was grateful for the help and concern, and yet the mother felt that this indicated some doubt about her trustworthiness in caring for the baby.

In contrast to the sameness of the physical setting, the emotional climate was characterized by difference. Almost all the mothers report a state of depression at the time they first began to care for their babies. In some cases this was manifested simply by a feeling of "tiredness." Other mothers had eating and sleeping problems, and a few developed more serious physical illnesses, such as ulcers or eczema. Most mothers tended to hide their distress, but a few cried openly. Thus, one mother stated, "Every time X cried, so did I."

In relation to their babies, the mothers' feelings were dominated by pessimism and uncertainty. A few still had the hope or the expectation that the baby might soon die. Others were concerned that they were beginning a lifetime of bondage; they felt that these children would never grow up and become independent, but would require constant care and attention. Besides such general anxieties, there were the many specific worries aroused by particular aspects of the babies' development.

This type of sadness and anxiety was similar to that manifested by the mothers during the prelude to maternity stage; in a sense, it can be considered the mourning of the mother's own deprivation. But a new type of anxiety became more prominent at this period, one that indicates the growing impingement of these babies on their mothers' consciousness. The anxiety here centered not on the mother's lack of gratification in this type of relationship, but on the child's possibilities for happiness. A number of mothers expressed this uncertainty in the form of a prayer: "Lord, let him live if he'll be able to be happy, but if he won't, please let him die." This new type of anxiety may have been a defense against the mother's own wishes, but it also exemplifies the double burden of guilt carried by these women. Not only were they beginning a maternity that was unwelcome to them personally, but they were also undertaking the rearing of children who might curse the day they were born, and blame their mothers for letting them live.

In general, the husbands were in the background at this time. As has been noted, many of the mothers report that their husbands were as upset and distressed as they were, but there appears to have been little communication or mutual support between husband and wife. The siblings, too, played a minor role. A number of mothers did mention that the siblings were distressed by this family tragedy, but they themselves were more often too preoccupied to pay much attention to this aspect of the situation.

Indeed, there was only one mother who devoted much time and care to introducing the other children to the new baby and to coping with their questions. This mother stands out, because she is a clear exception to the general way of handling the situation. According to her, she waited until the baby was three weeks old, and then, making sure that her face was smiling, gradually showed the stunted arms to the siblings. As she did so, she reassured them:

You'll see, you'll get a lot of pleasure from X. He's small now, but he'll grow up and be able to play and go to school like you. You'll see, he's going to be a lot of fun.

But even this mother became disturbed when the children voiced concern and worry, rather than pleasure, about this different baby.

In describing the early months of the babies' development, twelve of the fifteen mothers presented a surprisingly uniform picture. The words "easy," "quiet," "good," were the most frequent terms used to portray the children. A number of mothers commented that this was the easiest of their children. The rarity of crying was another characteristic frequently mentioned. For instance, one mother reported that a neighbor was moved to comment how happy she was to hear the baby cry one day, because she had been disturbed by the child's "unnatural" quietness. A description given by one mother of her child at this time summarizes the perceptions of many of the mothers:

X was a very quiet baby. She slept all the time till she was eight or nine months old. I had to wake her for meals. It was as if she were not in the house. She was the easiest of all my babies.

This almost universal description of a very quiet, undemanding child raises a number of puzzling questions. Did these mothers perceive their children as unusually quiet, because their initial expectations were of a very difficult child to rear, and any contraindication was, consequently, given undue emphasis? Was the perception of quietness related to the mothers' own depression and fatigue? Or were these babies, in fact, unusually quiet, and if so, why?

In describing the mothers' child-rearing practices at this period, there is one major factor that helps to explain the types of similarities and differences encountered. None of these mothers had been given any specific information about the possible effects of the deformities on the child's *current* behavior, or any advice on how to cope with these potential differences. They knew that these babies were different and that this difference would have serious, if still unknown, repercussions on their later development. But they didn't know how these differences would be manifested at any particular time in any specific area. Thus none of these mothers began the physical care of the child with the expectation that the deviance of the baby required any immediate change in her habitual child-rearing practices. The mental set was for "sameness"; where differences occurred, they were largely unintentional.[4]

In general, once the initiation had taken place, most mothers were not conscious of much anxiety about the actual physical care of the child. While some of the mothers of first children did manifest the jitteriness usually associated with new mothers, most assumed that the actual mechanics of caring for the child would not be grossly different, at least not at first. Here the experienced mothers could draw upon their familiarity with other children as a reliable guide. Thus, as one mother put it, "I may lack confidence in many things, but not in caring for a baby."

Nor were the mothers consciously concerned about their possible aggression toward these children. In spite of the almost universal hope, at first, that their children might die, only one mother reports that she was worried that she herself might harm the child. And even this mother quickly qualified her statement by limiting it solely to verbal aggression, that is, to the possibility of screaming at her child. If the mothers were, in fact, struggling with the problem of aggression, the indices of it are extremely subtle and have to be inferred from acts of omission or hints provided by the mothers. For instance, three mothers "forgot" or "never got around to" providing the customary immunization shots. Furthermore, some

---

[4] The one area where the mothers were confronted immediately by the problem of difference was in relation to prehension. However, because the development of prehension is so closely linked to the problem of the prostheses, we shall reserve our discussion of this topic until the chapter on the prostheses (cf. Chapter 5).

mothers had fears that may have been a displaced manifestation of aggressive feelings. One mother, for instance, was worried that her child might suddenly become "very sick"; a few were afraid that the baby might "fall out of my arms," or might suffocate during the night.

Thus the general picture that emerges is of mothers who were depressed and tired, felt pessimistic and uncertain about their babies, but were set toward rearing these very deviant children "as normally as possible." The abnormality of the child was not perceived as requiring either a different type of physical care, or as a factor that might provoke aggression from the mother.

The most important specific child-rearing technique characteristic of this chronological age is feeding. Here one finds a surprisingly uniform picture: All fifteen of these babies were bottle-fed.[5] But for eleven of the fifteen mothers, the use of the bottle as the feeding medium was based on past habit, or on choice made during pregnancy. Only four had considered breast-feeding as a possibility during their pregnancies. One mother changed her mind following delivery because, as she put it, "during the first few days when I wasn't sure whether X would live or die, whether I would take her home or not, breast-feeding was the last thing in my mind." For the three other mothers, the abandonment of the idea of breast-feeding was based on the belief that there was something "wrong" with their milk. One can only speculate here whether this constituted a defense against getting too close to the child, or whether the birth of a deformed child had led these women to believe that they, too, were somehow damaged.

[5] There are very few case histories available on the rearing of congenitally limb-deficient children. But one of the rare histories recorded (Lussier, 1960) mentions that the child in question was breast-fed. It is, of course, possible that the divergence observed here is due to a different social situation. The child described by Lussier was born in England, and it appears that the emphasis on breast-feeding in England, at that time anyhow, was much stronger than in Canada. It would be interesting to know how many of the thalidomide children in England were breast-fed, but here, too, comparative data are unavailable.

Thus, any relation between the baby's deviance and the preferred mode of feeding appears to involve only a minority of these mothers. In analyzing the data on this early oral period, however, another difference appears. Once again it involves only a minority of the mothers—in this case, six. These mothers mention that they were sufficiently concerned about their babies' deprivation in having no thumbs to suck that they turned to pacifers as a substitute. This practice is particularly interesting, both because it is one of the very few compensatory techniques spontaneously initiated by the mothers, and because it involves the use of an inanimate object as a substitute for the missing limbs. In a sense, the pacifier can be considered the first prosthesis.

Another major index of child-rearing practices at this stage is the amount of time the mother spends with the baby. Here the delineation of sameness and difference is far more difficult. As would be expected, the quantative amount of time devoted to the care of the child varied greatly, both in relation to the personality of the mother and to the extent of her other responsibilities. Some mothers report spending a great deal of time with the child, others much less. Nevertheless, underneath this apparent diversity a remarkably uniform qualitative picture emerges.

For almost all the mothers, the term "play" is very rarely used in describing this stage of their relationship with the baby. In fact, only two mothers mention at all playing with their children at this time. This may be related to the fact that the babies were very young, or to the mothers' perceptions of them as very quiet. Or this absence of play could be a direct result of the difficulty in fondling a deformed baby. To cite one example, a natural playtime of mothers and children at this age is the daily bath. But for many of these mothers this was an activity judged particularly stressful, because the nakedness of the child clearly exposed his deformities. Thus one mother reported, "For six months I bathed X without being able to look at her arms."

But if the mothers didn't play with their children, their anxiety, or desire to remedy the handicap, could lead them to spend a surprising amount of time with these babies. For some mothers, this time was devoted to watching for "positive" signs of development. For instance, one mother stated that when her older children were infants, she was usually very quiet about the house and tried to prolong their sleep as much as possible. With this child, however, she consciously dropped objects, flashed lights into the child's eyes, and so on, in an attempt to make sure that hearing, sight, and intelligence were "normal." In other cases, the mothers' desperation at the diagnosis of hopelessness they had been given about the child's stunted limbs led them to spend hours carefully exercising the feet or hands (cf. Chapter 5).

In summary, the mothers' perceptions of this transitional period presents us with a paradoxical situation. The bleak affective tone eloquently conveys how different and how difficult the mothers found this form of maternity. And yet, on the basis of our data, the mothers' feelings of difference appear to have had surprisingly few repercussions on actual techniques of child rearing. Faced with this deviant child, the mother did not provide either less physical care or, on the other hand, a different type of care specifically adapted to his needs. Most of the mothers, whatever their feelings, tried to do as much as they could for their children. If there was deprivation here, it lay not in the physical neglect of the child, but in the absence of joy, and the inability to deal creatively with the differences inherent in this type of child.

THE PSYCHOLOGICAL ONSET OF MATERNITY

In contrast to the two preceding stages each of which is demarcated by a specific event (that is, the birth of the deviant child began the prelude to maternity stage; the arrival of the baby home initiated the physical assumption of maternity), the transition to psychological maternity was not marked by any sudden, dramatic happening. Rather, this development was a slow, gradual one, and few mothers could pinpoint the exact moment at which it occurred. In general, however, there were two indices that this stage had been reached.

The first of these was the mother's gradual acceptance that her relationship with this child would be an enduring one. The child would neither die, nor be miraculously cured. Instead, the mother would be called upon to care for this particular child, normal or abnormal as he might be, for the foreseeable future.

For most mothers, this realization was brought home to them by the children themselves. As the months passed, it gradually became clearer that, regardless of frailty or illness, these babies had the physical stamina to survive. And, psychologically, the fact that these children continued to live became a justification for their continued existence. As one mother put it:

At first I wanted X to die. But once she passed three months, I knew she was going to live. She wanted to live, and I wanted her to.

In a sense, the fact that these babies were able to live, in spite of the pessimism and uncertainty that surrounded their birth, became their first victory. The mothers were no longer caring for completely helpless and hopeless infants but for babies who had fought the battle of survival and won it.

For some mothers, this gradual investment in their babies as children who were likely to live was only brought to consciousness by an event that threatened the relationship. Thus one mother remembers how disturbed she was when she read a newspaper article predicting the early demise of all thalidomide children. For six months she had lived with the hope that her daughter would soon die. Now she was faced with the realization that the death of her child would arouse not only relief, but also mourning. For better or worse, this woman had invested six months in caring for and worrying about a child. The death of this child would no longer mark the disappearance of an anonymous stranger, but the destruction of a human being with whom, in spite of herself, the mother had begun to establish a relationship.

The second major factor in this development was the appearance of some behavior in the child that was able to serve as a "critical releaser" of the mother's maternal feelings. For some mothers, this critical releaser was a type of behavior that is believed to serve the same purpose in the normal child. For instance, two mothers note that once the babies began to smile their attitude somehow changed. For other mothers, the critical releaser was more general; it could involve any index of "normal" behavior. The belief that the child had normal intelligence was particularly important in this respect; even an appearance of alertness could be viewed as confirmation of this crucial asset. And for some mothers, the awakening of maternal feelings was linked to the discovery that the child would be able to find a path to normality in spite of the barrier of the handicap. One mother describes the day that her daughter was able to place a digit in her mouth and begin to "suck her thumb" as a day of general rejoicing in the family. The mother was so excited that she phoned her husband long distance. "For the first time," she reports, "I had the feeling that X would bring us joy."

Retrospectively at least, it is impossible to trace the relationship of these two changes. Did the termination of the mothers' acute phase of mourning make them more responsive to the signs of development manifested by their children? Or was there, in fact, some change in the children that served as a releaser of maternity? Whatever the etiology, it is interesting to note that it is at this period that many mothers found their children becoming more alert and demanding. The process of maternity finally began to involve two living, active individuals in a reciprocal relationship.

In stressing the feeling of an enduring and satisfying relationship that marked the mothers' perceptions of the onset of psychological maternity, one must not ignore the many lacunae that this relationship still presented. For one thing, the mother-child relationship might be a continuing one, but it was one characterized by a remarkable absence of continuity. The mothers could gradually begin to assimilate the present reality of their babies, but this did not lead to an automatic integration of past and future. For instance, a mother might be willing to "make the best" of mothering this child, but still regret that the baby had ever been born. Even the mothers who were now able to believe that what had happened was "for the best," continued to be haunted by the pain and suffering they had undergone.[6] And the problem of what type of future awaited this mother and child remained an unsolved one. In fact, it is at this period that most mothers adopted the common stratagem of living on a "day-to-day" basis. The acceptance of this type of maternity implied the acceptance of living in a form of limbo; neither the past, nor the future, could be easily integrated with the present. It is in this context that the mothers' perceptions of their children's subsequent development, and the specific child-rearing techniques used, have to be understood.

The Period of Differentiation

The next stage of the mother-child relationship is one of growing differentiation, as the mothers began to make much finer discriminations about their babies' assets and liabilities, areas of normality and abnormality. This greater emphasis on the details of development formed part of the mothers' general shift from global concerns to "day-to-day" living. The onset of psychological maternity had not provided a final solution for the mothers' basic uncertainties about their babies, but it did mark an implicit bargain to continue with the job of maternity, in spite of these unresolved issues. Now the mothers turned their attention to the details of daily living. In addition, the children's continued growth also helped facilitate this process of differentiation. As one developmental milestone succeeded another, the mothers had a much better basis for evaluating the effects of the deformities on normal growth and development.

In assessing their children's development at this stage, the mothers tended to divide it into two distinct, if parallel, timetables. The first,

---

[6] Particularly in stress periods, the guilt and anxiety associated with this painful past were clearly apparent. The writer spent the long morning of a child's operation with the mother. As she and the mother drank innumerable cups of coffee and made careful small talk, the mother suddenly blurted out, "You know, I would be as sorry if X died now as if it were any of my other children. I really feel this, even though I wanted her to die at first." For this mother, the goodness of her maternity could never become something to be accepted at face value; because of her guilt at her past "badness," she had constantly to reaffirm and prove it.

which can be termed the area of normality, concerns those aspects of the child's development which were perceived as following an essentially similar course to that found in the normal child. The second, the area of abnormality, refers to those areas of development which were perceived as following a slower or different course because of the deformities.

There were three main areas of functioning which the mothers saw as developing normally: affectivity, intelligence, and speech. For the mothers, these three areas were not seen as distinct and separate functions but as part of a global picture of mental normality. Nevertheless, there were subtle differences in the initial expectations for, and criteria used for evaluation of, each of these functions.

As implicitly defined by the mothers, "normal" affectivity was manifested in three main ways: (a) the appearance of specific affects, for example, a smile, a laugh; (b) the presence of "personality" or "character," that is, will, spirit, initiative, and so on; and (c) the capacity to give and receive verbal and physical signals indicating that a strong attachment had been formed to an individual, for example, desire for cuddling, or responsiveness to praise. All the mothers judged that their children were normal in these respects.

In general, these signs of normal affectivity came as no great surprise to the mothers. Whatever had worried the mothers at the moment of birth, it had not been the possibility of lack of feeling in their babies. And yet the growing responsiveness of these children did serve as a form of reassurance. At first, the babies' unusual quietness and passivity had been a relief to these depressed and anxious women. Now, as the mothers grew more hopeful, they found that this change in themselves was matched by babies who could display a much larger range of feelings and desires. In particular, it was the appearance of positive affects and manifestations of initiative that pleased the mothers. Whatever the future held in store for these babies, they were not now showing a picture of helpless invalids engaged in a lifetime of perpetual mourning. On the contrary, they could manifest the same pleasure and willfulness as did all other babies. Significantly enough, it is at this period that the mothers first began to use the term "play" in describing their activities with their children.

The mothers were pleased, but neither unduly surprised nor grateful, to discover that their babies could follow an emotional development similar to that of normal children. In the area of intelligence, however, this appearance of normality received much more emphasis and served as one of the major factors in changing the mothers' conceptions of, and expectations for, their children. Without exception, all the mothers found that their children were as intelligent, if not more so, than the norm. The basis for their belief lay in such factors as "alert eyes," "interested expression," "good memory," and "responsiveness to my voice." Moreover, the mothers reported that this was the aspect of their babies' development most frequently commented on by the environment. If a mother at first did not attribute undue importance to these signs of intelligence, a grandmother or neighbor would be quick to point them out to her.

This greater emphasis on normal intelligence arose from its crucial role in resolving past doubts and in influencing future expectations. In spite of the fact that almost all the mothers had been reassured that their children would be intelligent, many mothers still had lingering doubts at the time they brought the babies home. Now this appearance of normal intelligence became a justification for the mothers' decision to rear these children in the family, and a reassurance that they were rearing essentially normal children rather than monsters. In addition, the possession of normal intellectual capacities opened the door to the possibility that these children would be able to find some way of compensating for their handicaps.

The third area of normal development, speech, is more ambiguous. Fourteen of these eighteen mothers claim that their children spoke their first words at an early age, that is, at anywhere from six months to a year. Four mothers, on the other hand, found that their children were much slower to speak. But even the mothers who report late speech (that is, first words at one and a half or two years), continued to believe that this was an area of normal development. As one mother put it, "X was so small that everything was going to be late." Moreover, just at the age when language development is usually greatest, most of these children were hospitalized for lengthy periods, and any deficits in language could be seen as part of the general regression produced by hospitalization. Thus, in spite of the fact that here the evidence was much less clear, all the mothers believed that their children manifested an essentially normal language development.

In assessing the relative contributions of nature and nurture to these areas of normality, most of the mothers placed the greatest emphasis on their children's innate capacities. As one mother described it, "X couldn't use her hands, so she used her head." Even the mothers who did feel that their child-rearing practices contributed actively to these attainments, didn't perceive themselves as using different child-rearing techniques for these children. The major difference, when there was one, was in the intensity of the stimulation and reinforcement given to these areas of strength. For example, some mothers claim that they talked *more* to these children, rather than in a different way. Others simply state that they spent more time watching for signs of progress and encouraging them when they appeared.

The most common and most important area of abnormal development noted by the mothers was not an unexpected one. It was in the development of motor behavior (for example, reaching, sitting, crawling, and walking) that all but two mothers found that their children differed radically from the norm.[7] While the extent and type of disability faced by each mother varied, there were three common types of problems.

The simplest and most common problem was slowness of development. For most of these babies, the usual developmental timetable of motor behavior was simply not applicable, because they lagged so

---

[7] The discussion of motor behavior here will be a general one and will largely ignore the specific problem of prehension. As previously noted, this topic will be discussed in detail in the chapter on the prostheses.

far behind the norm. Many of these babies didn't use their hands at all for the first months or year of life. Sitting, crawling, and walking could also show a severe lag. To cite only one example, a few children began to walk around the time of their first birthday, but others were two or more before they took their first step. In spite of the fact that retardation in this area was common and sometimes severe, it was not this aspect of the problem that proved most worrisome to the mothers. They perceived limb-deficiency as naturally influencing motor behavior, and while lags were manifestations of abnormality, they were expected ones.

A far more serious problem for the mothers than the quantitative difference in timing of motor development, was the qualitative difference in the type of motor behavior manifested. This difference could be shown in a number of ways. For one thing, the sequence of steps might be completely unexpected; for example, a child could learn to stand before he learned to sit independently. Or, the rhythm of learning might vary—a child could learn to sit easily, but take months learning to roll from stomach to back. Or, the motor behavior itself might take a very atypical form, that is, "crawling" for a limb-deficient child was very different from the form of locomotion to which this term is usually applied. In particular, the unusual forms of prehension manifested by these children aroused much anxiety and confronted these mothers with a number of painful decisions.

Even when the children did attain normal developmental milestones, these achievements could have a very different significance in the context of their total development. Thus, to cite only one example, the achievement of walking by these children (even those with upper-limb deficiencies) did not necessarily imply more independence. On the contrary, because of the impaired balance that led to frequent falls, it was at this point that the mothers had to face the conflict that good legs could easily lead to a broken head. While all mothers of toddlers have many potential dangers to avoid, these mothers had the additional problem that the child literally could not be left alone even in a "safe" situation.

By far the most serious problem faced by these mothers, however, was the fact that they had no precise knowledge of either the cause or the outcome of many of their children's atypical motor patterns. When a child with deformed hands did not reach for objects in the usual way, the mother was facing a difficult, but easily comprehended, situation. Because of the general lack of knowledge surrounding limb-deficiencies, however, some of the problems facing these mothers were far more puzzling. When a child with stunted arms showed a delay in walking, was it related to his arms, or did it mean that his legs, too, were affected? Was a lag in development only a delay, or did it mean that the child would never learn to do this activity? Until a child actually learned to sit, stand, and walk, none of these mothers could be absolutely sure that he would ever be able to do so.

The atypicality of motor behavior was the clearest evidence of their children's deviance faced by the mothers at this period. But even this well-demarcated difference did not lead to any radical modifications in the mothers' habitual child-rearing techniques. Faced with this problem, the mothers reacted mainly by passive resignation. The usual lore of child-rearing was not applicable to these children in this area, and there was nobody available to help them cope actively with this difference. Some of the comments made by the mothers in describing this period exemplify well the impasse they were facing:

I let X manage by herself. I would have helped if I could, but I didn't know what to do.

I tried to sit X up. But when she collapsed, I decided that she was simply not ready.

X didn't stand in her crib. People said she never would stand. I didn't know how to encourage her.

Even the two mothers who found that their children showed no serious lags in motor attainments (both children had relatively minor handicaps) attribute this achievement largely to their children's own capacities and initiative:

I let him manage and he did. I didn't know how to show him how to do things with his hands. *My hands are not like his.*

A few mothers, however, were not able to accept completely this role of passive spectator. They might not know precisely what to do, or how to do it, but they were determined to do something. Thus one mother of a child with upper-limb deformities massaged her child's legs for hours daily in the hope that this technique would lead to early walking. A few mothers of children with upper-limb deformities, when they discovered their children were not learning to crawl or walk independently, bought walkers and had the children use them as the major mode of locomotion.

Within this sample, however, there was one mother who was able, on her own initiative, to develop a number of ingenious techniques to facilitate her daughter's motor development. For example, in teaching her daughter to climb stairs (this child's major limb deformity was upper-limb phocomelia), she constructed a two-step staircase with broad steps, similar to that used at the RIM. To teach her daughter to fall, without hurting her head, she enlisted the aid of her older children. Because they were nearer the ground than she was, she had them practice "safe" ways of falling until the thalidomide child learnt to mimic her elder siblings. For this mother, the challenge of a deviant child became a stimulus for creativity; why it was specifically this mother, and only this mother, who responded in this fashion is one of the inexplicable findings in our data.

In summary, during the period of differentiation the mothers arrived at a surprisingly similar picture of their children. In terms of affectivity, intelligence, and speech, they considered these children to be normal, or above the norm. Their motor behavior, in contrast, was deviant, though it was difficult to be certain how extensive and how permanent this deviance would eventually prove. In responding to these areas of similarity and difference, the mothers could encourage the positive signs of development and hope that the children might find some way of eventually overcoming the area of disability. But in neither case did the mother perceive this child as eliciting a radically different type of child-rearing practice.

This modal picture raises two problems. The first, the mothers' general inability to respond actively to the deviance manifested by their children, has at least one facile explanation. Both the initial pessimism of the doctors about the deformed limbs, and the lack of knowledge about limb-deficiency, led to a situation where the mothers could only try to rear their children "as normally as possible"; where this proved impossible, the mothers were largely forced to resort to hope and prayer.

The second problem is a much more complex one. Without exception, these mothers perceived their children as developing normally in terms of affectivity, intelligence, and speech. And yet, the psychological evaluation done when these children were approximately two years old (O'Neill, 1965), showed that the mean I.Q. of the group was below average, a number of children were functioning in the retarded or borderline range, and almost all manifested some retardation in language. It is, of course, possible that by the time these children were evaluated they had undergone some regression in development because of prolonged hospitalization; particularly in the area of speech, most of the mothers claim that their children lost considerable ground during the period of hospitalization. Nevertheless, in view of the continued finding of below-average intelligence for some of these children (cf. Tremblay, 1967), the question remains whether some of these mothers did in fact overestimate their children's intellectual capacities, and if so, why.

One possible explanation is that the mothers tended to view their children as intellectually normal because of their intense emotional investment in normal intelligence. The major criterion for choosing to rear these children at home lay in the belief that, in spite of their limb-deficiencies, these children had good intelligence and, consequently, could benefit from and respond to a family environment. To abandon this hope, according to the mothers, was to render their maternity futile. In addition, the "theory of natural compensation" added strength to this hope. Most mothers, as did the environment, found it hard to believe that fate or God would allow a child so cruelly deprived in one area to be deprived in others. If these children had deformed limbs, then at least they would have good heads.

The second possible explanation lies in the ambiguity of the criteria for evaluating intelligence at this age. The clearest developmental milestones are the motor ones, but, for most mothers, these were outside the area of normality and, consequently, were not perceived as bearing any relation to the child's intelligence. Because of the absence of clear norms, the mothers could interpret any behavior of the child as indicating good intelligence. For instance, one mother, in explaining the basis on which she judged her child to be intelligent, simply stated, "X didn't do anything, but she followed us with her eyes."

A third explanation for this possible overestimation of intelligence lay in the revised expectations produced by the deviance of the child. Because these children had initially been viewed so pessimistically, every positive achievement was given a great deal of emphasis. As one mother explained it, "Everything X did was a tremendous accomplishment." Thus, in spite of the fact that intelligence was placed in the area of normality, the standards used to evaluate it were not necessarily those applied to the normal child.

The Impact of the Habilitation Program

As has already been discussed, the greatest impact of the habilitation program on the mother-child relationship lay in its modification of the climate of this relationship; by providing a social framework for the normalization of abnormality, the RIM helped provide a social rationale, as well as a personal one, for this form of maternity. But the RIM also impinged on the lives of these mothers and children in numerous other ways. In particular, there were three major dimensions added to the mother-child relationship by this new force: (a) the introduction of comparative norms by which to judge the progress of a limb-deficient child, (b) the provision of professional advice specifically designed for the needs of this type of deviant child, and (c) the experience of continued interruptions in the mother-child relationship due to the child's hospitalizations.

THE INTRODUCTION OF COMPARATIVE NORMS

By enrolling their children in a habilitation program that contained other children with similar handicaps, the mothers were
given their first opportunity to compare the development of their
children with that of others. Up to this time, the maternity of a limb-
deficient child had been a very solitary undertaking. The fact that
these children were deviant had made the usual standards for
judging progress invalid, but there were no substitute norms with
which to fill this void. Now that the mothers were able to observe
the development of a relatively large number of similarly handicapped children, they at last had a basis for evaluating their children
in comparison with others like them.

For most of the mothers in the sample, this was an extremely
welcome opportunity. Finally, they had become part of a main-
stream rather than isolated, atypical cases. Thus the mothers were
eager to hear how other children were progressing, whether they had
yet received prostheses, and so on. In fact, at the time of the research interviews, one of the complaints of the mothers was that
professional discretion prevented staff members from giving them as
much information about the other children as they would have liked
to have.

For some mothers, this comparison confronted them with the fact
that other children were doing more than theirs, for example, using
their hands, and walking earlier. But, initially anyhow, the impact
of this blow was softened by the possibility that lags in development
were largely due to lack of training. Consequently, at this period, the
faster progress of another child served as a stimulus for greater effort
rather than as a cause for pessimism.

Surprisingly enough, however, in one respect these new contacts
proved relatively fruitless. Except in a few isolated cases, the
mothers did not use this opportunity to share child-rearing techniques. In part, this lack can be explained by the fact that the
thalidomide mothers never formed a cohesive group. Even more
important, perhaps, was the fact that few mothers had developed

any special techniques to share with others. For help in this area, the mothers turned to the professionals.

THE RIM AS A SOURCE OF PROFESSIONAL ADVICE ON CHILD-REARING TECHNIQUES

There were two professionals on the staff of the RIM who were perceived by the mothers as occupying roles which made them especially useful in providing direct help and advice on child-rearing techniques: the occupational therapist and the psychological consultant. The mothers' perceptions of the respective functions of these two advisors corresponded remarkably well with the demarcation they had already established concerning their children's development; the occupational therapist was seen as a helper in the area of abnormality, that is, motor behavior, while the psychologist was regarded mainly as a consultant for the area of normality.

Not surprisingly, it was the occupational therapist who was regarded as particularly helpful at this time. Not only was she concerned with problems that were most relevant for the mothers (for example, teaching a child to feed himself, to walk, and so on), but she was an unusually stable member of the staff, and her work brought her into daily contact with the children and the mothers. Thus, for a number of mothers, the occupational therapist became their most valued friend and ally at the RIM. It was her help in overcoming some of the barriers of the handicaps that gave these mothers their first concrete hope of eventual physical independence for these children.

For a number of reasons, the benefits derived from the advice of the psychological consultant were less obvious. But in spite of shortcomings, the mothers generally welcomed her intervention, too. In some cases, the mothers perceived her advice as helping them to avoid pitfalls. For example, one mother recalls that it was the psychological consultant who pointed out to her how she was infantilizing and overprotecting her child. Even the mothers who didn't feel that they had yet faced any acute problems tended to see the psychological evaluations as a form of reassurance for the present and insurance for the future. In addition, the detailed attention given to these children emphasized again how "special" they were.

In one respect, however, the availability of professional advice made very little impact on the mothers' ways of perceiving or handling their children; there was little transfer of learning. During their exposure to the habilitation program, the mothers were taught a number of specific child-rearing techniques, for example, how to teach a child with deformed arms to dress himself, or how to prepare a child for hospitalization. The mothers were grateful for what the professionals taught them and their children, but, on the whole, this learning remained specific rather than generalizable. Few mothers could use this learning as a basis from which to derive new techniques to fit new problems. In relation to the habilitation program, they remained pupils rather than initiators of their own learning.

This characteristic of passivity may be attributable to some factor in the mothers, or in the program, or both. Nor do we know how possible or useful the opposite characteristic would prove.[8] Whatever the cause or the value, however, this characteristic continued to be a dominant motif in the mothers' child-rearing attitudes and behavior.

THE EXPERIENCE OF SEPARATION

For almost all the mothers in this sample the rearing of a deviant child in the family has been marked by periodic interruptions in the continuity of the mother-child relationship. All but one of these families have experienced anywhere from one to twelve separations of child and family caused by the hospitalization of the child.[9]

[8] One mother who appears to have attempted to generalize the psychological consultant's advice regarding hospitalization soon ran into considerable difficulty. This mother decided to make the RIM less strange for her daughter by insuring that she wore her own clothes during hospitalization. What may have been a valid technique psychologically produced a severe burden for the nurses (in keeping track of the clothes) and chaos in the laundry department.

[9] The one exception to this general rule of periodic separation is the family which was not affiliated with the habilitation program; at the time of the re-

According to the mothers' perceptions, these periodic interruptions constituted an essential element of their maternity. And yet the diversity of conditions under which they took place make any attempt at a general summary extremely difficult.

Even a few examples will highlight the many possible variations in the experience of separation. Some mothers began their maternity with a prolonged separation of mother and child (for example, the two institutionalized children), while for others the first lengthy separation occurred after the mother-child relationship had been established. For some mothers, the first hospitalization was voluntarily sought as a means of improving the child's condition, while for others it was an unforeseen emergency that brought additional misfortune in its wake (for example, the diagnosis of a hitherto unnoticed congenital cardiac anomaly). In addition, the child's age, the type of hospital, or the distance of the hospital from the home could all be very different for each of these families.

In view of this diversity, perhaps the easiest way of approaching the problem is to choose the hospitalization that was most similar for the largest number of mothers, and to use this common denominator as the prototype for the experience of separation in general. In this case, the experience of nine mothers during the initial hospitalization of their children at the RIM comes closest to providing a modal pattern. What distinguishes these nine mothers from the rest of the sample was that their children (a) had been reared at home since infancy, and (b) had manifested the more severe forms of limb-deficiency. Both these factors led to a situation where there had not been any prolonged separation of mother and child prior to this hospitalization.[10] In addition, the purpose (evaluation, pros-

---

search interviews the child had never been hospitalized. For this mother, her ability to avoid hospitalizations was a source of considerable pride. She kept insisting that she was the only mother in Canada who had not "abandoned" her thalidomide child.

[10] It will be recalled that almost all the mothers in the sample began their maternity with a period of physical separation of mother and child. For these nine children, however, this separation was terminated within six weeks after birth when the mothers became the main caretakers. Moreover, the lack of

thetic fitting, or surgery), timing (within a few months either way of the child's first birthday), and length (six to ten months) of this hospitalization were fairly similar for all nine cases. Consequently, the experiences of these nine mothers and children during the initial hospitalization at the RIM serve as a convenient vantage point from which to view the typical effects of separation and discontinuity on the mother-child relationship.

In choosing the initial hospitalization at the RIM as the prototype of separation, we are selecting an episode that tended to evoke feeling and behavior in a magnified form. Because of the particular circumstances surrounding this hospitalization, the mothers were subject to hope and despair in their more intense forms. For one thing, the strangeness of all hospitals was accentuated here, for the RIM was hitherto an unknown hospital for most parents, its patient population of the physically disabled was perceived as depressing and frightening, it was geographically remote from the homes of many of these mothers, the physical facilities for and psychological attitudes toward pediatric patients were grossly inadequate at the inception of the program, and the bilingual nature of the Institute posed a language barrier for many of the mothers. In addition, none of the mothers had any preparation for this prolonged separation. Most of the mothers were simply asked to bring their children to Montreal for an evaluation and assumed that they and their children would return home after a few days. Even the few who were given some advance warning that their children would be hospitalized had no inkling that the separation would last so long.

Balancing these negative factors, however, was the intense hope allied to this hospitalization. Up to this point, these mothers had not been able to find any medical facilities suitable for their children's condition. Hospitalization at the RIM provided their only chance of assuring some form of treatment and help for themselves and their children. Thus, whatever the anguish inherent in this hospi-

---

medical knowledge concerning treatment of severe limb-deficiency meant that these nine children had had either no, or only one, hospitalization prior to their arrival at the RIM.

talization, the mothers had a strong motivation for not terminating it.

The immediate effect of the child's hospitalization on the mother was the evocation of a state of disorganization and regression. Not only was the hospital environment itself strange and bewildering, but in relation to their children these mothers were suddenly transformed from powerful authority figures into helpless bystanders. A mother might feel doubtful about many of the child-rearing practices used in the hospital (for example, the abrupt removal of bottle and pacifier), but she was soon forced to realize that her habitual techniques were irrelevant in this new environment. In addition, the attitudes of some of the professionals reinforced the mothers' feelings that they were unwelcome intruders in the hospital world. As one mother put it, "She (one of the nurses) treated us like dirt; she made me feel small."

Besides this sudden loss of power in relation to their children, the mothers faced considerable conflict about how their children would fare in the hospital. Here there was a wide "credibility gap" between what the mothers were told about the hospital, and their own perceptions of this new environment. Doctors, social workers, and nurses were unanimous in insisting that this hospitalization was for "the good of the child"; once the mother left, the child would "settle down and be perfectly happy." And yet it was difficult for the mothers to believe that their children could be happy in an environment that made them feel so depressed and anxious, and in which many instances of inadequate staffing and organization were easily noticeable.

A few of these mothers stifled their doubts and retreated physically and psychologically from the scene. The others, however, initially refused to accept that hospitalization marked a complete (if temporary) severance of the mother-child relationship; instead, they attempted to continue their habitual relationship to the child within the hospital. Thus one mother recalls that when the nurse abruptly removed her child's pacifier, she went to the nearest drugstore, bought a dozen more, and proceeded to scatter them all over the child's bed. Another mother stealthily brought a humidifier into the ward to treat her child's respiratory ailment. Others insisted on being present for feedings.

Inevitably, this type of behavior brought the mothers into conflict with the hospital authorities. Sometimes this conflict took the form of an open battle. But the usual practice was to appeal to the mother's concern for the welfare of her child; to refuse to separate from the child became a characteristic of the "bad" mother.

Gradually, the mothers came to realize that they could not maintain their habitual relationship with their children under these new circumstances. For the out-of-town mothers, the practical necessity of having to return to their families hastened the loosening of the bonds, and even the Montreal mothers were soon confronted by the conflicting demands of husbands and other children. It was at this stage that separation became a psychological reality, as well as a physical one, for the mothers.

This return to the usual environment without the child led to a state of depression and mourning in the mothers. In describing their feelings at this time, the mothers mention frequently not only feelings of tenseness and irritability, but also sentiments of emptiness and loss of interest. One mother stated that although previously the demands of her child had interfered with her housework, she found that it took her much longer to complete her household routine in the absence of the baby. Another mother complained that both she and her husband were constantly "jumpy, as if something was missing." And another simply said: "I felt as if there was a big hole in my family."

The link between these reactions and the mourning phenomenon is exemplified by an interesting occurrence. In two cases, the communities assumed that the absence of the children from the families meant that they had been permanently institutionalized. Both mothers reported that they did not have "the heart" to contradict statements of this nature. It was as if the mothers' intellectual belief that the children would return home was not accompanied by any real emotional conviction. It is possible, too, that the mothers' general vulnerability regarding this maternity made them place less faith on the permanence and stability of the mother-child bond.

In relation to the children, too, there emerged an emotional separation that suggested that absent children might be treated as temporarily dead ones. Perhaps the clearest behavioral index of this change was the decreasing "visiting curve" manifested by the mothers. There were a number of reality factors that made visiting difficult for some mothers, but even those who were physically able to visit gradually stopped wanting to. In fact, by the end of the hospitalization, most mothers were visiting very rarely or not at all. Even the few who continued to maintain some kind of physical contact with their children throughout the period of hospitalization, tended, near the end, to limit these contacts to taking the children home (when permitted) for weekends and holidays; they did not choose to see their children within the strange territory of the hospital.

There were a number of factors leading to this decrease in maternal intervention. In general, however, one can ascribe it to the mothers' feeling that they were neither needed nor wanted in the hospital environment. Thus some mothers found that their telephone calls or letters went unanswered; the nurses and social workers were "too busy" to reply. Even when the mothers were given news of their children's progress, this was usually in terms of how well and how happy the child was in the hospital. Sometimes the mother would discover weeks later that her child had suffered an illness but that she had not been notified because it was considered unnecessary to "worry" her.

The nature of the visits, too, made many of the mothers willing to forego them. On the one hand, they strove to believe that what they were doing was for the child's welfare. And yet, what they saw were children who had "lost weight," "looked pale and sad," and so on. Moreover, the mothers wondered how much their visits disturbed their children and perhaps prevented them from being truly happy in the hospital. The usual way of resolving this conflict was by removing themselves from the disturbing situation. As one mother neatly summarized it, "I found the hospital a terrible place, but it was good for X."

Thus the mothers' reactions to this separation reveals a paradoxical situation. On the one hand, the mothers felt very intensely about this rupture; on the other hand, they expressed their feelings not by drawing closer to their children, but by a retreat to a private mourning. In one sense, the sequence of steps in the mothers' reactions is similar to the sequence that Bowlby (1960) has described for young children: protest, despair, and detachment. In this case, however, detachment was the reaction, not to the permanent loss of the desired object, but to the temporary suspension of the relationship. The mothers were able to maintain some hope that eventually they would be reunited with their children; for the time being, however, the best adaptation that they could make to these changed circumstances was to withdraw.

The mothers perceived their loss during the period of separation as largely expressed in terms of a changed state of feeling; for the children, however, the impact of the separation was perceived mainly in terms of physical deprivation and symptoms. Thus, while all the mothers believed that their children suffered some speech retardation, most attributed it to the fact that the nurses did not have much time to speak to the children or spoke a different language. The frequent loss of toilet training was also ascribed to the nurses' lack of time or to difficulty in comprehending the children's wants. It was as if the deprivation of hospitalization was seen as affecting the children's physical well-being rather than their emotional welfare.

There are a number of plausible explanations for this type of perception. It may be that the mothers considered the children too young to manifest the same emotions they felt, and, in fact, the younger the child, the more likely are feelings to be expressed by an altered physical state. It is also possible that the mothers' emphasis on physical causes and symptoms may have resulted from their desire to accept the hospital's reassurance that their children were happy there; they could see the physical inadequacies and effects of the hospital more easily than they could argue with the experts about emotional states. Or it may be that the mothers tended to deny the emotional impact of separation, because it was precisely this aspect that was most threatening. By deciding to rear physically handicapped children at home, these mothers hoped to compensate for the handicaps by developing the normal residuals of affect and intelligence. To acknowledge that it was precisely these areas that might be most damaged by hospitalization would be a very difficult admission.

The reunion of mother and child did not lead to an immediate dissolution of the psychological estrangement. On the contrary, the mothers again perceived themselves and their children as manifesting very different reactions. This time, however, it was the mothers who suffered physical hardship, while the children's distress was perceived largely in emotional terms.

Once the mothers were reunited with their children, they were ready to begin again where they had left off. Their emotional conflict and anguish had been resolved by the return of the child, and they were now ready to re-embark on maternity. The children who returned to them, however, were very different from the children they had left in the hospital. In some areas they had made distinct gains, for example, learning to sit alone, walk, and so on. But in many other areas they had definitely regressed to behavior typical of much younger children. Most mothers had neither an intellectual nor an emotional grasp of the concept of regression. What it meant to them essentially was a great deal of physical work in bringing their children back to their former level. Thus, as one mother described it:

Because of her hospitalizations, I toilet trained X three times and taught her to walk four times. I don't think I could begin again.

Moreover, if the mothers were themselves emotionally reassured by their reunion with their children, it was at this time that they perceived the children as beginning to manifest emotional distress.

Nightmares and clinging behavior were particularly common. In addition, some children showed additional distress linked to the changes in the family that had taken place during their absence. One boy left a younger sibling of three months when he entered hospital; when he returned, he was confronted by a nine-month-old child who had moved far closer to the center of the family stage in terms of demanding and attracting attention. In another case, the family had moved to a new house, and the child had not only to readapt to the family, but also to a different physical environment.

A few of these mothers were able to respond in a very intuitive fashion to their children's emotional needs. For example, one mother recalls that when her child would wake up crying during the night, she would go to the child's bed and slip her hand under the plaster cast that enclosed much of the child's body, in order to reassure the child by her physical closeness. For most mothers, however, the demands produced by the children's emotional distress (for example, refusal to let the mother out of sight) were perceived as adding to the already heavy physical burden they carried.

In selecting the experience of nine families during the initial hospitalization at the RIM as the prototype of the experience of separation, it can be argued that we have chosen an atypical example. Certainly not all the mothers in this sample were as attached to their children as these nine mothers were. Again, not all the mothers found the hospitalization as traumatic as these did, and even for these mothers subsequent hospitalizations were generally perceived as much less stressful. In fact, many of these mothers were insistent in emphasizing that this particular hospitalization constituted one of the most traumatic episodes in their experience of maternity.

And yet, if this particular hospitalization tended to present the problems of separation in an unusually dramatic form, it should be noted that at the time of the research interviews many of the problems connected with separation were still unsolved. For instance, many of the mothers were still uncomfortable in dealing with their children's manifest emotional distress during the period of separation. The common tendency was still one of "avoiding crying" by visiting infrequently or by not telling the children when they were leaving. Futhermore, the possibility of regression after the separation remained a difficult one to plan for; particularly where surgery or illness had occurred during hospitalization, the mothers preferred to treat symptoms appearing after the return home as part of the physical convalescence rather than as an emotional recuperation. Moreover, most mothers did not share the views of child workers (for example, Bergmann and Freud, 1965) who judge the effects of repeated separations to be cumulative, that is, the child becomes more vulnerable with each succeeding hospitalization. On the contrary, because the mothers themselves had become more habituated to separation, they tended to console themselves with the thought that the children, too, had "gotten used" to it. With the course of time, there may have been considerable improvement in the material and psychological circumstances of separation, as well as less frequent and less prolonged separations, but these improvements did not necessarily reflect any greater understanding of, or adaptation to, the general problem of discontinuity.

The Present: Living Day by Day

From the observer's point of view, the most striking change in the picture at the time of the research interviews was that, in relation to their current family situations, the differences between the mothers became much more apparent than the similarities. For much of this developmental history it had been possible to ignore the individual characteristics of each mother in favor of common problems and reactions. At this time and on this dimension, however, doing so meant denying more and more of the mothers' reality. One could no longer easily derive an image of the typical limb-deficient thalidomide child and his mother. Instead, there appeared to be eighteen different mothers interacting with eighteen different children in a multitude of ways.

There were a number of factors that could account for this growing diversity reflected in the mothers' perceptions. One is the fact that, except for the common tragedy of thalidomide, these women had always constituted a heterogeneous group. In the social area, and in the early stages of the mother-child relationship, the immensity of the problems they shared (for example, the social problem of the deviant child and his mother, the emotional trauma of bearing a deformed child, the stress of integration into the habilitation program) had imposed a certain uniformity of structure upon their different ways of life. But at this time, in the context of their daily routines in the home, individual personality traits and idiosyncratic family patterns became as salient, if not more so, than the common problem of a deviant child. In a sense, this reappearance of individuality among the mothers indicated how much the disruptive crisis of this birth had been assimilated into the texture of their lives. If the mother's life was very different from the way it had been before the birth, it was also very different from its characteristics immediately after the birth; a new equilibrium was in the process of formation.

Another factor making for diversity was that the mothers were no longer rearing similar children. As the children grew, the common diagnosis of limb-deficiency played an increasingly smaller part in explaining their total development. Even at birth, no two cases of limb-deficiency had been identical. Now, however, even small differences could become important ones. Thus two children sharing the same medical diagnosis of bilateral upper-limb phocomelia could have very different potentialities for upper-limb prehension, depending, among other things, on the length of their respective arms. In addition, the thalidomide syndrome had proved to be a broad and complex one; not all the anomalies had been diagnosed at birth, and it appeared that thalidomide could have affected each child in very different, and not always easily discernible, ways. At the time of the research interviews it had been established, with various degrees of certainty, that, besides the limbs, thalidomide could affect growth, general health, cardiac and kidney functioning, intelligence, sensory acuity, and speech. Added to the variations produced by the differential effects of thalidomide were the inevitable variations in hereditary endowment and environmental experiences. The result was a group of children whose intergroup differences were as striking as any common divergence from the norm. All the mothers might be engaged in rearing deviant children, but they were not rearing the same kind of deviant child.

Not only were the mothers and children becoming more different objectively, but the mothers' perceptions reflected their conscious awareness of this fact. When drawing comparisons between themselves and other mothers of thalidomide children, the women no longer referred solely to the type of child each had produced. Instead, more and more, the mothers stressed such differentiating factors as personality, age of mother, socioeconomic status, religious values, type of marriage, and so on.

Even more important, perhaps, was that the mothers' perceptions of their children had also shifted. At birth, these children had been unknown entities, and simple labels such as "monster" or "physically abnormal–intellectually normal" had been sufficient to describe them. In the early phases of the child-rearing process, the mothers had started to refine these categories somewhat, but even then the emphasis had continued to lie on the demarcation of areas of normality and abnormality. As the mothers continued to live and interact with their children, however, there was a gradual shift from the use of these categories to an emphasis on the individual child in the individual situation. Thus a mother might be concerned about a child's loss of appetite, not because it was perceived as a symptom of a general state of normality or abnormality, but because this constituted a specific problem of this particular child at this phase of his development. Or a mother was as likely to explain some aspect of her child's behavior on the basis of a family characteristic, or of his own temperament, as to view it solely in relation to the handicap. For the first time, statements such as "X is tall, but then so are all my children," or "X has always had an independent spirit" became frequent in the mothers' accounts.

At the time of the research interviews, therefore, this sample of mothers consisted of women who, in relation to their family situations, saw themselves as different individuals rearing dissimilar children. Moreover, this change reflected not only a shift of subjective focus, but there was a reality basis for the mothers' feelings of greater difference. In short, they felt more dissimilar, and they were, indeed, becoming more dissimilar.

From the researcher's point of view, this growing diversity among the mothers and children posed a serious problem. Up to now, the decision to ignore individual differences in favor of common problems and reactions had proved a fruitful one. Now, however, the conflict arose whether in continuing this procedure here we would be attempting to draw water from a dry well. In eliminating the factor of individual differences, was there anything left worth studying? Had the story of mothers of limb-deficient thalidomide children, in this area and at this time, become eighteen different stories completely, or were there any residual factors that still permitted us to speak in terms of modal patterns?

Certainly, it was evident that we could no longer follow our original plan of describing child-rearing practices in detail. On the basis of this diversity one would expect, and unfortunately the data confirmed this all too well, that the precise details of child-rearing practices were likely to be too varied to be meaningful. Nevertheless, beneath this striking diversity one common problem still remained. All these mothers might be rearing children who were dissimilar compared to each other, but, regardless of variations, these children still remained very different from any conception of the average or typical three- to four-year-old child. How did the mothers deal with this deviance in their general child-rearing values, attitudes, and techniques? In short, how did the deviance of these children affect the mothers' general feelings of sameness versus difference in the child-rearing process?

In addition, as we looked at the data, an unexpected problem came to the fore. One of the reasons for the growing diversity in the sample during this period was the increasing recognition that limb-deficiency was neither the sole, nor necessarily the most important, anomaly in the thalidomide syndrome. On the contrary, at this time many new facets of abnormality were being revealed. How would mothers who had already undergone the experience of living with one form of abnormality incorporate new types of difference? How did they react to and deal with a developmental prognosis that could become more, rather than less, complex and uncertain with time?

The attempt to answer the first of these questions immediately brought us face to face with a paradox. On one level, the difference of these children did appear to introduce considerable modification in the way the mothers perceived and treated them. On another level, however, the picture was one of sameness; in spite of the fact that these children were not average children, the mothers didn't feel or act as if they were dealing with a different type of development.

The area where the child's deviance appeared to make the greatest impact was in tolerance for and adaptation to his physical limitations. Usually, this took the form of the mother's giving him extra care, overlooking his inability to meet usual expectations, or performing tasks for him that a child his age might ordinarily be expected to do for himself. Thus, a child who was perceived as needing more sleep was given an afternoon nap, and a child who had a tendency to fall in the snow was not sent out to play alone. Or, a mother might agree to overlook the primitiveness of a child's table manners. Most often, however, it meant that the mother would assume responsibility for such routines as dressing, toileting, and so on, if she felt that the child was unable to handle them.

Because emotion, speech, and intelligence are much more intangible factors, and perhaps because this type of deviation was more threatening, the mothers had greater difficulty in recognizing and adapting to deficiencies in these areas of development. But even here, some mothers could be quite sensitive and intuitive. Thus a number of mothers mentioned that they delayed the onset of toilet training, not only because of the physical difficulty in removing clothing, but also because the children's slowness in speech made it hard for them to understand the mothers' demands, or for them to voice their desire to go to the toilet. Some mothers, too, recognized that, because of their children's physical limitations, they were constantly meeting frustration, and took pains either to provide extra consolation, or to see that the child didn't become "too frustrated."

And yet when the mothers described their daily routines, they constantly gave voice to the fact that the rearing of this child was not essentially different from the rearing of any other child. It might impose an extra physical burden on the mother, be harder and longer, but it was not qualitatively different. In fact, compared to the anxiety manifested in relation to the social problems, and the emotional difficulties encountered during the early phases of the mother-child relationship, the current job of child rearing was one that the mothers appeared to be taking in their stride. It was not perceived as either a particularly complex or traumatic task.

It is possible, of course, that much of the mothers' sense of mastery resulted both from habituation and from the comparative normality of the present compared with the past. The physical limitations of these children had existed since birth, and in comparison with the mothers' earlier anxieties (for example, whether the child would ever be able to walk or grasp), the present problems could be treated as relatively minor ones. If the present reality of the child was contrasted with the initial one of "hopeless invalid," some measure of physical dependency could be easily assimilated and tolerated.

But the mothers' perception of "little difference" also bore witness to a present reality. The deviance of these children might be introducing many changes into the child-rearing process, but it was not significantly modifying either the mothers' usual teaching techniques, or their final goals and values in relation to these children. Thus, to cite one example, confronted by a child who had physical difficulty in removing clothing and also speech difficulty in voicing his wants, a mother might delay the onset of toilet training and change her expectations of how soon or how perfectly it should be accomplished. For most mothers, however, this developmental lag was not seen as one requiring the mother either to learn different teaching techniques, or to abandon her final goal of independent toileting. Rather, the problem became one of waiting until maturation and development permitted the child to "catch up." The timing was different, but the mechanics and goals remained unchanged.

The problem of parental teaching techniques for exceptional

children is one that has been studied extensively in a recent work (Barsch, 1968). Here, his conclusion accords closely with our own findings:

> The child-rearing practices employed with these handicapped children did not differ significantly from those used with their siblings. . . . Confronted with children manifesting a variety of perceptual confusions, language deficiencies—both receptive and expressive, various motoric abilities, etc., the general child-rearing approach reflected in the data is largely one of employing the same techniques with the handicapped child as were used with the normal siblings (pp. 344–45).

In interpreting his findings, Barsch places considerable weight on parental ignorance, both in recognizing that an exceptional child may have a different learning process and in knowing what techniques to use. Certainly this factor is worthy of consideration. Nevertheless, some of the data made us doubt whether this constituted the sole, or necessarily the most important, explanation, and whether the problem of techniques could be viewed independently of the problem of values. For in a number of areas, where professionals or the children themselves did suggest alternative techniques, the mothers were not always willing to use them.

At the time of the research interviews, over one-third of the children were being partially or completely fed by the mothers. This situation did not result from the children's complete physical inability to feed themselves; rather, the mothers preferred to feed these children because the modes of prehension open to them (for example, the use of feet) were considered bizarre and abnormal. From the mother's point of view, it was better to treat the child as younger than his chronological age than to let atypical patterns of behavior develop. Or, to cite another example, one mother, in spite of her guilt at being "over-protective," preferred to dress her daughter rather than to let her wear the "ugly velcro clothes" which the child could put on herself.

This attitude became much clearer when we turned to an examination of the values that these mothers brought to the child-rearing process. In general, the deviance of the child did not lead to any gross modifications in child-rearing values and goals. For instance, all these mothers were rearing children who were more physically dependent than most children their age, and who were expected to manifest some measure of physical dependency for the rest of their lives. And yet, while many mothers remarked admiringly, "X is so independent; he wants to do as much as possible for himself," none was heard to say that "X accepts dependence so gracefully." It would appear that in the rearing of different children very little premium was accorded for the development of different values.

Another area where the mothers preferred to ignore the expected difference in outcome was in relation to their children's current phantasies about marriage and parenthood. As has been noted, many of these mothers had serious doubts about whether their children could or would marry or reproduce. And yet, when their children talked about "marrying Jane one day," or "having a baby in my tummy," most of the mothers responded with conventional reassurance or uneasy silence. Only one mother in the sample reported suggesting to her daughter that marriage and parenthood were not necessarily possible, or even ideal, goals for all people.[11]

An interesting illustration of the mothers' desire to avoid any recognition of difference could be seen in their attitude toward exceptional attributes that could be considered positive rather than negative. As has been stressed, normal intelligence constituted a fundamental value for these mothers. And yet two mothers who were told that their children departed from the norm, in testing very high on formal intelligence tests, were far from jubilant. Both preferred to believe that their children were simply average, that is, normal.

---

[11] The analysis of the data on the mothers' perceptions of their children's current sexuality revealed another interesting finding. One of the clearest direct effects of the handicap was that many of the children in the sample were physically incapable of masturbating, at least not in the usual way. Because of their general disapproval of masturbation, however, the mothers did not view this lack as a deprivation. Certainly, none reported developing or wishing for any compensatory techniques in this area. Once again, the fact is brought home that the consequences of physical handicaps are defined as much by social values as by any functional limitations.

Even too much of a positively valued attribute could raise the danger of deviancy.

But it was in relation to the second issue raised, the problem of incorporating new forms of difference, that the mothers' attitudes about sameness versus difference in development were most clearly exposed. At the time of the research interviews, not only were the mothers confronted with the necessity of adding new problems to the list of known anomalies, but also the broadening of the thalidomide syndrome raised the possibility that even more anomalies might be present or develop, though not yet diagnosed or foreseen. Instead of becoming simpler, the child's development could increase in complexity and unpredictability.

Here it became evident that the mothers' past history of living with abnormality had not constituted either a psychological preparation, or a mental set, for incorporating new forms of difference. Whatever the adaptations made in the past, these had not led the mothers to develop a general way of perceiving their children as individuals who would continuously exhibit a complex and varying admixture of normality and abnormality. On the contrary, much of the mothers' present adjustment seemed to be based on viewing the area of abnormality as a clearly delineated and constantly diminishing one. When the mothers were confronted by the possibility of new facets of abnormality, they reacted either by splitting the new problem from the old ones, or by denying the significance of these defects.

For a few mothers the situation was a relatively easy one, because no new medical problems had been added to the original diagnosis. Nevertheless, their attitude is interesting, because it reflects the adaptation made to a possible, but as yet abstract, danger. Some of these mothers would not discuss the issue at all. Others would, but only to assert that this "couldn't happen to me." In fact, one of their major sources of consolation lay in their belief that, compared to parents of normal children, they had faced "all the difficulties right at the beginning." One of their frequent refrains was that "others don't know what misfortune can happen to them in the future." It was as if having been punished once by fate, they believed that they were henceforth entitled to be spared further misfortune.

For other mothers, however, the added anomalies or dysfunctions were no longer an abstract possibility but a present reality. Depending on the nature of the new problem, the mothers' techniques of adaptation varied. Where the diagnosis involved a "physical fact," for example, kidney dysfunction, the mothers were able to accept this finding as part of their reality. But usually the mothers did not integrate this problem with the pre-existing ones. On the contrary, these newly discovered illnesses or dysfunctions tended to crowd out the old problems, and the mothers focused on the new areas of concern to the exclusion of all else. As a result, a mother whose child manifested bilateral upper-limb phocomelia and a cardiac anomaly could say, "If only his heart would be all right, everything would be fine."

Where the deficiency was more intangible, for example, speech or intelligence, the mothers' response was different; here the typical reaction was one of denial. This denial took two main forms.

Some mothers used the general complexity of the child's development and experiences as a means of exempting him from comparison with any scale of normal or abnormal development. There were so many factors that could explain why a child's behavior was deviant that the significance itself of the deviance could be explained away. Thus, to cite one example, a child who was not toilet trained at the age of four could manifest this lag because (a) he had a kidney dysfunction or other physical anomaly which might or might not be linked to the thalidomide etiology, or (b) he had a functional difficulty in lowering his pants or climbing on the toilet, or (c) he could not speak well enough to tell when he wanted to use the toilet. This speech difficulty, in turn, could be interpreted as produced by (a) a hearing loss, or (b) a generally low intelligence, or (c) the negative effect of numerous hospitalizations. In the case of these children, the various alternatives were not simply abstract possibilities but had all been present in one or more cases. Thus, there were so many atypical qualities about these children's development and experience that the mothers were able to use them to cancel each other out. On the basis of this complexity, the mothers were able to avoid any attempt to distinguish the real deficiencies from the pseudodeficiencies and could treat everything but the limb-deficiency as belonging to the second category.

The second major technique for explaining deviation in the areas of speech, intelligence, and so on, was by altering the conception of the relationship between past, present, and future. Here a wide gulf existed between the mothers' and the professionals' view of development. For the mothers, a gap of one year between chronological and mental age was not seen as a relationship that would widen as the child grew older. On the contrary, a retardation of one year in intellectual development was given the same significance as the repetition of a school grade. The child would always stay one year behind or even, hopefully, make up the lag by more intensive training. The fact that the mother could see continuous growth was given more importance than the rate of growth.

Moreover, in equating difference with simply slower development, the mothers were helped by two factors in their reality. One was the chronological age of the children at the time of the research interviews. In contrast both to the periods of infancy (where motor milestones are clearly demarcated in popular folklore) and latency (where the school experience imposes a comparison between children), the developmental milestones of the preschool period are less clear and less well known. In addition, three-quarters of these children were the youngest or the only children; in these families, there were no younger siblings who would make pointed comparisons inevitable.

In summary, the mothers' feelings about rearing a deviant child in the family indicated that, while they found the difference of the child added to their physical burden, the child-rearing process itself was viewed as neither particularly stressful nor particularly different. In part, this feeling of sameness resulted from the mothers' ability to maintain their habitual or expected child-rearing techniques, values, and goals globally, if not in every detail. In part, too, this attitude resulted from the mothers' perceptual set that the current differences did not indicate a qualitatively different type of development, and their belief that many aspects of this difference would be resolved through time. And, finally, the ways in which the mothers reacted to the possible or actual discovery of new ramifications of the abnormality suggested how much their current adaptation to the deviant child in the family rested on stressing the *ultimate* normality or sameness of the child and the child-rearing process.

The Future

The mothers' anticipations of the future development of the child in the family can be summarized very briefly. Indeed, there is little to say because most mothers were either unwilling or unable to commit themselves on this topic. As has been described, this same reluctance was found in relation to social expectations, too. There, however, external forces imposed a timetable, even on reluctant mothers; whether a mother liked it or not, school entry became a problem at the age of six. In this area, however, the mothers did not feel the same external pressure and, consequently, were better able to use the technique of "wait and see."

This did not mean that the mothers had no hopes or anxieties in this area. Many mothers did express concern about specific issues. For instance, some mothers were hopeful that their children would remain very close to them through adulthood and that the protective alliance of mother and child would serve to cushion the stresses of the handicap. Others, in contrast, were worried that the child's discovery of the etiology of the handicap would create a gulf between mother and child. There were even more concrete worries. For instance, one mother focused on the problem of how she would handle a menstruating daughter who would be physically unable to manipulate sanitary napkins or tampons.

Not surprisingly, the problem most frequently mentioned was the fate of the child once the parents, and particularly the mother, died. A few mothers remarked, half-seriously, that maybe the child would always stay the same age, and there would be no problem of the future. Others, particularly the wealthier parents, had made some concrete provisions for the future in terms of insurance, trust programs, and so on. Many mothers, too, expressed the hope that these children would become relatively self-sufficient adults, and that any minor needs remaining would be supplied by the government or siblings.

In the final analysis, however, most mothers' anticipations of the child's future relations with his family were closely allied to the social and medical expectations. If the prostheses could reduce the functional disability, if the child could obtain a good education, if he could find a satisfying vocation, then the child would be able to find his way. The future development of the child in the family ultimately depended on his future development outside the family. What would happen if this proved a failure was a topic too anxiety-provoking even to be considered.

Conclusions

The addition of another dimension to the description of the mothers' perceptions of the bearing and rearing of a congenitally limb-deficient thalidomide child has led, not unexpectedly, to an increase in complexity as well as understanding. Before looking at some of the new questions arising from the data, however, it is necessary to consider the original question posed. The aim of this chapter was to focus on the history of the thalidomide child in the family with particular reference to the mothers' perceptions of sameness versus difference. Was there a common developmental pattern? And if so, how much was this pattern one of sameness or difference?

On the basis of our data, it would appear that, in spite of the many individual differences among the mothers and children, the history of the thalidomide child in the family can be described in terms of a common developmental pattern. And, as in the social area, the typical pattern is one of increasing normalization. The rearing of a visibly deviant child began on a note of stark abnormality, but gradually the mothers became able both to perceive and to treat the children more and more within the framework of their individual and familial conceptions of normality. To conclude this is not to deny the many differences and problems in development that the mothers perceived and reacted to. It is simply to note that even though the mothers initially found the prospect of rearing a child like this so traumatic as to threaten the very basis of the mother-child relationship, eventually the child-rearing process became increasingly comfortable and familiar.

Evidence for this conclusion is available on many levels. In part, it can be derived from the problems that did not occur in the course of the history of the child within the family. No mother killed or physically harmed her child, no family in the sample broke up as a result of the presence of the deformed child, and no mother viewed the actual mechanics of child-rearing as creating an unbearable strain. And even where the presence of the child did lead to some changes in family structure or functioning (for example, a decision not to have any more children, the mother's termination of outside employment), these were rarely solely determined by the abnormality itself.

Even more important are the mothers' perceptions of the impact of the handicapped child on child-rearing attitudes and practices. On the perceptual level, the mothers did not develop an image of these children as embodying a totally different type of development. Rather, the usual tendency was to view the area of abnormality as separate, limited, and improving. In fact, the few times the mothers did appeal to a concept of different development, the motive for this emphasis on difference (for example, with respect to different speech development) lay in the desire to affirm the children's inherent normality. On the level of child-rearing practices, the differences manifested by these children led to many changes in daily routine. The mothers did more for these children than they would ordinarily do for children of the same chronological age; they worried more, and they expected less. But neither their teaching techniques, nor their basic goals and values, showed any significant modifications.

In describing the mothers' perceptions of social development, it was possible to isolate a number of factors that permitted and shaped the transformation of the initial trauma into a process of normalization. Were there any factors specific to the family situation that could account for the normalization process within the family? Most evident were three "practical" factors: (a) the functional effect of this type of abnormality on the activities of daily living, (b) the chronological age of the children at the time of the research interviews, and (c) the changes manifested by these children in the course of their development.

Actually, at the time of the research interviews, the functional impact of the anomalies on the activities of daily living was more one of degree than of kind. None of the children in the sample was a totally helpless, mute, bedridden invalid. On the contrary, compared to the impact on the daily routine of many other forms of handicap (for example, cerebral palsy, blindness, deafness, severe retardation), the effect of limb-deficiency was relatively minimal. A limb-deficient child might fall more easily, but he could walk; he might not be able to handle very heavy or unwieldy objects, but he manifested considerable capacity for prehension and surprisingly good manual dexterity. And even those children who showed intellectual or speech defects in addition to the limb-deficiency usually did not manifest them in a sufficiently severe or a sufficiently total fashion to really affect the mother's global image (many children, for instance, were retarded in speech, but none was mute or completely unable to understand language). Thus one of the major factors permitting the mothers to normalize the children within the family was that there were as many similarities to normal children as there were differences.

Secondly, at the time of the research interviews the children were of preschool age. All preschool children require some help in dressing, feeding, and toileting, and the range of normality here is a wide one. Thus, in dealing with the problem of dependency, the mothers were not confronted with a situation in which their children's total dependency had to be contrasted to the complete independence of others. Rather, the context here was one of relative dependency, and these children's needs could be viewed as forming part of this normal continuum, instead of as completely different.

And thirdly, in rearing these children the mothers were dealing with a development that was neither static nor deteriorating, but one that, on the whole, showed continual improvement. The problems arising from the limb-deficiencies had, in most cases, proven far less severe than originally anticipated. Even if in certain areas (for example, intelligence) the professionals became more pessimistic about the prognosis for some children, the mothers were able to deal with this by refuting the significance of the lag, and by the consolation that, regardless of the rate of growth, there was still evidence of continuous change and improvement.

But while these factors help to explain the relative ease with which the process of normalization took place, they do not provide a satisfactory understanding of the psychological and social mechanisms underlying this process. In a sense, the mothers' perceptions of sameness versus difference can be considered analogous to the situation of a man who is faced by a half-filled glass of water and can choose to view it either as half-full, or half-empty. The mothers, in stressing the dimension of sameness, took the option of viewing their maternity as half-full. Why?

One possible explanation for the mothers' growing normalization of the children within the family can be found by relating this history to the social development described in the previous chapter. Certainly, the mothers' child-rearing attitudes and expectations within the family cannot be divorced from their social expectations outside the family. And, as we have seen, the social dimension was a crucial one in this form of maternity. Much of the birth crisis can be explained in terms of the social conflicts it posed, and a good deal of the subsequent resolution of this conflict was in finding a social *modus vivendi* for this deviant child and, by extension, for the mothering of this child.

In particular, the fact that the major mode of social resolution took the form of seeking to integrate these children within the normal community helps to explain many of the mothers' attitudes and practices within the family. Thus the mothers' rejection of some forms of atypical behavior (as, for instance, in the child's custom of using his feet to feed himself) can be seen as one way of rearing children who would be able to accomplish the social goal of becoming part of the normal community. Similarly, the areas in which the development of special skills were encouraged (such as unusual facility in languages) were those in which the achievements would be valued by the standards of the normal community.

In addition, participation in the program of the RIM not only helped the mother to see her child as an essentially normal human being, but also may have been influential in helping her to feel like a normal mother. One of the major problems in the rearing of a deviant child is not simply the problems and stresses encountered, but also the fact that these problems are very different from those confronting most mothers. A mother who is struggling to adjust to the complete dependence of the new-born baby, or who is learning to deal with the tantrums and "no's" of the two-year-old, is also living in a stress situation. She, however, can derive some consolation from the fact that others, too, have undergone these normal crises of development. In contrast, the mother of a different child is isolated. In interpreting the significance of her child's behavior, she has no conceptual framework for judging what is normal or abnormal, temporary or permanent. Here the presence of professional advisors, to whom many of these bewildering phenomena were familiar and understandable, may have provided considerable help in diminishing the strangeness of the situation.

And yet, while the manifold influences of habilitation program may have been very important in stabilizing and normalizing the mothering of a deviant child, this, too, does not fully explain the process. For one of the puzzling elements in our data is that the development of a strong mother-child bond antedated the impact of the habilitation program. For only two mothers in this group did formation of a habilitation program constitute a necessary condition for maternity; the others underwent a complex process of "growing into" maternity even before their children's entry into the program. If the mothers were able to find some satisfaction in their maternity even before receiving the social support of the habilitation program, it would appear that the establishment of a mother-child relationship has other dimensions besides the social one.

Few mothers were fully conscious themselves of what exactly permitted them to rear children who initially had repelled and shocked them. And yet, if the data on the early phases of the mother-child relationship are looked at, not from the perspective of the abnormalities inherent in the situation, but as the beginning of the process of normalization, a number of elements existed that could have served as the precursors of later development. The period of the birth and its aftermath was a crisis situation characterized by discontinuity, but it also may have contained elements of continuity.

Looked at from this perspective, the decision to bring the children home may have constituted a very positive and very significant action psychologically rather than simply a passive resignation to the lack of feasible alternatives. As has been stressed repeatedly, in very few cases was the mother's decision to take her child home accompanied by any real psychological commitment to this child. The mothers still found their children strange and frightening, and the child's return home did not end the mother's hoping for his death. But if the mother's decision to begin caring for the child was not an affirmation of her love for him, it did mark an important affirmation of her trust in herself as a mother. The mothers who took their babies home were able to believe that, in spite of their hostility, they would not kill or harm these children. Thus one of the first elements of continuity in the discontinuity provoked by these births may have been the mother's ability to risk physical proximity to the child on the basis of her faith in herself as a reliable and trustworthy caretaker of even an unwelcomed child.

Similarly, the period of physical maternity was not necessarily one devoid of psychological meaning. Emotionally, the mothers might still remain very anxious and uncertain about the mothering of these children, but in terms of behavior they were thrust into a familiar or expected situation of caretaking. Partly because they didn't know what else to do, the mothers, confronted with the necessity of caring for these children, began to use their habitual or expected child-rearing techniques. A child with deformed limbs still had to be fed when hungry and diapered when wet. Moreover, like all children, these children did eat when hungry, sleep when tired, and so on. This physical routine might have been largely devoid of emotional gratification, but the mother's ability to do the same things for this infant as for any other child, as well as the child's responsiveness to these familiar techniques, provided the mother with her first concrete reassurance that this infant was a baby, as well as deformed.

A third major step may have been the baby's capacity to manifest behavior indicating that psychologically he shared a common human heritage with his mother. This time it would be the mother who would have to recognize and respond to the signals provided by the baby. As described by the mothers, these critical signs could be very different for each child (for example, a smile, alert eyes, the ability to perform an action resembling thumb-sucking), but the important message they communicated was that the child was as similar as he was different. Once the mother was able and willing to interpret these signs, the identification with the child that had been threatened by the abnormal nature of the birth could then be established. The maternity of a deviant child involved not only an adaptation to difference, but also a recognition of similarity. Significantly enough, it is at this period that most mothers recalled that they first had the hope that this child would bring them joy as well as sorrow.

Thus, if we review the data on the early stages of the mother-child relationship, the psychological dimension, as well as the social and practical ones, becomes an important factor in understanding the normalization of the deviant child. Moreover, this dimension in itself contains many interwoven strands. The beginnings of the mother-child relationship involved the mother's ability to risk her own trustworthiness, the physical familiarity of the caretaking process, and the mother's ability to recognize similarities in the midst of difference.

As we look at these various elements, it is tempting to speculate how large a role each of them played not only in the establishment of the mother-child relationship, but also in its subsequent unfolding. To attempt to reinterpret our data from this new vantage point may be to read more into the "facts" than actually existed. And yet one of the fascinating characteristics of complex psychological relationships is that they may contain many truths simultaneously. To interpret the later development of the mother-child relationship in terms of the mother's capacity to risk her own reliability, the importance of the physical presence of the child in the family, and the mother's ability to recognize similarity in her child, may not yield the whole truth, but it does provide a plausible explanation for some aspects of our data.

Thus one of the qualities of this form of maternity that has puzzled us most has been its seeming ability to flourish in the absence of any integration of past, present, and future. The mothers were rearing children largely, as they themselves expressed it, "on a day-to-day basis"; regardless of the satisfactions of the present, the past remained traumatic, and the future uncertain. Granted that the mothers' ability to at least hope for a better future played a large role in maintaining their present stability, was this in itself sufficient? What else contributed to the stability of this form of maternity? Here one can wonder whether the element that later permitted the mothers to function so well was not already revealed in their initial decision to take the children home, that is, at the point in time when the mother affirmed her belief in her own capacity to be a reliable mother to an unreliable child. The beginnings of this form of maternity were founded as much on the mother's faith in herself as on her faith in the child. Was the mother's continuing ability to trust her own continuity and stability one of the major counterforces to the chaos and disorganization created by the unpredictability of the child's development?

Similarly, the extent of the trauma experienced by these mothers during the prolonged hospitalization of their children, and their reaction of distancing themselves from the point of conflict, can be explained as an exaggeration of the "normal" reaction to separation, caused in this case by the rather unfavorable circumstances. And yet, when we consider the importance of the physical presence of the child in the home (and the familiar process of caretaking) in cementing the mother-child bond initially, we are led to speculate whether the removal of these basic props of maternity did not explain at least some of the trauma of hospitalization. Was one of the basic factors in the normalization of a deviant child the simple fact that he could be reared like any other child in the home? If so, might not the mothers' later placing themselves at a distance from their children during the hospitalization be based, at least partially, on the fact that if this child was so abnormal as to need this type of hospitalization, then it became difficult for the mother to continue to view him as a "family" child? A question arises here as to whether hospitalization had the same meaning for these mothers as it does for mothers of normal children, or did it carry a more serious threat?

Most important of all is the role of recognition of similarity in the adaptation to difference. Throughout this history, we have emphasized the fact that the mothers never really developed a different style of mothering, or even an image of their children's development as something radically different from the norm. Was this lack due to ignorance or rigidity, or did it represent the mother's attempt to preserve an even more vital quality in her maternity, her capacity to identify with the child as an essentially similar human being? In stressing the quality of sameness in their maternity, were the mothers using the mechanism of denial as we usually understand it, or were they expressing one of the basic truths that made their maternity possible?

There are no conclusive answers to these questions because the history of the thalidomide child in the family permits no single interpretation. It is a history of abnormality, but also of normality, a story of discontinuity, but also of continuity, a record of the remarkable capacity of these mothers to adapt, but also of their refusal or inability to adapt. And throughout, the history of the child in the family is interwoven with the social climate in which it took place.

Chapter 5

The Normification of Abnormality: The Prostheses

The aim of this chapter is to present the developmental history of the bearing and rearing of a congenitally limb-deficient thalidomide child from still a third perspective: the mothers' perceptions of the successes and failures inherent in the attempt to normify [1] the abnormality by means of prostheses. Although all three accounts of this history concern a process of change, here the focus of change is a different one. In the two previous chapters, the emphasis was mainly on how mothers changed their own perceptions to assimilate the handicap; here, in contrast, the focus will be on how mothers perceived and reacted to an attempt to change the nature of the handicap itself.

At first sight, the decision to devote a separate chapter to a specific habilitation technique—and at that one used for only thirteen of the twenty children in the sample—might appear surprising. But for a number of reasons, the prostheses occupied a central role in the history of thalidomide limb-deficiency, at least as it developed in the Province of Quebec. For one, the decision to use prostheses

[1] As used by Goffman (1963), the terms "normify" and "normification" refer to the attempt of the stigmatized person to shape his behavior so as to present himself as much as possible as a normal person. In applying this term to the prostheses, we are, of course, using it in a different context; here the behavior in question refers not to an action initiated by the thalidomide children themselves, but to a habilitation procedure introduced by medical specialists. Nevertheless, we have chosen to use this term, because we believe that it conveys very aptly the meaning and goals underlying the particular use made of prostheses for this sample.

for these children was far from being a purely medical one; on the contrary, the original choice of prostheses as the main habilitation technique was heavily influenced by social considerations and, in turn, influenced the future development of social policy and expectations. Secondly, as used for the thalidomide limb-deficient children, prostheses were never conceptualized solely as the replacement of missing limbs. Rather, the prostheses were intended and expected to change the *whole* appearance and functioning of the child. Thus, in addition to their role as a specific habilitation technique, the prostheses became an important force in the general history of thalidomide limb-deficiency.

In retrospect, it is difficult to appreciate the revolutionary nature of the decision to fit prostheses for very young phocomelic children. On the practical level, the age of the children, the most common type of limb-deficiency manifested, and the lack of trained personnel all posed severe problems. It was only in the five or ten years preceding the thalidomide tragedy that medical opinion had gradually shifted the optimal age of fitting prostheses from ten to twelve years of age to two years of age or earlier, and practical experience with such early fitting was very limited (Hall, 1963). The fact that the most common limb-deficiency was bilateral upper-limb phocomelia increased the difficulty on three counts: (a) bilateral amputations are more difficult to compensate for than unilateral ones, (b) upper-limb functioning is more difficult to compensate for than lower-limb functioning, and (c) the shortness of the "stump" in phocomelia might make some form of external power necessary to operate the prostheses. Furthermore, the decision to use prostheses was made at a time when trained personnel for manufacturing and fitting appliances were very scarce in Canada.

In addition to these practical difficulties, the functional utility itself of the prostheses for cases of phocomelia was open to question. The view of the RIM, which led to the adoption of prostheses, was expressed by its Executive Director:

Certains thalidomidiens présentent des doigts reliés directement à l'épaule; ces doigts ne leur permettent cependant pas de porter leur nourriture à leur bouche. Il leur faudra donc des appareils pour manger, se vêtir, se laver, écrire, etc. *Les appareils sont essentiels* et, avec le temps, deviennent partie intégrante du corps.[2]

In contrast to this point of view, habilitation experts in England suggested that, in cases of phocomelia, prostheses might actually *decrease* the child's functional capacity, because they deprived him of "direct manual contact." [3] They believed that, on the whole, it might be better to leave the children without prostheses. The major value of prostheses, if such were to be used at all, would be their cosmetic function.

But it was in relation to the possible psychological benefits to be gained from the early fitting of prostheses that the most crucial conflict existed. The rationale for fitting prostheses as early as possible was based not only on the functional usefulness of this compensatory technique but, more importantly, was intended "to help the child incorporate the presence of an artificial arm into his body image" (Gingras *et al.*, 1964, p. 72). On the other hand, Hall (1963, p. 965), quoting an American expert, claimed that previous experience in this area had been so limited that the "psychic influence of early prosthetic fitting cannot be evaluated at this time."

Underlying much of this controversy about the optimal mode of prehension lay a basic issue of social policy. The children's use of certain modes of prehension (for example, the feet) would obviously make it more difficult to integrate thalidomide children into the normal community, while others (the prostheses) would, hopefully, facilitate the process. Though rarely stated as explicitly, the policy

---

[2] "Some thalidomide victims have fingers attached directly to the shoulder; nevertheless, these fingers are insufficient for carrying food to their mouths. Therefore, they will need mechanical devices for eating, washing, dressing, writing, etc. *These mechanical devices are essential* and, with time, will become part and parcel of the body." (Emphasis mine.) This statement forms part of a press release issued by Dr. G. Gingras on June 16, 1966.

[3] The point of view expressed in this paragraph is contained in a booklet entitled "Notes on the Prosthetic Management of Upper Extremity Congenital Defects arising from Thalidomide." This booklet was "prepared by the Minister of Health, England, for guidance of directors of limb-fitting clinics" and issued on August 15, 1962.

of the RIM in adopting the use of prostheses was to help thalidomide children—through the better functioning, more normal appearance, and intact body image provided by the prostheses—to function as members of the normal community. It is in this sense that the
prostheses became a way of normifying the abnormality.

In spite of the practical difficulties, and unresolved theoretical
issues, thirteen [4] of the children in the thalidomide limb-deficiency
group at the RIM were fitted with prostheses (see Table 2).[5] It is

---

[4] There were 14 children in the habilitation program for whom prostheses
were recommended. One family refused both the prostheses and affiliation
with the program.

[5] Since much of the discussion in this chapter will hinge on the merits and
disadvantages of the prostheses for upper-limb deformities, a brief description
of the various types used or considered for thalidomide children may be helpful. It is understood, of course, that this description will not enter into all
the subtleties of this highly technical and complex subject; rather, the perspective used here is that of the layman. Basically, there were three kinds of
upper-limb prostheses that were discussed in connection with thalidomide
children: conventional, CO_2, and what came to be called the "Russian arm."

Both conventional and CO_2 prostheses are fabricated of hooks attached to
a plastic or leather body harness; the difference between them lies mainly in
the source of the power used to activate the hooks. Conventional prostheses
are operated by cables, that is, the energy is provided by the movements of
the wearer himself, while CO_2 prostheses, as the name would indicate, are
powered by the gas.

Each of these types has advantages and disadvantages. Conventional prostheses have been used very successfully with below-elbow amputees. Most
thalidomide children, however, lacked arms and, consequently, had difficulty
in performing the shoulder movements necessary to activate the hooks. CO_2
prostheses, in providing an external source of power, largely eliminated this
problem, but contained the disadvantages of being heavier and having a
cylinder of gas that had to be refilled daily. In addition, the cylinder that
had to be carried on the body in some fashion was awkward and bulky.

The "Russian arm" terminates in a hand, in contrast to the usual hook, and
operates through electrodes placed on the muscles; it was considered, at least
at one time, to most closely approximate the functioning of the normal arm.
But although frequent reference was made to thalidomide children during the
campaign to raise the money to buy the patent from the Russians, it was never
actually used for any thalidomide child. Instead, an adaptation combining a
"hand" with the more conventional switches of the CO_2 prostheses was tried
on one child. It proved so heavy and cumbersome, however, that it was
abandoned.

the mothers of these children who became the sample on which this chapter is based. It should be noted that while these mothers constituted only two-thirds of our total sample, their children were among the most handicapped ones.

Table 2. Classification of thalidomide children wearing prostheses according to site of major limb-deficiency, and past and present placement

		Placement year following birth		Placement at time of research study	
Site of major deformity	Number of children	Number institution-alized	Number at home	Number institution-alized	Number at home
Upper-limb deficiency	9	1	8	1	8
Lower-limb deficiency	2	1	1	0	2
Multiple-limb involvement	2	2	0	1	1

The nine children with upper-limb deformities were all cases of phocomelia. For the other four children, however, the classification of the type of deformity is far more complex. Three had originally been cases of phocomelia (two cases of bilateral lower-limb phocomelia, and one case of tetraphocomelia), while the remaining child manifested nonphocomelic involvement of all four limbs. But prior to being fitted with prostheses, the two children with lower-limb phocomelia had their phocomelic feet amputated. Thus at the time the prostheses were fitted, ten children continued to have terminal appendages (that is, digits) on their deformed limbs, while three had never had, or no longer had, these appendages. What makes this factor particularly significant is the fact that there was a strong correlation between the presence of terminal appendages and the site of the major limb-deficiency. The children with upper-limb deformities all had terminal appendages, while those with lower-limb or multiple-limb deformities did not (except for

the one case of tetraphocomelia). Thus the difference between
the two groups involved not only the site of the main deformity
but also the type of deformity.

The Global Birth Crisis

Paradoxically, it was for these thirteen children, the most
severely handicapped children in the sample, that possibilities for
habilitation of the limb-deficiencies were least discussed during the
global birth crisis. In part, this situation can be attributed to the
rarity of the type of limb-deficiency most of these children manifested (phocomelia) and consequent lack of medical knowledge
concerning treatment. In part, too, the lack of emphasis on treatment resulted from the fact that these children, in general, posed
the most severe emotional and social problems for the mothers
and attending physicians. There were so many global conflicts
and uncertainties attached to this form of birth (Would the children
live or die? Should they be taken home or institutionalized?) that,
for the moment, treatment of the deformed limbs themselves constituted a relatively minor issue.

The possible use of protheses some time in the future was mentioned to some of these mothers, but discussion concerning them
was usually very vague; indeed, only six of the mothers recall hearing any mention of prostheses in the week following birth. The
sources from which they obtained such information ranged from
orthopedic surgeons and pediatricians formally consulted, to casual
reference by a passing resident interested in pediatrics, or a visiting
nurse. The mothers were told that the age for fitting prostheses
ranged from the third to the tenth year, but there was no detailed
information on what the equipment was like, what functioning it
permitted, or where it could be obtained. It is significant that none
of the mothers at this time considered consulting, or was advised
to consult, a specialist in rehabilitation medicine.

Moreover, the deformed limbs themselves were largely written
off. In spite of the fact that all but one of these children were cases
of phocomelia, the doctors and mothers perceived the children to be

in the same category as were amelics, that is, here the deformed appendages were considered to be without any future usefulness for prehension or locomotion. Instead, the search for compensatory functions was focused on whether or not the child was intelligent rather than on any residual functioning in the deformed limbs themselves.

In summary, the birth crisis was a crisis provoked by visible limb-deformities, but, for these children anyhow, the potentialities of the limbs themselves played a surprisingly small part in the attempted resolutions. The mothers and doctors did not see the deformed limbs as having any role in future development. And the possibility of prostheses at some time in the future was only one of many vague possibilities (such as hope for the death of the child, miraculous cure, grafting of limbs) competing for attention. Even when prostheses were explicitly mentioned, it was as a vague comforting device rather than as a practical habilitation technique.

Child-Rearing before the Prostheses

There were nine mothers within this group who took their children home in the weeks following birth. At first, there was still very little mention of and information about prostheses. Instead, as we have seen, the primary concern for the mother became one of rearing the child as he was in the best way she could.

Eight of the nine children taken home at this time were children with upper-limb phocomelia. Because the mothers were not given any advice on how to treat the deformed limbs, most, as we have seen, resorted to rearing these children as they would any other child. Only in one area was there a significant difference. In the vacuum created by the absence of professional advice on how to substitute for the missing arms, these mothers all spontaneously transferred the usual stimulation of the hands to the feet and, less frequently, to the mouth. In concrete terms, this meant that light toys were placed near the feet, the feet were massaged, and so on.

For all the mothers, this procedure aroused considerable anxiety, particularly when they anticipated how visually abnormal this would look as the children grew older, for example, a child at school writing with his feet. But the mothers' basic feeling can be expressed as "the feet were there while the hands weren't and something was better than nothing." Only one mother mentioned that when the baby was three months old she changed techniques and started to stimulate the deformed hands; this followed the visit of a friend, an orthopedic surgeon, who advised the change. Nevertheless, four of the babies spontaneously began to use their hands, at ages varying from five to eight months. The day the mother first realized that the infant was using his hands was usually a dramatic one, as evidenced by the mother who phoned her husband long distance to announce that his daughter was sucking her thumb. But, while the emotional impact of this event was strong, the practical utility was still uncertain.

There is only one mother of a child with predominantly lower-limb phocomelia who took her child home directly from the hospital, making generalizations difficult. From her account, however, it appears that while the emotional turmoil was the same for her as for the others, the immediate necessity to compensate for the handicap by using the remaining limbs was less urgent. For one thing, locomotion is a developmentally later achievement than prehension and the issue therefore did not arise as soon. For another, while the mothers of children suffering from upper-limb phocomelia considered prehension with the feet possible, albeit anxiety-provoking, the mother of the child with lower-limb phocomelia considered locomotion with the hands so bizarre and animal-like as to exclude it from the realm of consideration (though in fact children with deficiencies of the lower limbs were among the first to learn to displace themselves, using their hands as aids.)

Gradually, as the months passed and most of the mothers became aware that the deformities were caused by thalidomide, there was increasing mention of a government program, and some mothers began to read reports of what was being done in Europe, particularly in Germany and England. Here began the first focus on prostheses as a possible solution and, simultaneously, the anxiety of waiting for something to happen. All of the mothers who thought of prostheses at this point considered them favorably and were impatient for the program to begin. But detailed information about the prostheses was still lacking and, basically, the prospect of artificial limbs assumed the mystique of a magical dream—another chance at normal functioning. Certainly some of the publicity that surrounded prostheses at this point helped to encourage this viewpoint; for instance, there was talk that the children could learn to use and treat the prostheses like the normal arms they lacked.

While newspaper reports do not necessarily accurately reflect what the doctors concerned actually said, it was from the newspapers that the mothers derived their first knowledge of the prostheses. A picture of the type of publicity current can be gained from the following excerpts:

Le **Dr.** Gingras a révélé que les membres artificiels sont maintenant tellement perfectionnés que les bébés de quelques mois apprennent à s'en servir plus utilement que ce que peuvent accomplir des bébés normaux avec leurs membres normaux! (Dimanche Matin, July 12, 1964, p. 8) [6]

There is no reason why the thalidomide child cannot within his limitations look forward to a full and useful life. There is no reason why he cannot go to school, train for a profession, and marry. The ease of his adjustment will depend to a large extent on how soon he is fitted with prosthetic appliances (artificial limbs). The sooner the better. (Report of interview with Dr. M. Mongeau, *The Montreal Star,* December 17, 1963, p. 14)

In summary, while this stage presented fewer dramatic and overt conflicts than the first period of global crisis, it was during this time that the ground was laid for many of the future conflicts about the prostheses—conflicts that would only become apparent months later. This is particularly true in the case of the mothers of the children with predominately upper-limb phocomelia, and, in fact, it is in this period that we can observe the genesis of the

[6] "Dr. Gingras revealed that artificial limbs are now sufficiently perfected that babies of several months are learning to use them more effectively than normal babies can use their normal limbs!"

distinction between mothers of upper-limb phocomelic children and those of children with lower-limb phocomelia or multiple-limb deformities.

The area of potential conflict for the mothers of upper-limb phocomelic children can be summarized very simply as a question of the relative value of deformed arms versus intact feet or potential prostheses as the best means of achieving the goals of optimal functioning and the most normal visual appearance. As we have seen, even within this period there were a number of shifts of position between these various modalities. But the implications of each, and the potentialities for conflict, were still far from being clearly seen. In the sole case of the lower-limb phocomelic child living at home, on the other hand, there seemed to be less conflict, both because there was less urgency and there were fewer alternatives.

The Fitting of Prostheses

In spite of the fact that all of the children had had at least one previous medical consultation and two had undergone surgical procedures, for most of the mothers the habilitation program formally began with the children's arrival at the RIM at ages varying from eight months to thirty months.

At this time the distinction between the reactions of mothers of predominantly upper-limb phocomelic children and those of children with lower- or multiple-limb deformities becomes even clearer. While the handicaps are more varied in this latter category, the psychological reactions appear simpler. Regardless of any initial disappointment in the unavoidable awkwardness of the prostheses, all of these mothers accepted them as being absolutely necessary, especially so for two children with solely lower-limb phocomelia who had their feet amputated, thus removing any conflict between limbs and prostheses, and for two others who had such multiple anomalies (in both cases all four limbs as well as other deformities were involved) that prostheses offered the only hope for a semblance of normal functioning. Indeed, two mothers in this category were able to consider the possibility of permanently raising their children at home only after they knew they would receive prostheses or had actually received them.

For the mothers of children with predominantly upper-limb phocomelia, the situation was psychologically more complex. Even those mothers whose children were not yet using their hands were able to observe in the hospital that other upper-limb phocomelic children had learned to use theirs. In addition, during the children's hospitalization for evaluation and prosthetic fitting, the policy of the nurses and occupational therapists was to encourage the use of the hands for self-care activities. This marked a considerable reversal of orientation and placed the mothers in a very unclear position; in a short period of time they had to accept the futility of their previous efforts to stimulate the feet, turn their present attention to the hands, while focusing their hopes for the future on the prostheses.

The actual fitting of the first prostheses occurred for these upper-limb phocomelic children at ages varying from 15 to 26 months (one child was fitted at 15 months, one at 16, two at 21, one at 22, two at 24, and one at 26). The age at which the child was fitted seems to have been determined mainly by the fact that the prostheses only became available at a certain date and, consequently, the children born first were fitted at older ages. Within this restricted age range, there is no discernible relation between the age of fitting and the mothers' perceptions.

When shown the actual upper prostheses that her child would receive, two mothers continued to be pleased, but six were disappointed. The reasons given for this disappointment are expressed similarly by all the mothers, that is, they found the prostheses to be cold, hard, artificial, and cumbersome. But it is possible that these negative attitudes were founded on a much more basic disappointment, one which the mothers had difficulty in verbalizing, both on first seeing the prostheses and during the research interviews. From the way they described their earlier anticipations of the prostheses, and their hopes for the future, it is clear that what the mothers were looking for were prostheses whose terminal devices resembled hands. But the prostheses that had been described in such glowing terms, and on which so much hope rested, did not end in hands, but in hooks.

Nevertheless, in spite of their reservations, they all accepted the prostheses. There seem to have been three fundamental reasons for this acceptance: (1) The government program stressed prostheses, and the mothers felt dependent on this authority. (2) Regardless of the present utility of the hands versus the prostheses, the mothers remained uncertain about the future; for example, they had to consider that even if the child was managing well now, he might need prostheses for school. This viewpoint was strengthened by the medical opinion that it was essential to fit prostheses early in order to integrate them into the body image. Thus, even if they disliked the present prostheses, the mothers considered them an essential prerequisite for the wearing of the future "good" prostheses. And (3) there was considerable guilt attached to the refusal of the prostheses since (more or less explicitly) the good mother was considered to be the one who accepted them.

All the mothers whose children were to be taken home following the fitting came to the hospital for a period of training in learning how to help the children use the prostheses. Whatever their underlying feelings about the prostheses, the reaction to the training program itself was unanimously positive; without exception, the mothers considered this training excellent and, in fact, many formed a very strong attachment to the occupational therapist involved.

In summary, while the difficulties experienced by the mothers of lower-limb and multiple-limb deformed children during this period were numerous, they were relatively manifest and, consequently, they could be dealt with more or less realistically. The concerns of the mothers of upper-limb phocomelic children, on the other hand, were far more difficult to manage, because there were issues involved that had never been explicitly expressed.

In some ways, the mothers of upper-limb phocomelic children faced a mourning crisis at this time that was similar to that experienced in the first period. Their early hopes for a normal or miraculously cured baby had been transformed, for most of them, into a hope for prostheses that would look and function like normal arms. Instead, they were confronted by prostheses that were radically different from their ideal. Though able to express some of their disappointment, they felt too guilty and too uncertain to really work through the basic issue involved, which was that of almost-real arms versus plastic and steel hooks; while accepting tentatively the present prostheses, the emotional investment was once more displaced to some future potential prostheses. These were to be the "real" prostheses, in contrast to the present only preliminary ones. And yet, if the future prostheses were to be truly integrated into the body image, they were told the process would have to start now; thus, the present prostheses were essential and had to be valued.

The other basic problem that had not yet been faced was the relative hierarchy of values to be attributed to the feet, the phocomelic hands, and the prostheses. It was relatively simple to evaluate such matters as present functioning of the hands versus the functioning permitted by the existing prostheses. But the issue was far more complex in that not only functioning, visual appearance, and tactile qualities had to be included in this evaluation, but in each case present possibilities had to be balanced against future potentialities that were still very uncertain.

Given the number of dimensions involved, it is not surprising that even the carefully devised and generally sensitively executed prosthetic training program carried out by the Institute did not lead to a definite solution. Instead, the end of this first phase of the formal habilitation program can be seen as merely a prelude to the mothers' attempts to come to terms with the prostheses.

Present Perception of Prostheses

At the time the research interviews were conducted, the children had been fitted with prostheses for a period of approximately two years. All had returned to the Institute for prosthetic adjustment, and a few had even undergone a change of prostheses, that is, from conventional-style prostheses to CO_2-powered types (see note 5 above), but, according to the mothers' perceptions, no radical advances had yet occurred in the type of prostheses available. Thus the judgments expressed during the research period were largely the fruit of their experiences in learning to live with the first prostheses, both psychologically and practically, and with their attempts to incorporate use of the prostheses into the daily routine in the home.[7]

The dichotomy between the perceptions of mothers of upper-limb phocomelic children and those of children with lower-limb or multiple-limb deformities concerning the prostheses had grown to the point where, at the time the research interviews were conducted, two psychologically distinct groups were formed. There are a number of areas involving the prostheses that illustrate the differences between these groups, but Siller and Silverman (1962) have suggested, in their research project on acceptance of prostheses by upper-limb amputees, that there are three main factors that determine whether or not a prosthesis will be used: (a) the static qualities or appearance of the prosthesis, (b) the dynamic qualities or perceived functional utility, and (c) the intensity of the social situation in question. Since our concern is not with the patients themselves, but with the mothers' perceptions of the children, we have somewhat modified the operational definitions of these dimensions. Thus, as our measure of the appearance of the prostheses, we have used the criterion of whether or not the child

---

[7] For the specific problem of the mothers' perceptions of the prostheses in daily living, our sample is further reduced to the mothers of those children who were living at home at the time of the study (involving eight cases of predominantly upper-limb phocomelia and three cases of lower- or multiple-limb deformities). The mothers of the two children who remained in hospital had neither the necessity nor the opportunity to form the type of discriminative judgment under discussion, partly because they had relatively infrequent contacts with their children. Thus one of the mothers only discovered that her child was wearing prostheses on one of her infrequent visits, weeks after they had been fitted.

looks more "normal" or "abnormal" to the mother while wearing them. Functional utility is evaluated by whether or not the mother perceives the child's level of independence to be increased while wearing prostheses. And since one of the crucial elements of the early mother-child relationship is physical expression of affection, we have used the mother's perception of its facilitation or hindrance by the child's wearing the prostheses as a measure of whether the prostheses are useful in an intense social situation. The results obtained on visual appearance can be summarized as noted in Table 3.

Table 3. Mothers' perceptions of the children's appearance while wearing prostheses

Site of main deformity	Number of children	Visual appearance		
		More normal *N*	No difference or mixed feelings *N*	Less normal *N*
Upper-limb involvement	8	1	1	6
Lower-limb or multiple-limb involvement	3	3	0	0

The two mothers, in the upper-limb phocomelia group, who found that the children looked more normal or no different with the prostheses introduced further distinctions. Thus both agreed that the children looked more normal to them without prostheses, but they based their reply of "more normal" or "no difference" on their belief that when wearing long-sleeved clothes in a situation involving strangers the children would appear more normal with prostheses. The six mothers who found that the children looked more abnormal with the prostheses complained that the wearing of prostheses made the child appear to have four hands.

With respect to the degree of independence achieved by children wearing prostheses, the response of the mothers of the upper-limb

phocomelic children was unanimous (see Table 4). It is significant, too, that while all the children in the lower- and multiple-
limb categories had achieved relative independence in putting on
and removing the prostheses (two completely and one partially),
none of the children in the upper-limb category was able to do this.

Table 4. Mothers' perceptions of the children's level of independence
while wearing prostheses

Site of main deformity	Number of children	Level of independence		
		Increased independence N	No difference N	Decreased independence N
Upper-limb involvement	8	0	0	8
Lower-limb or multiple-limb involvement	3	2	1	0

In discussing the functional utility of the prostheses, the mothers
of the upper-limb phocomelic children pointed out another disadvantage which they considered important. Because of the restriction in activities imposed by the prostheses, all were forced to devote considerable time to cajoling, devising activities, and amusing
the children while they were wearing them. While some of the
mothers were quite ingenious in planning activities that would encourage the children to wear prostheses (for example, one mother
permitted her young daughter to put on lipstick while wearing the
prostheses, four made favored activities, such as visiting, depend-
dent on the child's agreeing to wear the prostheses), all resented
the effort involved. From their point of view, these children in general required much more attention and time than normal children
their age, and the effort demanded by the prostheses was an added
burden.

The same pattern is found when we examine the mothers' perceptions of the role of the prostheses in facilitating or hindering
their ability to express affection toward the children (see Table 5).

Table 5. Mothers' judgment of their ability to caress children wearing prostheses

		Ability to caress		
Site of main deformity	Number of children	Easier N	Same N	Harder N
Upper-limb involvement	8	0	1	7
Lower-limb or multiple-limb involvement	3	1	2	0

Thus we find a high correlation between the mothers' perceptions of these three dimensions of the prostheses. The mothers whose children wear only upper-limb prostheses found generally that the children, while wearing the prostheses, looked more abnormal, were more dependent, and were harder to caress. On the other hand, mothers of children with lower, or upper and lower prostheses judged that the children, while wearing them, looked more normal, were more independent, and were no more difficult to fondle. In accord with Siller and Silverman's results, we also find that the mothers' evaluation of the prostheses on these three dimensions tended to correlate highly with wearing time (see Table 6).

Table 6. Mothers' estimation of children's daily wearing time of prostheses

		Wearing time daily		
Site of main deformity	Number of children	Not at all N	Less than two hours N	Six to eight hours N
Upper-limb involvement	8	1	7	0
Lower-limb or multiple-limb involvement	3	0	0	3

The most apparent conclusion that one could draw from these findings is that in the case of children with lower- or multiple-limb deformities the attempt to fit prostheses had proved largely successful, according to the mothers' perceptions, while in the case of children with upper-limb phocomelia, the reverse was true. This would certainly accord with previous research findings mentioned in the literature; in general, lower-limb prostheses are much more easily accepted by the patient than are upper-limb prostheses (Dean, 1958; Gingras *et al.*, 1964). One would simply make the further generalization that this is true not only for adult patients, but is applicable as well to mothers of child patients.

And yet there are a number of contradictions in our data that are not easily explained in this fashion. For instance, given the fact that all prostheses, both upper- and lower-limb, are fabricated of plastic and metal, why did the mothers of upper-limb phocomelic children find that their cold metallic quality made it difficult for them to caress the children while they were wearing prostheses, while for the mothers of children with lower-limb or multiple-limb deformities this factor was not an issue? Or, given the fact that all the mothers of upper-limb phocomelic children found that the prostheses actually decreased the level of independence, and most found that they made the child look more abnormal, why did all but one insist that the child wear them for at least a limited amount of time each day? (And even in the one case where the child was not wearing them at all at the time of the research interviews, the mother had not discarded the prostheses but expected the child to resume wearing them once certain adjustments were made.)

In order to understand both the surprising homogeneity of perceptions found within each group and some of the contradictions elicited, it is necessary to explore the psychological situation of the mothers in each of these groups. For the mothers of the children with upper-limb phocomelia, the choice had never been simply one for or against prostheses, but had always had to include the alternatives of the other possible modes of prehension, the various dimensions of each modality, and the major periods of time. An example of the multiple evaluations necessary can be seen by portraying graphically what could be the responses of a hypothetical mother of an upper-limb phocomelic child if she had to rate the visual appearance, functional utility, and tactile qualities of the hands, feet, and prostheses in the past, present, and future (see Table 7). Even if we completely ignore such important factors as personality variation, cultural influences, and so on, and use categories that are much too global to indicate some of the subtle differentiations possible and necessary, there still remain a minimum of twenty-seven combinations that a mother of an upper-limb phocomelic child would have to consider in order to evaluate the optimal mode of prehension.

Table 7. Hypothetical rating of visual appearance, functional utility, and tactile qualities of hands, feet, and prostheses

	Hands			Feet			Prostheses		
	Past	Present	Future	Past	Present	Future	Past	Present	Future
Visual appearance	—	+	+	—	—	—	—	—	+
Functional utility	—	+	?	+	—	—	—	—	+
Tactile qualities	+	+	+	+	+	+	—	—	+

This already extremely complex situation is further complicated, for the mothers of upper-limb phocomelic children, by the inherent and inevitable conflicts contained in some of these alternatives. To take only a very simple example, originally the feet were seen as the most useful, and at that time the only available, mode of prehension, but the increase in "normalcy" achieved in functional utility conflicted with the greater "abnormality" in visual appearance. Or, consider how the perception of the greater utility of the hands in most activities, in the present, conflicts with the expectation that the prostheses will eventually prove more useful, while yet recognizing that it is necessary for the child to use them as the main mode of prehension now, if they are to be useful eventually.

Thus we can assume that the psychological situation of the mothers of upper-limb phocomelic children concerning the optimal mode of prehension had always contained a high level of conflict, and that it continued to contain this conflict at the time of the research interviews. For certain of these alternatives, attempts at dissonance reduction had been successfully made, and it was possible to observe other attempts at dissonance reduction at the time of the research interviews, but the general situation remained a conflict-laden one.

The change in attitudes toward the use of feet as a mode of prehension represents probably the most successful attempt at dissonance reduction. Although this mode was originally favored by all the mothers of the upper-limb phocomelic children, anxiety concerning its implications, the policy of the RIM in discouraging the use of the feet, and the development of more acceptable alternatives, had all combined to make this alternative one of relatively minor importance at the time of the research interviews. The children had not changed as much as their mothers' attitudes had. Some of the children had achieved considerable dexterity with their feet and, upon direct questioning, the mothers would hesitantly admit that the children sometimes sought to use them and, in fact, were sometimes permitted to do so in play situations. But, in spite of the dexterity that the children manifested with their feet, the mothers were unanimous in ranking the functional utility of the feet very low. Most of the mothers would occasionally permit the use of the feet for solitary play, but the conditions for such use were that it be neither frequent nor public. For focal activities such as eating, and in all social situations, the use of the feet was strongly tabooed.

To a similar extent, we could find some attempts at dissonance reduction at the time of the research interviews regarding the merits of the hands versus the prostheses as alternative modes of prehension. The finding of greater utility of the hands had been generalized by the mothers to all activities and manifested no correlation with the varying lengths of the phocomelic arms. In the same way, we found a very high correlation between perception of utility, visual appearance, and tactile qualities, although these later two categories are not inherently functions of the first.

Nevertheless, in spite of the overwhelmingly superior rating given to the hands, no final decision was possible for these mothers. For one thing, their perceptions conflicted with their understanding of RIM policy; they believed, with some justification, that the Institute considered the integration of the prostheses into the body image possible and necessary, that the achievement of this goal depended on the mother's success in fostering the wearing of the prostheses now, and, consequently, that the good mother was one who insisted on the wearing of the prostheses. They realized, too, that they were unable to judge accurately the future development of the hands and the prostheses, and the ultimate relative efficacy of the two. Thus the conflict continued and was manifested in such contradictions as the mothers finding the prostheses of very limited value, but insisting that the children wear them at least some of the time.

For the mothers of children with lower- or multiple-limb deformities, the situation had always been simpler, because the alternatives had been much more restricted. Two of these children only returned home after amputation and, in one case, after the fitting of prostheses; the rearing of these children in the family, then, began after prostheses had become the main mode of prehension and locomotion. Even in the one case of a lower-limb phocomelic child taken home after birth, the feet were later amputated. Although this child was almost three at the time his feet were amputated, the mother completely denied any phantom limb sensations, or any sense of loss on the child's part at the removal of his "silly little feet." Whatever the difficulties encountered with the present prostheses, for these mothers they were so much better than anything else available that one of the mothers, at least, completely denied that the prostheses were not as good as "skin legs" and, in fact, found it very hard to touch her child when he was not wearing his artificial legs.

Future Expectations

Any discussion of the future [8] necessarily involves definition of the time element involved; depending on the perspective from which it is viewed, the future may mean tomorrow, next month, or ten years hence. And yet the surprising fact is that when considering the prostheses, the time dimension used by all the mothers was extremely vague and uncertain. There was remarkably little attempt to link expected changes in the prostheses with life stages they considered important, for instance, school, adolescence, and so on. Nor was there much emphasis placed on the future as a developmental process involving constant resolution of conflicts and adaptations to new situations. Rather, here is where was seen the continuation of the magical wishes that were so predominant during the first stage; the hope was for a final outcome that would settle all issues and resolve all conflicts once and for all. In this context, it is not surprising that four of the mothers began the discussion of their future expectations concerning the prostheses by spontaneously reviving their earliest hope—that arms could be transplanted or grafted.

Regardless of their present conflicts about the prostheses, all the mothers expected their children to wear prostheses for the rest of their lives. Moreover, they implicitly accepted the view of the RIM that these prostheses were essential for schooling and jobs. They even hoped that the prostheses would make possible a large range of activities not usually considered accessible to people with this type of handicap, for example, tennis. There was no difference in this area between the opinions expressed by mothers of upper-limb

[8] At the time the research interviews were conducted, the RIM had bought the patent for the Russian electronic arm and was in the process of adapting it for children. But none of these mothers had seen the arm or knew exactly when it would become available, nor had the name of the child chosen as the first one to be fitted been publicly announced. While only three mothers explicitly mentioned this electronic arm, it is highly probable that all had some degree of awareness of it.

phocomelic children and those by mothers of children with lower-limb or multiple-limb deformities.

Two of the mothers of children with upper-limb phocomelia did show some questioning of the general attitude that prostheses could and should be integrated into the body image. One, at one point, suggested that perhaps the prostheses should be treated like a sweater: put on when needed and removed when unnecessary. Another half-jokingly remarked that maybe the prostheses should continue to have hooks; they were artificial, so why should one try to make them look real? But even these two mothers did not maintain this point of view consistently.

Instead, the major hope for all the mothers of upper-limb phocomelic children was for prostheses that would terminate in hands, rather than hooks, and tend to be indistinguishable visually from normal arms. Given prostheses with hands, all the mothers believed that the children would readily accept them because they would work better, look more normal, and, presumably, feel more comfortable. All the mothers assumed, too, that any wearing tolerance developed with the present prostheses would be automatically transferable to any future ones.

Thus, for the mothers of the upper-limb phocomelic children, the end of the present conflict was envisaged by the attainment of prostheses with hands. They showed remarkably little desire to consider some of the contradictions inherent in such a view. For instance, the present dislike of the prostheses was expressed mainly as a result of the greater utility of hands versus prostheses. Three of the mothers explicitly mentioned that they hoped the arms would continue to grow in proportion to the body, but none would entertain the possibility of future conflict between hands and prostheses. Again, most of the mothers rated the prostheses low in visual appearance because the children looked "as if they have four hands" while wearing them. How would the provision of prostheses with hands resolve this conflict? And, finally, the mothers claimed that it was harder presently to fondle the children while they were wearing the prostheses, because of their cold, metallic quality. How would the plastic and metal characteristics of even ideal prostheses permit them to be used in situations of intense physical contact—for example, in sexual intercourse in adulthood? And yet, the criterion they used to measure the success of any prostheses was precisely that of becoming "like a part of the body."

For the mothers of the children with lower-limb or multiple-limb deformities the situation was, as usual, much simpler. They hoped for prostheses that would be lighter, more comfortable and, in one case, have knees. But, in general, the future was seen as a process of gradual improvement upon the present.

In summary, the future expectations of mothers of upper-limb phocomelic children, contrasted with those of children with lower- or multiple-limb deformities, presents us with a paradoxical situation. The mothers of the upper-limb phocomelic children, who placed very little value on the present prostheses, anticipated an almost miraculous change. They expected ideal prostheses that would provide a solution for most of their present conflicts. Even though they had been sadly disappointed in the usefulness of the prostheses contrasted with the hands, all assumed that prostheses would be essential for future activities. On the other hand, the mothers of children with lower-limb or multiple-limb deformities, who were relatively satisfied with the present prostheses, hoped for some improvement but expected few radical innovations.

One could interpret this paradox rather simply; considering how little satisfied the mothers of the upper-limb phocomelic children were in the present, they were the ones who saw the most room for improvement. And yet this explanation does not help us understand why the mothers continued to place their faith for the future in prostheses and completely ignored present disillusionment in predicting future possibilities. Perhaps this overevaluation of the future can best be understood as one more attempt to reduce the conflict these mothers experienced. Given the present situation in which the mothers found the prostheses of very little value, but believed it necessary to make the children wear them because of future benefits, it was not surprising that they tended to hope for ideal prostheses that would somehow make the present struggle and disappointment worthwhile.

Conclusions

The attempt to describe the mothers' perceptions of the prostheses unexpectedly presents us with a double problem. It is impossible to discuss how mothers perceived and reacted to the prostheses without including some questions about how the professionals concerned perceived them, and how they communicated their perceptions to the mothers. Here the questioning must be rather cautious since our knowledge of the policy decisions involved in the choice of the prostheses as the instrument of normification is based solely on a layman's reading of some of the literature. Nevertheless, as a psychologist, it is legitimate to pose questions about how a technique that raised doubts even among the experts concerned came to be perceived and used virtually as a "magical cure-all" for the problems of thalidomide limb-deficiency. Did the popular press oversimplify the complex issues inherent in the use of prostheses, or did those who initially made the policy decision themselves undergo a conversion that led them to underemphasize the reservations expressed by their colleagues who were less enthusiastic about this technique? How much were those who were charged with implementing the policy and communicating it to the mothers aware of the issues involved in the original policy decision? Even more basic, how much of the professional uncertainty concerning a given technique or medicine should be communicated to the patient concerned? If too much, will this prevent a patient from accepting a potentially useful procedure? If too little, will this eventually lead to disillusionment and loss of trust in the professional involved?

It is ironic that a study which at its beginning became involved with questions concerning medical practice and communication should also end with similar questions, though in a different context. In both cases our knowledge of the medical point of view is too limited to permit us to do more than raise these questions.

Nevertheless, this type of problem again brings to the fore two basic characteristics of the history of the maternity of a limb-deficient thalidomide child. The first is that many of the problems encountered in the history are far more general than the unique historical circumstances of the thalidomide situation itself; in many cases, the particular story of thalidomide only highlighted long standing, but still unresolved, issues. Secondly, and perhaps more important, the mothers' perceptions and reactions cannot be viewed in isolation; throughout the history, there was a complex, ongoing interaction between the mothers and their environment. To attempt to understand what happened, solely in terms of the individual mother's personality or perceptions, is to deny a considerable part of the reality confronting these mothers.

But, once again, while the environmental factor adds to the complexity of the original problem posed—How did mothers perceive and react to the prostheses?—it, in itself, does not offer a complete explanation for this problem. On the basis of our data, it seems clear that in relation to the prostheses the mothers can be divided into two distinct categories: the mothers of children with multiple-limb or lower-limb deformities who liked and used the prostheses, and those whose children manifested upper-limb phocomelia as the major limb-deformity who were very ambivalent. Why?

In our discussion of the difficulties encountered by mothers of children with upper-limb phocomelia, there is one basic issue that may easily escape our attention. It is possible that these mothers were in a more conflicted state, not only because the reality they faced was more complex, but also because these were the mothers who appeared to have most drastically modified their original perception of their children. Thus the disillusionment these mothers experienced with some of the modes of prehension (feet, or prostheses) was not necessarily the result of their disillusionment with or rejection of their children; on the contrary, it may have been directly attributable to the fact that they currently perceived more possibilities in these children than they had ever anticipated.

In order to understand these mothers' changes in perception, it is necessary to attempt to reconstruct the developmental process that they had undergone. At the time these babies were born, the mothers shared the environmental viewpoint that classified them as grossly handicapped. Indeed, their original conflict centered on this necessity to raise an "incomplete" child. Even the choice of the feet as the original mode of prehension, and the anxiety aroused by this choice, can be viewed as the mother's uneasiness with a situation that fulfilled neither her expectations nor her anticipations of what society would judge normal. Gradually, however, the originally devalued phocomelic hands began to assume greater usefulness. However, this greater valuation of the hands did not simply remain a judgment of the functional utility of a mode of prehension, but became generalized to the point where these mothers judged that the children looked, acted, and felt more normal as they were, and the prostheses were rejected as an added artificial encumbrance. And yet, for a variety of external and internal reasons, they felt impelled to try to integrate prostheses—which they judged to neither look, feel, nor function like normal arms—into the child's body image.

Seen in this light, the problem becomes a much more general one than simply the choice of the optimal mode of prehension. Instead, it involves the whole question of what constitutes normality. These mothers psychologically were in a very different situation from those whose children have suffered amputations some time after birth, or even from that of mothers of children with congenital limb-deficiencies where the children are completely amelic or hemimelic. While at birth they perceived these children as suffering a loss, when they compared them with themselves and with other "normal" children, their emotional investment had been in children who were "born that way," who had suffered no subsequent loss, and who did have some form of hands. One mother expressed this dilemma very poignantly when she said, "I know that my child is handicapped and yet when I look at other children I somehow feel that it is their arms which are too long." Thus one can legitimately raise the question whether the conflict of these mothers at

the time of the research interviews, concerning hands versus prostheses, was simply due to the fact that the hands had been found to
have unexpected usefulness or whether, on the contrary, the greater
utility perceived in the hands resulted from a changed perception
of the whole child.

Here one must be very specific as to what this changed perception
of the child by the mother entailed. The "negative phocomelia"
examinations carried out by the occupational therapists at the
RIM (Hutchison, 1967) showed that all these children manifested
some impairment of functioning compared to normal children of
the same chronological age. From the description given by the
mothers of what their upper-limb phocomelic children could not do,
it was clear that none of these mothers was denying the restriction
in functioning. On the contrary, these mothers were very explicit
in pointing out activities that could not be performed by their children. What had changed, however, was the point of reference from
which they viewed these limitations. There was no longer a comparison of the child with an external criterion of normality, but
instead a perception of the child that recognized his differences,
and yet still considered him essentially "whole" in his functioning
as a unique individual. In some ways the situation was analogous
to that of the mother who recognizes that Susan is prettier than
Mary and that Johnny is smarter, but that Mary is essentially
herself regardless of what assets or liabilities she possesses.

In this situation, the aim of integrating the prostheses into the
body image became a goal of attempting to add something to a
child whose image was already whole. In short, it constituted a
deformation. If this was so, however, why were the mothers so insistent that this could and must be done? Regardless of the external
pressure, there must have been strong internal forces that impelled
the mothers to violate their own perceptions of the children. While
none of the mothers was able to state explicitly these reasons, from
their remarks we can infer some of the possible reasons. The basic
difficulty seems to have been that the perceptions these mothers
currently had of their children were still very personal, partial solu-

tions, and they were very unclear about the future and the social implications of such a view.

For one, the mothers were unable to predict whether they themselves would continue to hold this point of view in the future. At the time of the research interviews the children were still comparatively young and, when viewed from the adult perspective, all children are so different and limited that small differences are less relevant and more easily tolerated. In the case of the upper-limb phocomelic children, they could perceive the arms as whole, because they did end in hands, and all children's arms are much shorter than those of adults. But they did not know how they would feel as the children grew older when it would become necessary to start to judge them as men and women like themselves.

A second consideration was that the mothers did not know how the environment would perceive these children. A handicapped child may be "cute," but how would his peers judge him at school, at work, and so on.

And thirdly, the mothers did not know how these children would perceive themselves as they grew older. The mothers experienced much uneasiness even at this age when they were occasionally confronted by their children with the fact of their difference, and, as we have seen, most anticipated the problem of "telling" as a very difficult one. To the degree that the mothers expected that the children would experience a loss and reproach them for this loss, the prostheses were viewed as a form of reparation which they could offer the children as a substitute for the missing arms. And, in fact, in spite of their own present dislike of the prostheses, the mothers generally tended to praise these artificial arms to their children and to describe their future benefits in glowing terms.

For the mothers of children with lower-limb phocomelia or multiple-limb deformities, the situation has been very different. These mothers also perceived their children as suffering a loss at birth, and this perception had not been radically modified. Two of these children, in fact, did suffer a subsequent loss—the phocomelic feet were amputated. In the remaining case, the child suffered from such multiple injuries that the mother stated "his prostheses are part of him; without prostheses he would not be a human being." For these mothers, prostheses were the only possible means of reparation for a very evident loss. Added to this was the realistic factor that leg prostheses more closely approached the functioning and appearance of normal legs. This point of view certainly contained the possibility of future psychological difficulties, as in the case of one mother who denied her child's loss and kept insisting that "it depends on him; his artificial legs can work as well as skin legs." But certainly it facilitated the stated goal of integrating the prostheses into the body image.

Considering the complexities of the situation, there appears to be no simple way of alleviating the conflicts of mothers of upper-limb phocomelic children. Certainly, both for humanitarian and practical reasons, no one would suggest amputating the phocomelic hands so as to avoid the issue of hands versus prostheses. Instead, the problem becomes one of attempting to reduce the dissonance for the mothers between the implications of the two alternatives.

There are at least two main fashions in which this might be attempted. One might be to develop more specific role definitions for each of these modes of prehension in the hope of making them complementary rather than conflicting. This would involve abandoning the goal of integrating the prostheses into the body image, replacing it instead by one of accepting the children as they are, and perceiving the prostheses mainly as a tool, useful for certain specific activities. Thus the prostheses would be seen not as a substitute for missing arms but as a complement to existing arms.

The other alternative is a radically different one. To the degree that we assume that judgments of functional utility, visual appearance, and so on, are not completely independent, but instead are derived from global perceptions of "goodness" or "badness," one can wonder if radical improvement in one dimension of the prostheses, for example, its functional utility or its visual appearance, would be sufficiently generalizable so as to modify the global perception. Thus, if the prostheses could be made more useful, or visually more like normal arms, would this cause the mothers to perceive them as generally better than the phocomelic hands and, consequently, serve to reduce the conflict between the two?

Neither of these alternatives would solve all problems. Gingras *et al.* (1964) have pointed out that certain upper-limb amputees fitted with prostheses as adolescents do tend to view and use them mainly as tools. But if this were the goal for prostheses formulated for these children, what would be the optimal age of fitting? How would this affect the mothers' utilization of prostheses as a form of reparation to the children? Would prostheses in these circumstances be sufficiently invested by the mothers and children to make them willing to undertake the long, arduous training program?

On the other hand, if the attempt is made to develop prostheses that will be perceived as globally better than the phocomelic hands, is the crucial dimension that of visual appearance or that of functional utility? The mothers of these children expressed the hope for prostheses with hands, but currently none of the existing prostheses of this type for children, including the Russian army (see notes 5 and 8 above), is without functional disadvantages (cf. Boivin, 1968). Fishman and Kay (1964) have found that, in general, an artificial hand will be better accepted by young children and their parents than prostheses ending in hooks, even with some loss in utility. But, unlike the children studied by Fishman and Kay, the thalidomide children have bilateral anomalies. How much loss in functioning could be tolerated for the sake of prostheses with hands?

As usual, there are no conclusive answers available at this time. But in tolerating the uncertainty apparent in this and other areas, it may be helpful to remember that the perceptions of mothers of children with limb-deficiencies are part of a developmental process. The situation has undergone many changes in the time interval between the birth and the research interviews, and the only certain prediction we can make is that it will continue to change. Moreover, it is precisely in this factor of change that we find the element common to mothers of both normal and thalidomide children. Whatever the difficulties caused by the developmental process, it is this capacity for growth and change that defines the human condition. Dead children do not change, and their mothers do not have to; living children and their mothers must—whatever the number and type of limbs the children possess.

Chapter 6

Summing Up

In this final chapter we should like to abandon our microscopic perspective in favor of a macroscopic overview. Ignoring, for the time being, the qualifications that are the inevitable accompaniment of the conclusions, what in the broadest and most general sense does this lengthy study permit us to say about the maternity of a limb-deficient thalidomide child? And what relevance does the knowledge gained from the study of a particular form of maternity have for the general problem of the mothering of a physically handicapped child?

The second issue that concerns us in this summing up is the evaluation of the study itself. Here we must deal not only with the content of the results, but also with the approach used to obtain these results. For, as will be recalled, in searching for an appropriate conceptual model from which to view the maternity of a limb-deficient thalidomide child, we became increasingly dissatisfied with the approaches used in the existing studies on the mothering of physically handicapped children. Thus instead of adopting one of the customary ways of looking at this type of problem, a rather different approach was formulated. In a sense, we wanted not only to learn more about an unexplored phenomenon, but also to find a better way of understanding the issues involved in the maternity of a physically handicapped child. To what degree has our approach proved successful, and where and how has it failed?

This summing up, therefore, concerns both the results of the study and the attempt to evaluate the study itself. Although both

277

aspects are inevitably interrelated, for purposes of convenience we shall focus on each separately.

The Maternity of a Limb-Deficient Thalidomide Child

The clearest finding to emerge from this study is that there is no distinct and unique form of mother-child relationship that can be labeled "thalidomide maternity." There is no separate species of "thalidomide mothers" whose reactions can be classified as a function of a single factor—be it the childrens' distorted limbs or their own distress. Nor is there a species of thalidomide children neatly ranked by length of limbs or level of intelligence. Instead, there are mothers and children whose interaction manifests all the richness, complexity, and change that characterize the usual mother-child relationship.

Having said this, one must also note that while the mothering of a thalidomide child is not completely different from the mothering of any other child, it is not exactly the same either. Thalidomide mothers may be dealing with the same basic issues that confront all mothers but, because their children are different, much that is ordinarily taken for granted here poses acute and difficult conflicts. In a sense, theirs is history "writ large"; the elements are the same, but they appear in a magnified and more intense form.

THE DEVELOPMENTAL ASPECT

In this study of the mothers' perceptions of their maternity, the theme of change often reoccurred; throughout the history, mothers, children, and environment were continuously changing. And yet, while the history was one of change, it can be questioned whether it was one of development, at least in the conventional sense of the term. For what seemed to be lacking was any sense of teleology, or even continuity, in this change.

The most obvious example of the mothers' difficulty in treating development as a process of change within a framework of continuity lay in the way they developed, or rather failed to develop, a time perspective. In presenting the developmental history of their maternity, the mothers were emphatic in insisting that this experience could only be lived and assimilated on a "day-to-day" basis. As has previously been described, the most traumatic aspect of the research interviews for the mothers lay not in the content of any one of the questions posed, but in the attempt to relate their present situation with their past experiences and future expectations. Moreover, this difficulty was manifested not only in their relationship with the interviewer, but also in the way in which the mothers dealt with the children. It is significant that for these mothers two of the most anxiety-provoking questions which could be raised by their children were precisely those that attempted to link the present with the past and the future: "Mummy, what was I like when I was born?" and "Mummy, what am I going to be like when I grow up?"

This did not mean, of course, that the past and the future played no role in the mothers' perceptions of the present. On the contrary, this was a maternity that sometimes appeared to be dominated by the shadow of a traumatic past and by an ambivalent mixture of fear and hope about an uncertain future. But because it was so difficult for these mothers to integrate what had happened, what was happening, and what might happen, into any cohesive design, the major use of time became a flight into the present.

What made the maternity of a thalidomide child a developmental history without continuity was that these mothers were rearing children without being able to develop any image of the child's life as a whole. The infant he had been, the child he was currently, and the adult he might become could not be viewed as meaningful and necessary parts of a cohesive whole, but remained discrete, isolated entities. And, in the absence of the unifying structure provided by the concept of a life span, the element of time became a disorganizing factor rather than an integrating one. There was no continuity, but only unceasing, unpredictable change.

It is suggested that it is this lack of continuity, rather than the specific problems of any single time period, that constituted one of the basic elements of stress in this form of maternity. As Roth

(1963) points out, the ability to organize time into a meaningful and defined sequence of steps is one of the basic orientation techniques in our culture. The eagerness with which Gesell's work has been popularized and devoured would indicate that this need is shared by mothers engaged in child-rearing. But it is precisely this that the mothers of thalidomide-deformed children lacked.

In trying to understand why the discontinuity was so prominent in the maternity of a thalidomide child, the unique circumstances of the situation deserve consideration; among other things, these mothers were rearing children in a world which contained no adults quite like them. But it was not only the unknown qualities in their physical development that made it so difficult for the mothers to visualize a life span for these children; the problem of integration over time was caused as much by the children's uncertain social status as by their medical prognosis. Given the fact that the problem of social status is one shared by all different children, discontinuity would probably be a basic characteristic of the maternity of any deviant child.

Here the reader may object that the problem of discontinuity is far from unique to handicapped children. Sociologists have long recognized that families who, geographically or otherwise, have broken from their cultural roots may be sharply confronted by the difficulty of rearing children with a discontinuous past, present, and future. Recently, observers of the contemporary scene have suggested that in a society changing as rapidly and unpredictably as our own all mothers may face this problem to some degree. But the problem is far more intense for the mother of a physically handicapped child, for she is dealing not only with the instability of society as a whole, or of a particular subgroup within it, but also with the very uncertain development of this child as an individual within the society. To the degree that the handicapped child is an exception, the usual life plans within a given society may not be accessible to him. How, lacking this external structure, does a mother build an image of the relationship of past, present, and future for her child? And what significance does her difficulty in doing so have for the way she perceives and treats her child at different stages of his development?

Surprisingly enough, the maternity of a physically handicapped child has rarely been studied from this perspective. As has previously been noted, very few studies are developmental in outlook; it is the problems or attitudes of the parents at a given moment in time that have been the focus of most of the work done in this area. Even in relation to the physically handicapped individual himself, the major treatment of the discontinuity in his existence has been in terms of selected crisis points, such as, for example, the period when vocational placement becomes a necessity. However, one can question whether the problem of finding a school or a job is in reality an isolated crisis, or whether, in fact, it does not form part of a far more general problem of finding a framework of continuity for those who do not follow the usual paths of physical and social development. One can also question whether the well-known traumatic identity crisis of the physically handicapped adolescent really marks the emergence of the problem, or whether the groundwork for this crisis has not been laid years earlier in his mother's difficulties in dealing with time in relation to him. Similarly, the questions posed by the mother of a two-year-old handicapped child about his ultimate future, and usually dismissed by professionals as useless rumination or neurotic anxiety, may reflect a very vital issue that is already shaping the form of her maternity. In short, the void in the literature does not necessarily indicate the nonexistence of the problem; it can simply indicate that researchers, too, may prefer to avoid the difficulty of integrating past, present, and future.

Moreover, it is doubtful whether the existing clinical services for those who will require a lifetime of aid adequately take into account, either in planning or structure, the concept of a total life span. In recent years there has been a move to integrate services in space. Thus, for example, the mother of a preschool retarded child may no longer have to deal with a variety of professionals individually but may be fortunate enough to have access to a comprehensive program. However, such programs focus only on a short segment of the child's total life span and do not help the mother deal with anything beyond immediate problems, such as, for instance, her image of the child ten or twenty years hence. Nor is there provision made, by and large, for integrating the service offered a child of one age with the later services he will require. In short, these programs do not reflect, either in their philosophy or in their structure, a way of dealing with a continuous problem in a context of continuity. The fragmentation here is evident in the "graduation" from one comprehensive program that must immediately be followed by a frantic search for the next one.

The habilitation program formulated for thalidomide children offered an unsual degree of continuity both because it was, presumably, a long-term one, and by virtue of the fact that it was centered in an institution whose services cover the complete age range. And yet even here the problem of time was rarely dealt with. It can be argued, of course, that the multiple uncertainties arising specifically from the thalidomide situation made any detailed planning for these children's long-range future particularly difficult. But even the way the structure of the program was presented to the mothers was "nondevelopmental" in approach. The time basis of the program itself was uncertain; because the government had made no commitment regarding time, it could, presumably, stop it at any moment. Nor did the specific aspects of the habilitation program, at least as far as the mothers were concerned, follow a developmental sequence over time. Examinations were ordered, prostheses were changed, hospitalizations were advised, as the mothers perceived it, solely on a "day-to-day" basis. They could not build up expectations of how one step led to another, even over a period of two or three years. Thus the mothers were dealing not only with children whose physical and social development fitted into no defined time structure, but also with a habilitation program that appeared not to integrate its services into any time sequence.

The basic problem of building an image of a life span for an individual whose deviance places him outside the usual structures of society is one which, like the handicap itself, is probably not totally curable by the available clinical techniques. The uncertain social prognosis is too basic an issue to be solved simply by evolving programs that deal with the problem of continuity over time in a more adequate fashion. And yet it can be asked whether the emphasis in clinical services on the present does not represent a professional form of denial; by ignoring the problem of building an image of total development, are we not simply echoing the mothers' fragmentation in time rather than providing a model for integration?

THE PSYCHOLOGICAL ASPECT

Our knowledge of the psychological aspect of the maternity of a thalidomide child suffers from a limitation in our approach: the absence of any study of the individual personalities of each of these mothers. For it is in this area that individual differences become most salient; the common problem of bearing and rearing a deviant child interacted with the unique attitudes and expectations that each of these mothers, as a result of her own developmental history, brought to the task of maternity. Thus, once again, the complexity of the problem is highlighted. The study of the maternity of a deviant child involves more than the personality of the mother, but one cannot eliminate this variable completely without some restriction in understanding. Even this rather broad study is far too narrow in scope.

Within the limits of our data, however, it is possible to make one broad assumption about the psychological basis of the maternity of a limb-deficient thalidomide child, in that the recognition of similarity was as crucial in the mothering of these deviant children as the adaptation to difference. The mothers never saw their maternity as the rearing of children who were totally foreign beings. On the contrary, it was because they could see these children in their own image that the multiple differences manifested could be assimilated and tolerated. Throughout, the maternity of a thalidomide child was influenced by the search for factors that would make it possible for the mother to view the child as "like me." And it is this psychological dimension, as well as the problem of social normality, that made such issues as normal intelligence, the child's capacity to respond to habitual child-rearing techniques, and so on, play such a crucial role in this maternity.

In short, we are suggesting that the essential threat psychologically to the mother-child relationship arose not solely from the mother's need to adapt to a different child, but from the fact that these differences, by concealing what was similar to mother and child, could weaken the mother's capacity to identify with her child. And it is only at the time and to the degree that the mother became able to view the differences in a framework of similarity that maternity became psychologically possible. Thus, when some mothers, on first viewing their children, stressed the "alert eyes" or "untouched face," rather than the stunted limbs, they were not simply engaging in denial. Rather, this can be seen as an attempt to focus on that which was vital if a relationship was to exist. Similarly, the later emphasis on the "normal" aspects of these children's development can be seen as an attempt to preserve this essential condition for identification. The maternity of a thalidomide child was not simply a triumph of maternal feelings over abnormality; on the contrary, it was based on the mother's ability to find sufficient common ground between mother and child, in spite of the differences.

Once again, there were unique factors in the thalidomide situation that made this element emerge in a very clear fashion. As has been noted before, the limb-deficiencies characteristic of thalidomide children were difficult to assimilate, not only because they were congenital, but also because they were clearly visible at birth. In other words, the deviance of these children emerged at a time when the mother had not yet established any identification with this child as an individual. Thus the mother was confronted with the differences before she had established any firm basis of similarity. In this sense, the situation here was different from the problem of the mother whose child becomes different (from, say, polio or traumatic amputation) and who must then maintain, rather than build, a relationship under these circumstances. But would not the capacity to find similarities enter into the maternity of any deviant child? It is hard to imagine how any mother under any circumstances could rear a child who is perceived as completely different from her.

On one level, this emphasis on the importance of similarity in the maternity of a deviant child may appear so self-evident as to seem platitudinous. What makes it worthy of discussion, however, is that the perspective of the mother may be very different from the perspective of researchers and clinicians in the area. Professionals become involved with deviant children because they are different, and the usual emphasis is on the extent of the difference. For example, in trying to establish the impact of a physically handicapped child on the mother, the usual variables measured are type of handicap, or severity. Essentially, our outlook here is in terms of the degree or type of abnormality. But it might be more relevant psychologically to investigate not the extent of the abnormality, but the elements that are crucial for the mother in finding a basis for similarity. It is possible that a severe handicap might be tolerable if it did not affect an area that the mother considered vital, and a minor one traumatic if it did. In short, we have a defined way of measuring what can be absent in the child; it may be equally important to have a similar measure of what must be present if the identification of the mother with the child is to take place.

The importance of similarity in the mother-child relationship also has implications for clinical practice. For instance, it is possible that the mother's ability to see the child as "like her" may be one of the best predictive signs of her capacity to mother this child. Even more important is the role of the professional in fostering this identification of mother and child. Thus the choice of specific habilitation techniques may have to depend as much on the mother's feelings as on medical opinion. The mother who rejects a given technique as "bizarre" or strange is not necessarily being simply balky or neurotic; on the contrary, she may be trying to express what is to her a threat to her maternity. Similarly, it may be necessary and desirable, in terms of the general mother-child relationship, to place less emphasis on correcting the abnormalities (for example, minimal improvement of the child's anomalies by surgical interventions requiring lengthy hospitalizations), and more on developing and strengthening the child's "normal" capacities.

A more delicate problem is the fact that a certain dose of denial may be a necessary condition for the rearing of a deviant child. Given the mother's need to identify with her child, there may be a certain limit beyond which she can neither tolerate nor adapt to difference. Thus it may be asking too much to insist that a mother adopt radically different child-rearing practices and goals. It may also be possible that where the difference is too profound and traumatic (for example, discussing with a child the possibility that he may never marry), the task may have to be assumed by someone besides the mother.

In essence, our point here is that the advice commonly given to mothers of handicapped children to treat the child "as normally as possible" may be based on sound psychological premises. However, the validity of this philosophy lies neither in the fact that it assures the child's optimal development (it may have a contrary effect), nor with its ability to provide the mother with a meaningful guide for resolving the many dilemmas of child-rearing (it definitely does not). Instead, the major value of the "as normal as possible" viewpoint is that it permits—and may be a necessary condition for— a mother to feel and act like a normal mother.

THE SOCIAL ASPECT

It is the most difficult aspect of our subject that we have reserved for discussion last. For if there is a single theme that has dominated the developmental history presented here, it is the crucial importance of social factors in the maternity of a **limb-deficient thalidomide** child. Regardless of whether the problem under discussion was labeled "social" (for example, school entrance), "psychological" (the mother's identification with the child), or "medical" (the prostheses), we were inevitably dealing as much with social factors as with psychological or medical ones. And yet, in spite of its overwhelming importance, it was the social dimension of the maternity that could not be satisfactorily analyzed in the terms in which we had originally conceptualized this study. In fact, as we struggled to understand why we could not understand the social problems in this maternity, we became increasingly disturbed by the possibility that perhaps it was our general approach to this topic that was faulty.

In setting out to describe the mothers' perceptions of the mothering of a limb-deficient thalidomide child, our belief was that we were dealing with a clearly delineated, if complex, clinical problem. What kind of maternity develops when the child is congenitally abnormal? It is true that here we rejected, as being simplistic, the common approach of treating the difficulties in the mother-child relationship solely in terms of the mother's "acceptance-rejection-overprotection" syndrome. Instead, we suggested that many of the problems in this maternity might originate as much in the child's partial normality and partial abnormality as in anything inherent in the mother. Thus instead of conceptualizing the problem as an individual's, we sought to study it as a relationship between two individuals.

But, as the work proceeded, the description of the course of events continuously implicated a third party. At the time of the birth crisis, we had not only to describe the anomalies of the children, and the mothers' reactions to these deformities, but also, and equally as important, the influence of the attending physicians and the environment. Later on it was the habilitation program that became crucial in understanding how the mothers reacted. And when we tried to describe the mothers' anticipations of the future, whether it was in terms of schooling, vocational placement, friends, or marriage, we were again dealing not solely with a mother, or a mother and child, but with a third entity: the society in which the mother and child lived. Unlike a mother or a child, a society is not embodied in a single person; instead, it could be represented by a series of individuals (among them, the doctors who delivered the babies, families, religious authorities, friends, or neighbors), a number of institutional structures (the hospital, habilitation program, government, school), or even abstract ideas (such as social norms, social values). But it was always there and always important. Moreover, this third entity could not be considered simply as the background against which the mother-child relationship took place; on the contrary, our data strongly suggested that society (in its various representations) played as vital a role in shaping the meaning and course of events as did the mothers and children themselves.

It was this fact that made us question whether we had not been using the term "mother-child relationship" as a misnomer for what was actually a triangular relationship involving mother, child, and society. Certainly, empirically it had been proven impossible even to describe the relationship of mother and child without continuous reference to the society in which it existed. And logically, it could be asked whether to speak of an individual's social problem was not a contradiction in terms; did not the existence of a social problem necessarily depend upon a troubled interaction with a society? And yet, throughout this work we had, in effect, described the interaction of three entities, while using a model based only on the interaction of two.

In a sense, the problem that now confronted us was of finding a way of describing the triangular relationship of mother, child, and society during the initial birth crisis and the subsequent attempts at resolution. If the crisis provoked by the birth of a visibly deformed baby depended as much on the social meaning of this event, as on its medical or psychological significance, how did these three elements interact to create the disorganization, distress, and frustration that was so evident in our data? Who produced the failure and who suffered from it? Was it the child who failed by being "monstrous," and, if so, what was the impact of this both on the mother and on society? Was it the mother who failed by being unable to cope with the birth of a deformed child as one of the possible results of pregnancy, and, if so, what were the implications of her failure both for the child and for society? And if it was society (here represented by the attending physicians, families, religious authorities) who somehow proved inadequate, how did this affect mother and child?

It can be suggested that the crisis provoked by the birth of a visibly deformed child is not attributable to a failure in any one entity, be it child, mother, or society. Rather, this type of birth creates a unique type of social breakdown by upsetting the delicate network of interlocking needs and obligations—child's, mother's, and society's—on which the successful rearing of a child depends. And what makes this event so disruptive and so difficult to treat is that the failure does not occur on one level, or in one partner. Instead, there is a chain reaction in which the needs of mother, child, and society, rather than working in harmony, become embroiled in a complex conflict of interests.

The precipitating event in this chain is the birth of a child who is sufficiently sick or deficient to be immediately recognized as different from the normal. But the meaning of this difference is then supplied by society which, validly or invalidly, considers physical abnormality as a form of social deviance and which, as a consequence, has no defined place in the existing social structure for this child. The mother may then decide that in this situation neither the child *nor society* fulfills the necessary conditions for maternity; to rear a child whom society considers socially deviant is to assume a social task without the support and rewards that society usually gives to maternity. But if the mother refuses to act in her habitual role as intermediary between child and society, then society is forced to intervene more directly and intensively than usual in the rearing of a child whose needs as an individual may be in direct conflict with the needs of the society as a whole.

In a sense, the disruption of one part of this network leads to a situation where other parts, too, become unable to operate in the usual manner. The child is doubly endangered because neither society nor the mother is willing to treat him in the way infants are customarily dealt with. The mother, too, is dealing with a double problem in that neither the child nor the society is able to fulfill her expectations of maternity. And society is confronted by a mother and a child who refuse to or cannot fit into the usual scheme of things.

What accentuates the problem is the fact that this breakdown cannot be ignored. At stake is the fate of a helpless infant whose physical survival depends upon the willingness of someone to rear him. Either mother and society must agree to let the child die, society must convince or coerce the mother into rearing him, or else the mother must convince society that in this situation her usual obligations are no longer in force, but that alternative provisions must be made for the child's welfare.

In conceptualizing the birth crisis of the thalidomide child in this manner, one is, of course, grossly oversimplifying. Neither the child's abnormality, the social perception of him as deviant, nor the mother's rejection of maternity was absolute; on the contrary, much of the anguish in this situation centered on trying to define and decide the degree of each of these. But in terms of our hypothesis the essential point is that this form of crisis must be considered not as the sickness or failure of any one person or entity, or even of two, but as a conflict of interests involving three parties. And it was the nature of society's involvement in this crisis that was, in our opinion, the issue that was never adequately dealt with, or even recognized, in the subsequent attempts at resolution of the thalidomide problem.

Initially, it was the attending physicians, "healers of the sick," who were placed in the position of having to treat mothers and children as patients. It was they who were expected to formulate diagnoses, prognoses, and recommendations that would "cure" the dilemma, if not the anomalies. But the initial diagnosis of "monster" was not purely a medical one; it was based, at least partially, on a perception of social deviance. Nor can the mother's reluctance to mother a child like this be understood solely in terms of ignorance, mourning process, or neurosis; this reluctance was based, at least partially, on the mother's recognition that the physical abnormality of the child changed the social basis of maternity. The physicians' recommendations (whether to institutionalize or take home the child) were as much social as medical ones. In short, we are arguing that the conflicts of the birth crisis were as much social as medical or psychological ones. Moreover, for these conflicts there was no optimum solution that would maximally satisfy the needs of all three partners. Instead, each of the possible alternatives necessarily involved a consideration of the relative benefits versus the costs to each of those involved. And it was hardly in the context of the doctor-patient relationship—where they were placed—that these social conflicts and decisions could be handled most appropriately.

Eventually, society (represented here by the government) became concerned about the fate of thalidomide children. The etiology of the deformities, the nature of the anomalies, and the large number of such children born, all contributed to the sense of urgency. But the habilitation program so quickly formulated for thalidomide children was also motivated by the fear that, unless some sort of intervention was undertaken, these children would be abandoned by their mothers. Consequently, although the program was to be conducted under medical auspices and in medical terms, its scope was seen as a broad one in that thalidomide children would not be permitted to be sacrificed either by their mothers or by society. Instead, by safeguarding their right to a family upbringing, and by the provision of the best available medical care, these children would be prepared and equipped for lives as useful, productive members of normal society. In pursuit of this aim, the mothers would be offered psychological and financial support to help them rear their children.

If the habilitation program is judged on the basis of whether it managed to prevent the maternal abandonment of thalidomide children, this program must be considered a brilliant success. Most of the children were kept in, or brought back to, their families, and, at the time of the research interviews, the mothers were managing to rear them more or less adequately. Moreover, the mothers did perceive the RIM as providing considerable help in this task.

But the question can be raised whether even this habilitation program ever dealt openly either with the issue of the children's social deviancy, or with the conflict between mother and society concerning who was responsible, and to what degree, for the rearing of a social deviant. For the child's deviancy became subsumed under his patient status: if this child could be given adequate medical treatment and a good family upbringing, then somehow he would be able to find his place in society. But the mothers were reacting not solely to the physical deficiency of their children; they were also confronted by the dilemma of a maternity which, because of the child's social deviancy, lacked the usual social substructure. Not even the best of medical treatment furnished by a segment of society could ensure that society as a whole would be willing to treat this child as normal. And since the deviancy was as unamenable to total cure as the anomalies themselves, it is doubtful whether even the most intensive psychological treatment of the mother could re-establish a "normal" mother-child relationship. In short, the original breakdown in the mother-child relationship had not occurred solely because of medical and psychological problems; the "abnormality" of the mother-child relationship was due at least as much to the atypical social role of each of the partners. How was this factor recognized or dealt with?

Far from ever being clearly enunciated, it can be suggested that the social conflicts inherent in the situation and the program became concealed under the medical framework of the program. The diagnosis of the "illness" was primarily in terms of the children's physical abnormality and the mothers' psychological reaction to these deformities, the "patients" were thalidomide children and their mothers, and the indicated "treatment" was medical for the children and psychological for the mothers. Moreover, the nature of government intervention in the thalidomide program was never made clear. Was the government here simply treating a mother-child problem, or, in throwing its moral and financial weight behind the policy of keeping these children in their families, had society, in effect, agreed to share the responsibility for rearing them? [1]

---

[1] Some idea of the conflict that could arise from this lack of clarification can be seen in the bitterness that later developed concerning the financial aspects of the program. Most of the mothers, far from being grateful, protested that it was inadequate. The staff of the RIM tended to view this as a

In particular, it was the mothers who became most exposed and vulnerable in this system. Because the problem was conceptualized largely in terms of the mothers' "acceptance" of the children, the prostheses, and the habilitation program, not only did they become the primary patients, but any failures could be most conveniently attributed to their present inadequacy, or even their pre-existing pathology. The mothers could and did respond with bitterness and resentment, but the power to define who was "sick," and the sophisticated nomenclature with which to do it, lay with the professionals.

In conceptualizing the thalidomide problem as a mother-child-society dilemma, we are, of course, dealing with a situation that contained many unique elements. In particular, the fact that these children's anomalies were visible at birth meant that their social deviance emerged at a time when the mothers had not yet embarked on their maternity. Thus the crisis here was much more acute and visible than it is likely to be in the case of children whose physical handicaps occur or are revealed later.

Nevertheless, it can be suggested that many of the issues raised here would be equally relevant to the maternity of any physically handicapped child. For surprisingly enough, although numerous studies have dealt in detail with the ambivalence and hostility that the physically handicapped individual can arouse in the community at large, the issue of the social deviance of the handicapped child has rarely been placed in the context of the mother-child relationship. This does not mean, of course, that specific social problems have not been described (for example, mothers' changed social transactions, parents' unrealistic social expectations, concern about

---

sign of ingratitude toward a government that had been unusually generous. The mothers, in turn, pointed with resentment to the much greater financial aid received by foster mothers rearing thalidomide children. The basic issue here seemed to be who was responsible for the rearing of the child. If this mother-child relationship is conceptualized in the usual terms, then the government had given these mothers more than it gives to most. If the nature of the government intervention had made it responsible, at least partially, for the rearing of these children, then the mothers' feeling of being cheated becomes more understandable.

school facilities). But in dealing with these problems, the omissions in the literature would lead us to believe that two assumptions have generally been made. First, the question of the child's social identity only becomes crucial when he himself begins to engage in prolonged interaction with the environment, for example, at school entrance time, and second, in handling the conflicts evoked by the child's deviancy, the mother will automatically view the child's social interests as identical to her own. It is as if the early years of the child's life were seen as a period of grace in which the mother-child relationship could develop largely uncontaminated by social conflicts. Whatever problems exist between mother and child at this time are on the psychological level rather than the social one.

But these assumptions are not necessarily valid ones. It is doubtful whether a mother can care for even a year-old child without taking into account his present and future social identity. If nothing else, the mother's awareness of the social implications of physical abnormality would probably make this a vital issue in her maternity from the moment the deviancy is revealed. Thus one of the basic problems in this type of maternity might arise as much from the mother's social deprivation as from her psychological one. Moreover, if the professionals continue to insist that the later social and emotional adjustment of the handicapped child depends in large measure on his early family environment, the mothers can claim, and with equal justice, that successful family integration of a child usually depends on a social substructure that is not present here. In short, even the mothering of a child whose abnormality occurs or is discovered later is likely to be characterized by multiple social conflicts linked to deviancy.

There is no facile solution, and perhaps not even an optimum one, for the complex problem of the deviant child. But it can be questioned whether this problem is best viewed or treated in conventional clinical terms. For the issue at stake is not solely the treatment of illness (be it physical or psychological); it involves as well a problem of social justice concerning who is to bear the burden of deviance. And it is hardly fair to ask the mother to assume the major burden for resolving an issue of social deviance in a society that provides neither adequate machinery for handling, nor even appropriate labels for recognizing, the basic conflicts involved. In our zeal to save the handicapped child, are we perhaps simply substituting the mother as scapegoat?

At this point, the objection can be raised that in shifting the locus of the problem from mother to society one is solving nothing, but simply substituting another scapegoat. One could even question whether this shift might not make therapeutic intervention more difficult, since society is a "patient" that is notably difficult to treat. These objections are not without merit, but the recognition of the element of social deviancy would appear to have more advantages than disadvantages.

For one, the recognition that the problem they face is at least partially a social one may prevent much needless guilt and suffering by parents of handicapped children. The poor may not have become richer, the blacks whiter, nor women liberated by the redefinition of their problems as social ones, but it has given them a new pride in themselves and a new orientation for their efforts. Thus, instead of spending their time and energy teaching their members how to "adapt to" or "accept" their disadvantaged status, organizations of the poor, the black, and women have focused increasingly on identifying and removing what they consider to be the real sources of their problems. Associations of parents of retarded, brain-damaged children, and other groups have existed for a number of years, but in many instances they have functioned as company unions, founded and directed by the "establishment." It is possible they could profit by studying carefully the lessons to be learned from their more militant confreres.

If nothing else, this shift in emphasis may eliminate some of the unwitting victimization of parents by professionals. Faced with a situation in which neither the child's physical deficiency nor his social deviancy is easily correctible, professionals have been tempted far too often to restrict their interest and intervention to the fertile territory of the parents' psychological problems. It is stating the issue baldly, but not necessarily unfairly, to suggest that exploration of the parents' psyches has sometimes been used as a substitute for adequate schools, sheltered workshops, and so on. One function of more effective parents' groups might be to reverse this process. First provide realistic help and only then label and treat as neurotic the parents who cannot profit from it. In fact, the efforts of such groups may help us to remember—particularly those of us who have used the insights of psychoanalysis in support of our indiscriminate "psychologizing"—that even Freud fed his hungry patient before trying to analyze him.

A second implication of this point of view would be a re-examination of whether the habilitation of handicapped children should necessarily, or even ideally, be primarily under medical auspices. Thalidomide-induced limb-deficiency provides only one illustration of a fairly large group of conditions (such as minimal brain damage, retardation, cerebral palsy) to the improvement of which medical science, in its current state of knowledge, can contribute only minimally. On the contrary, most of the breakthroughs in the treatment of the retarded or minimally brain-damaged child in recent years have come from the fields of education and social welfare, that is, from knowledge gained in special classes, sheltered workshops, and so on. And yet the traditional model of having the treatment team headed by a physician has often gone unquestioned. Historically, the provision of medical care may have constituted the only alternative to neglect and abandonment. But in this day and age is this the only, or even the most viable, solution? Could not, instead, the program be under the Minister of Social Welfare, and medical consultants used as necessary?

While the transfer of sponsorship is unlikely to provide a magical solution to the many problems posed by the deviant child, it does offer certain advantages. Perhaps most important, the vast majority of doctors have neither the training nor the inclination to handle social conflict; their orientation is in terms of patients and illness. And doctors have come under sufficient attack recently for not doing adequately what they are supposed to without demanding that they assume roles which they may neither want to handle nor perhaps are capable of performing. It is also possible that if social workers were placed in a situation where their primary responsibility was to their clients, rather than, as so often happens now, to the medical staff, some fresh and innovative approaches to the problems of the handicapped might result. Rather than continuing to function as an uneasy intermediary between doctor and patient (which, in effect, may mean striving to keep the patient "cooperative" so that the doctor may carry out "treatment"), the social worker may become more useful and more creative if he is directly confronted by, and given the responsibility for handling, some of the basic problems troubling his clients.

But the most radical implication of the recognition of the social component of the problem might be the adoption of schemes of shared parenthood under which the government would recognize that it had an obligation to provide special help in rearing such a child, because the parents were operating under a role disadvantage and were deprived of many of the tangible and intangible social props provided for parents of normal children. Thus a program like that provided for thalidomide children, instead of being an unusually generous gesture precipitated by guilt and anxiety, might be considered as a basic minimum. Direct financial aid to parents in the form of monthly allotments might also be a possibility. The establishment of a network of day-care centers, foster homes, and residential facilities might also reflect this concept of shared parenthood. Thus, instead of parents having to choose between home-rearing or institutionalization, it would be possible to move the child in and out of these various facilities as his needs, and those of his family, changed.

There are numerous experiments that could be tried. The basic premise underlying them all is the recognition that the problem of the handicapped child is caused as much by society as by his own deficiency or his mother's reaction to it, and that any attempt at resolution that does not include all three partners is incomplete and inadequate. The thalidomide tragedy provides us with a case history of how a society could intervene actively in the fate of a group of handicapped children without fully recognizing, however, the reasons for and the implications of its participation. In a sense, it was a program combining an innovative use of money and manpower with a traditional philosophy and structure. It is tempting to speculate how similar resources, combined with a more socially aware philosophy, might be used differently for the benefit of the deviant child and his family.

The Study of this Maternity

If one compares the final product with the aims with which we began this study, the results, inevitably, are disappointing. The usual ideal of understanding behavior sufficiently to predict and control remained as far as ever from our grasp. In fact, it was not always possible to provide a smooth, integrated description of this maternity. On the contrary, we continuously had the impression of working with a jigsaw puzzle in which many pieces were missing, and where even those that were present could not easily be fitted into an ordered relationship. In a sense, the problem appeared more, rather than less, complex and baffling as we worked with it.

In part, the difficulty lay in the nature of our approach. Rather than restricting this exploration to a single question, we sought to describe a number of facets of this maternity. The penalty paid for this approach was the dearth of simple, clear answers. No sooner had we established one "truth," than the consideration of other elements in the situation led us to question the adequacy of our initial interpretation. In fact, at times even the "facts" themselves were contradictory.

But the most serious difficulty lay with the incompleteness and inadequacy of our conceptual model. The original conception of the problem of thalidomide maternity in terms of the child's partial normality and abnormality, and the mother's reaction to this marginality, was useful to a certain degree, but obviously insufficient.

For, far from being solely a quality inherent in the child himself, the nature and meaning of the child's abnormality depended in large measure upon the eye of the beholder. But to understand fully how the child was perceived involved taking into account a host of determining influences ranging from the mother's personality as an individual to the structure of society as a whole. And it was only very tentatively and very partially that we became able to structure a model that would take into account these multiple elements.

And yet, while the gap between our level of aspiration and our achievement has left us considerably humbled, it has also left us rather unrepentant for seeking a new way of studying the maternity of a handicapped child. The approach used here led to much complexity, but, while some of the difficulty lay in our lack of clarity, the phenomena that we were trying to describe and explain were complex and baffling ones. And it may be more productive, in the long run, to admit the inadequacy of our understanding of the maternity of a handicapped child than to keep on using approaches whose major distinction is that they provide simple answers to oversimplified questions. In fact, it is possible that one of the major merits of this work lies precisely in the willingness to look at a multifaceted problem from a number of perspectives.

Moreover, if this study has not yielded a cohesive theory of the maternity of a handicapped child, it has provided us with suggestions of where to look for it, and perhaps more important, where not to look for it. If nothing else, this study has confirmed our initial belief that mothers of handicapped children should not be viewed in terms applied to psychoneurotics. The "acceptance-rejection-overprotection" model has long been proven both theoretically and clinically meaningless, and it is about time that it be given a decent burial. Rather, it is in the psychology of stress, the sociology of deviance, and our understanding of normal developmental psychology that we would seek to understand both the normality and the abnormality of this form of mother-child relationship.

In fact, it is this bringing together of the developmental, psychological, and social viewpoints that we consider the most original and most valuable aspect of the approach used.

The best consolation for the lack of omniscience, however, is the belief that research is a continuous process. This study was based on, and profited from the mistakes of, many previous researchers. Now there is the hope that it will serve as a stimulus for someone else to follow, broaden, and improve, the trail we have laid down.

APPENDIXES, GLOSSARY,
BIBLIOGRAPHY, *and* INDEXES

Appendix A

Reproduction of Interview Schedules[1]

I. SOCIOECONOMIC QUESTIONNAIRE

Current family status

1. First of all, how many children do you have?
   Name.   Age.   Sex.   School year.   Medical problems, if any.
2. When were you married?
3. How old are you?   How old is your husband?
4. Is this your first marriage?
   If not
   a) How was earlier marriage terminated?
   b) Were there children by the previous marriage?
5. What is your husband's occupation?
   Kind of work.   Place.   Length of time employed.
6. Where would you place your husband's annual income?
   Under $3,000, $3–$5,000, $5–$7,000, $7–$9,000, $10–$15,000, $15–$20,000, Over $20,000.
7. What positions has your husband held in the last ten years?

[1] The schedules presented here are faithful to the originals in terms of content, but differ slightly in format. In the originals, a large space was left after each question so that responses could be recorded directly on the sheet. The mother's name and the subject heading were reproduced on each sheet so that the pages could be separated for the analysis of data. Both these techniques made the interview schedules rather lengthy; a complete interview schedule is 150 pages long. In order to reduce the bulk of this work, the spacing of the text has been modified.

Only the English version of the schedules is presented here. This, too, was done to save space. It should be noted, however, that the English and French versions are direct translations of each other.

Type of work.   Place.   Length of time employed.
8. What about you? Do you work outside the house now?
   a) *If so*
      Type of work.   Place.   Length of time employed.
   b) *If not*
      Did you work after marriage?
      Type of work.   Place.   Length of time employed.
   c) Do you plan to return to work?
   d) Who cares for the children when you are out?
9. What religious denomination do you belong to?
10. Did you go to church during the past year?
    W: A few times, once a month, every week, more than once a week.
    H: A few times, once a month, every week, more than once a week.
11. How long have you lived in this community?
12. Do you own your own house?
13. Do you plan to move in the next year or so?
14. What is your favorite recreation?
    W.   H.
15. Do you belong to any clubs or organizations?
    W.   H.
16. Are you on the Executive Board or an officer of any clubs or organizations?
    W.   H.
17. Are your parents still alive?
    Wife's mother, wife's father.
    Husband's mother, husband's father.
18. Did you see them during the past year?
    W: Not at all in past year, a few times, once a month, every week, more often.
    H: Not at all in past year, a few times, once a month, every week, more often.

Past history

19. Where were you born?
    W.   H.
20. What did your father do?
    W.   H.

21. What was education of father?
    W.   H.
    What was education of mother?
    W.   H.
22. What was religion?
    W.   H.
23. How many children in family?
    W.   H.
24. What was your rank in family?
    W.   H.
25. How far did you get in school?
    W.   H.
26. How long did you live in the place of birth?
    W.   H.
27. Where have you lived since?
    W.   H.

II. THE PRESENT [2]

Physical appearance and health of child

1. It's been how long since you were here last? How has X been doing since then?
2. What about X's health?
   a) Compared to other children, do you find X a frail or robust child?
   b) In what way?
   c) To what do you attribute this?
   d) In what ways do you think X's handicap influences his health?
3. How is X's eating now?
   a) Have you any problems about X eating enough or the kind of food X eats?
   b) How do you think X's handicap might influence his eating?
   c) Do you ever buy or prepare any special foods because of X's handicap?
   d) Does X take any vitamins? Do you consider this very important or something that is not really essential for X? Why?

[2] Questions marked with a "P" are those designed specifically to test the mothers' attitudes toward the prostheses.

4. What do you expect from X in the way of table manners?

 a) Do you expect X to eat at the table with the family or do you prefer to feed X separately?

P b) Does X usually wear his prostheses while eating or do you find it easier without them?

 c) Does X eat completely by himself or do you have to help him? How do you feel about it?

 d) Does X ever try to pick up food with his fingers? How do you feel about it?

 e) Has X ever tried to use his feet to eat? How do you feel about it?

 f) Has X ever tried to pick up food with his mouth? How do you feel about it?

5. How is X's sleeping in general?

 a) Would you say that X needs more or less sleep than most children his age? Why?

 b) Does X have a regular bedtime or does he go to bed when tired? What time does X usually go to bed?

6. Who usually puts X to bed?

 a) What about sleeping arrangements? Have you put X in an adult bed yet or does he sleep in a child's bed? Up to what age did X sleep in a crib?

 b) Does X share a room with anybody or does he sleep alone?

 c) Some families have a definite bedtime ritual such as a story or a song, while others treat bedtime much more casually. How is it with X?

 d) If story, is there any special one?

 e) Some children have a special doll or animal they like to sleep with at night. Does X? What?

 f) Many children have special ways of helping themselves fall asleep; they suck their thumbs, or rub their noses, or rub their heads against the pillow. Does X do something like that before falling asleep?

P g) At night, where do you usually keep X's prostheses? Do you have a special place or do you put them where it is handiest?

7. Many children X's age have bad dreams at night. Does X?

 a) Do you think X dreams?

8. Does X manage to stay dry at night or does he wet his bed? If yes, how often? How do you feel about it?

9. What time does X usually wake up in the morning? What does X usually do when he first wakes up?

10. Is X the type of child who loves to get into bed with you in the morning? How often? With whom?

11. Let us talk of some aspects of X's development now. How many teeth does X have?

   a) Would you say that X's teething was fairly easy or were there any special problems? If so, what?

   b) Has X seen a dentist yet or have you felt it was not necessary? If no, at what age would you take X?

   c) Do you think X would have any special problems with his teeth? What?

P d) Does X use a toothbrush yet? If so, with his prostheses?

12. Does X have any special problems with his sight?

   a) Do you think X is likely to need glasses when he is older? Why?

   b) (If yes) How would you feel about it?

13. How do you find X's hearing?

   a) Do you anticipate any problems with X's hearing? Why?

14. What about X's height? Is X taller than or shorter than most children his age?

   a) (If different) Why?

15. How do you find X's weight? Is X thinner or fatter than most children his age?

   a) (If different) Why?

16. Does X resemble any person particularly in your family? Who?

   a) Does X take after you or your husband more?

17. In terms of appearance, what do you think is X's greatest asset?

18. What about X's handicap? Would you rate it as very noticeable, noticeable but not striking, or barely noticeable?

P 19. Do you find that X's handicap is more noticeable to you with his prostheses or without them?

   a) What about your husband?

   b) What is it like to strangers?

20. In general, is X a healthy child or does he often get sick?

   a) What illnesses has X had the past year?

   b) Are there any special precautions you feel are necessary for X? If so, what?

   c) When X gets ill, do you find that there is any difference in the severity or duration of illness because of the handicap?

    d) What special problems do you have because of X's handicap when he gets ill?

21. When X gets ill, do you usually call the doctor or do you prefer to manage most illnesses yourself?
    a) Who is the doctor you usually use for X? Is he your usual family doctor? If not, who?

Intelligence

22. How do you find X's intelligence? Is X more advanced, average, or slower than most children his age?
    a) (If different) In what way?
    b) (If different) To what do you attribute difference?
23. How do you find X's speech in general?
    a) How would you compare it to most children X's age?
    b) (If different) How?
    c) To what would you attribute the difference?
    d) Do you think that X's hospitalizations helped or hindered his speech? If so, in what way and why?
24. Does X use baby talk? If so, how do you feel about it?
25. What does X call you?
    a) What about your husband?
    b) Does X have a special name for himself? What is it?
P   c) Does X have a special name for his prostheses? If so, what is it? How did X start it?
26. Would you say that X has a very good memory or just average?
27. Can X concentrate on things for a long time or is he usually distractible?
    a) (If so) Why?

Personality

28. How would you describe X's personality in general?
29. Do you find that X is shy or does he make friends easily?
    a) Does X demand a lot of attention or is he content to play by himself?
30. Does X like to be cuddled or does he not show his feelings easily?
    a) What about toward your husband?
    b) Does X have a special time or place he likes to be cuddled?
P   c) Do you find it easier to cuddle X with or without prostheses?

31. Do you find in general that X is a happy child or is he often sad and angry?
    a) What makes X happy?
    b) What makes X sad?
32. Is X easily frustrated, or is he stubborn in doing what he sets out to do?
    a) What frustrates X the most?
    b) What happens to X when he gets frustrated?
    c) Does X have temper tantrums? How often?
33. Do you find that X is an easy child, or is he difficult?
    a) Is X usually obedient, or does he often not listen?
    b) What is your greatest problem in getting X to obey?
    c) How do you usually punish X when it is necessary?
    d) Do you prefer to do most of the punishment yourself or is this one of your husband's jobs?

Play patterns

34. What kind of toys does X like to play with most?
    a) Has X any favorite games? What?
35. *Girls*
    Does X like to play house or with dolls or has she not reached that stage yet?
    a) (If yes) What kind of games does X play?
    b) Is X the kind of child who enjoys helping you around the house or is she not particularly interested?
    Boys
    Does X like to play policeman or fireman or is he not interested in these things yet?
    a) Is X interested in your husband's work? Does X ever like to play Daddy?
36. Are there any particular toys or games that you feel are unsuitable for X because of his handicap? What?
37. Are there any particular things like T.V. or books that you would consider especially important for X because of his handicap?
38. Does X usually like to play alone or does he like to play with other children?
    a) With whom does X usually play?
    b) Where does X play?

39. Would you go out of your way to help X make friends or do you just let things happen naturally?
    a) Has anyone ever refused to let his child play with X because of his handicap?
    b) (If yes) What did you do?

40. When there are fights between X and his friends, do you usually prefer to step in or do you let them settle arguments themselves?

41. Is X the kind of child who likes to stay at home or does he enjoy going out?
    a) Does X often go to the park or do you prefer to have him play near home?
    b) What about visiting?
    c) Does X enjoy going shopping with you?

42. Does X enjoy playing with his daddy or does your husband not have much time to spend with him?
    a) What do they play?
    b) When?
    c) Does your husband like to take X out? Where?

43. Does X have a pet? How do you feel about the idea of X having one?

P 44. When X plays alone, does he usually wear his prostheses or is he more comfortable without them?
    a) What about when X plays with other children?
    b) How is it when you take X out?
    c) What about when X's daddy takes him out?

45. Would you consider it important for X to meet with and play with other handicapped children or would you not make a point of it? Why or why not?
    a) Would you go out of your way to tell X stories about handicapped people or do you not think this is especially important?
    b) When X was in hospital, he came into contact with many types of handicapped children. Do you think that this on the whole was a good thing or a bad thing?
    c) Does X know any adult who is handicapped? Who? How does X feel about it?

46. When X plays alone does he ever use his feet? How do you feel about it?
    a) What about when X is playing with others?

Psychosexual development

47. Some children are much more aware of their bodies than others. What about X?
    a) Is X a thumb sucker?
    b) Does X have any other ways of consoling himself when he is tired or sad?
    c) How do you feel about it?

48. Do you find that X is very much of a little (woman) (man) yet or is (she) (he) still too young for that?
    a) (If yes) In what way?

49. Do you think that X knows the difference yet between girls and boys?
    If yes
    a) What makes you think X has noticed it?
    b) Has X ever asked you where babies come from?
    c) What have you told X?
    If no
    a) Do you think you would prefer to have X bring it up or would you like to tell him?
    b) At what age would you like to tell X?

50. Many children X's age are very curious about other boys or girls and play games like doctor or house. Does X?
    a) How do you feel about it?
    b) What did you do?

51. Does X ever play with himself?
    a) How do you feel about it?
    b) What did you do?

52. Many families have strong feelings about modesty, e.g., not walking around undressed, privacy in bathroom, while others are pretty casual about these things. How is it in yours?
    a) Does X ever see you or your husband undressed?
    b) Does X ever like to run about the house without his clothes on?
    c) How do you feel about it?

53. Many children X's age talk about marrying their (mummy) (daddy) when they grow up. Has X?
    a) (If yes) What have you told X?

54. Has X ever talked about having babies of his own?
    a) How do you feel about it?
    b) What have you told X?
55. Would you say that X is closer to you or his daddy? In what way?
56. Do you feel that a handicap like X's is worse for a girl or a boy? In what way?

Self-help

57. Do you find that X is pretty self-reliant or is he still quite dependent on you?
58. Is X toilet trained?
    a) (If yes) When and how did it happen?
    b) (If no) How do you feel about it?
    c) Can X manage to go to the bathroom by himself?
P   d) Does X need his prostheses to do so or can he manage better without them?
59. What about dressing or undressing?
    a) What can X do?
    b) What does X need help with?
    c) Do you just buy X usual clothes or do you find that there are special requirements because of his handicap?
P   d) Can X put on his prostheses himself?
60. Are there any special precautions you have to take about the house because of X's handicap? What are they?
61. Does X go out to play alone or do you find that you prefer to go with him?
    a) Does X have to stay in the yard or would you let him go around the neighborhood alone?
62. Do you think that X's handicap has made him more or less self-reliant than most children his age? In what way?

Demands on mother

63. Do you find that X makes more demands on your time than most children his age?
    a) In what way?
    b) What, in terms of time, is the biggest demand that X makes on you?
64. Do you ever get a chance to go out without X or do you find that you spend most of your time with him?

    a) About how often do you get a chance to get out?

    b) Who baby sits?

65. Is your husband the kind of man who is helpful with the children or does he prefer to leave most of their care to you?

    a) How is he with X?

    b) Are there any particular times of day or particular activities that he likes to do with X?

66. Is there anybody else you find that you can call upon to help with X? Who?

67. Do you find that your social life has changed since X's birth? In what way?

68. Do you think that X's coming has changed your relationship with your other children in a particular way or no more than any other baby would?

    a) (If yes) In what way?

69. When X is in hospital, do you notice any change in your family? In what way?

Impact on environment

You know that one of the problems mothers of handicapped children often face is the attitude of others toward the child. I would like to talk a bit now about how things have been with you.

70. How does your husband feel about X?

    a) Do you think his attitude has changed or has it always been the same?

    b) If changed, in what way?

71. What about X's brothers and sisters?

    a) What have you told them about X's handicap?

72. What about your family?

    a) Has anyone ever made remarks about X?

    b) What did you do?

    c) What bothers you most about their attitude to X?

    d) What do you find most helpful?

73. What about your husband's family?

    a) Has anyone ever made remarks about X?

    b) What did you do?

    c) What bothers you most about their attitude to X?

    d) What do you find most helpful?

74. How do your neighbors react to X?

a) Have you ever had any unpleasant incidents?
b) What did you do?
c) Has anyone been particularly helpful? In what way?
75. What about strangers who meet X for the first time?
76. What about other children?
77. Has anyone ever told you that X would be better off dead or in an institution?
    a) Who?
    b) What did you tell them?
78. Do most people know that X's handicap is due to thalidomide or do you prefer not to talk about it?
    a) How do you think that the publicity about thalidomide babies has affected their attitude?
P   79. How do you find that most people react to the prostheses?
80. When taking X to a new place for the first time, would you tell people about his handicap in advance, or would you prefer to let them find out for themselves?

Awareness of handicap

81. Do you think that X realizes yet that he is different from other children?
    If yes
    a) In what way?
    b) When did X first notice it do you think? Did X say anything?
    c) How did you feel? Did you pretend that you had not noticed anything?
    d) Has X ever asked you why he was different?
    e) What did you or would you say?
    f) Did you use the word thalidomide or drug in explaining it to X?
    g) Has X ever talked about his missing (arms) (legs) growing when he is older? What did you say?
    h) Does X ever talk to his daddy about the handicap, or does he find it easier to ask you?
    If no
    a) Would you wait for X to ask first or would you tell him?
    b) At what age?
    c) Have you thought yet what you would tell X?

d) How does your husband feel about telling?

P 82. How do you think X feels about his prostheses?

    a) Do you ever talk about it or do you prefer not to emphasize it?

    b) What about the other children? How do they feel about the prostheses? Have they ever wanted to try them? What did you do?

83. How do you think X feels about coming to the hospital this time?

    a) What did you tell X?

84. Do you think X remembers any of his previous hospitalizations?

    a) Does X ever talk about them?

85. Do you think X behaves differently in the hospital? In what way?

86. If you could do things over, is there anything you would have changed about X's hospitalizations? What?

Evaluation of professional help

Since X's birth, you have been in contact with many professional people who have given you advice about X. I would like to spend some time talking about your feelings about some of these people.

87. When you have a problem about X to whom do you usually turn for advice? Why?

88. Of all the people with whom you have been in contact, who has been most helpful? In what way?

89. Who has been least helpful? In what way?

90. Do you think the fact that X has been a thalidomide baby has changed the reaction of others or the kind of help you get? In what way?

91. Looking over the government's program for thalidomide children, what do you think was its greatest advantage?

    a) What do you think was its greatest weakness?

    b) Are there any services you would have liked that were not provided?

92. Many parents of handicapped children have formed parents' groups, but there is not one for thalidomide parents in Quebec. Why do you think this is so?

    a) Would you be interested in joining one if it was formed? Why?

    b) What about your husband?

    c) What do you think the aims of such a group would be?

93. When X was here last time, we had the opportunity of discussing

the psychological test report with you. Do you remember what you were told at that time?

    a) How did you feel about it?

    b) In what way do you think it might have helped or made you worry?

    c) What are some of the things that were not helpful?

    d) What are some of the things that you would like to know as a result of this evaluation of your child?

94. Looking over the time since you were here last, would you say the situation has gotten easier or harder? In what way?

95. If one of your friends had a handicapped child today, what is the advice you would like most to give her?

III. THE FUTURE

I know that often we are so caught up in day-to-day problems that it is hard to think of things that might or might not happen a long time from now. Today, however, I would like to spend a little time talking with you about plans for X's future.

1. Do you ever think of X's future or are you content to handle things as they happen?

    a) (If yes) What do you think about?

    b) When you are feeling optimistic, what is the best thing you can imagine that will happen to X?

    c) What is the thing that worries you most?

    d) What about your husband?

2. Sometimes parents of handicapped children find it hard to talk of the future, because they are afraid that the handicap might so affect the child's health that X might die younger than most people.

    a) What kind of worries, thoughts, ideas, like this have you had?

    b) Why?

    c) How do you feel about it now?

    d) What about your husband?

3. When you think of X's future, do you see him at home, or do you think that he will be better off in a residential school, or in a place especially planned for handicapped people?

    a) Why?

b) (If this involves change) At what age?

c) What about your husband?

4. What about the more immediate future? Have you given any thought yet to X's schooling?

 a) What type of school have you considered? Why?

 b) At what age do you think X should start school?

 c) Would you expect the teacher to treat X like any other child, or do you think it would be necessary to make allowances for his handicap? In what way?

 d) How do you expect X to do in school? Why?

 e) How far would you like to see X go? Why?

 f) How far do you think X will go? Why?

 g) Is there any special course you would like to see X take? Why?

5. Apart from regular school, many families feel it important that their child have a religious education, while other families do not consider this that important. How is it in your family?

 a) Would you consider Sunday school or church attendance particularly important for X or not that essential?

 b) Why?

 c) What about your husband?

6. Children these days seem to have lots of activities outside school hours such as clubs, sports, etc. Do you think X will be able to participate in most of these or that some of them would be impossible for him because of his handicap?

 a) What are the kinds of things X will be able to do?

 b) What are the things you feel will be impossible for X?

 c) If some things are impossible, what would you like to see X do instead?

 d) What about your husband?

7. Have you ever thought of the possibility of a summer camp for X?

 a) What kind would you choose?

 b) At what age?

8. Do you think it will be easier or harder for X to make friends as he grows older?

 a) Why?

 b) Would you go out of your way to help X make friends or would you let things happen naturally?

 c) If yes, in what way?

    d) If some children act unkindly to X because of his handicap, would you step in or let him handle it himself?

    e) What would you or X do?

    f) How does your husband feel about this?

9. What about adolescence? Are there any special problems that you think will come up then?

    a) (If so) What?

    b) How would you like X to handle them?

    c) Do you think X will date?

    d) Do you think at adolescence that it will be particularly important for X to get to know other handicapped children? Why or why not?

    e) What does your husband think of this?

10. Do you think that X's handicap will influence the usual mother-child relationship when he is an adolescent?

    a) In what way?

    b) What about X's relationship to your husband?

11. When you think of X as a grownup, do you think he will be able to work at a regular job or do you think he will still need special care?

If work

    a) What kind of work would you like to see X do?

    b) Why?

    c) What about your husband?

If care

    a) What kind of special care do you think X will need?

    b) Where do you think X will be best cared for?

    c) What about after you and your husband are gone?

12. Have you thought yet about X's marrying?

    a) What have you thought about it?

If yes

    a) At what age do you think X might marry?

    b) What kind of person would you like X to marry?

    c) How would you feel if X wanted to marry a handicapped person?

    d) Why?

    e) Do you think X will manage by himself once he is married or do you think he will still need help? In what way?

If no

a) Why?
b) Do you think it will make a tremendous difference to X? Why?
c) What do you see X doing instead?
13. How does your husband feel about X's marrying?
14. What about children?
   a) Why?
   b) How does your husband feel about this?
15. Let us talk a little bit about the medical care that X will need in the future. Do you think that X's handicap is likely to get better or worse as he grows older?
   a) In what way?
   b) Do you think that there might be new medical discoveries that would help X as he grows older?
   c) What?
   d) What type of medical care do you think X will need as a grown up?
   e) Why?
   f) Do you think X's handicap is likely to affect his general health?
   g) Why?
   h) What does your husband think about these things?
16. You know that medical treatment can be pretty expensive. Up to now, the government has helped pay for some of it. What kind of financial help would you like to have that you have not received?
   a) What about the future? Do you think X will need financial help in the future?
   b) Why?
   c) What kind of help would you like to see?
   d) For how long?
17. You know a lot of things have changed since X was born. In some ways, things have been easier than you expected and in some ways, harder. How do you think things are likely to be as X grows older? Do you think it will be easier or harder?
   a) In what way?
   b) Why?
   c) How does your husband look at the future?
18. If a friend of yours were to give birth to a handicapped child, what would you like to tell her about what to expect?
   a) What do you think is the hardest time for a mother of a handicapped child?

   b) In what way?
   c) Why?
19. What about X's feelings about his handicap? Do you think X will find it easier or harder to accept as he grows older?
   a) In what way?
   b) Why?
20. Do you think X's brothers and sisters are likely to change their feelings about him as they grow older?
   a) In what way?
   b) Why?
21. Do you think there is likely to be any change in society's attitude toward the handicapped person in the future?
   a) In what way?
   b) Why?
   c) What about your husband?
22. As an adult, would you like to see X belong to an association of thalidomide children or do you think he is not likely to have much in common with them? Why?

IV. THE BIRTH PERIOD [3]

Pregnancy

1. *Family situation at time of pregnancy*
   Age.   Financial status.   Number and ages of children.
2. *Feelings about pregnancy*
   Mother's feelings.   Father's.   Reaction of immediate environment, if any.
3. *Mother's expectations of child*
   Sex.   Choice of name.   Father's expectations.   Worries about normality.
4. *Mother's medical and psychological state during pregnancy*
   Who took care?   How got pill?
5. *Knowledge of effects during pregnancy*
   How?   Father?   What difference?

---

[3] Because this interview was fully recorded and was much less structured than the others, only a schematic outline of the topics to be discussed was prepared.

Birth

1. *Queries as to when, where, who delivered, type of delivery*
2. *Immediate perception of doctors and nurses*
3. *Knowledge of abnormality*
   Who told?   How?   What said about future?
4. *Reaction of mother—psychological and somatic*
5. *Reaction of father—psychological and somatic*
6. *Contact with baby in hospital*
   Mother seeing, feeding, dressing.   Father.   Other relatives or friends.
7. *Mother's initial perception of handicap*
   Hopelessness vs. cure.   Effect on intelligence.   Medical help. Future of baby.   Home vs. hospital.   Possibility of unknown injuries.   Sex.   Type of handicap.
8. *Father's initial perception of handicap*
9. *Perception of attitudes and behavior of doctors and nurses*

The social significance of baby

Name.   Religious ceremonies.   Telling—who, when, what?

Asking for help

Who?   When?   What type of help?

Perception of environmental reaction

Knowledge of thalidomide link

V. THE BABY COMES HOME

1. Now I would like to talk with you a bit about the first few months after the baby came home. Did X come home with you from the hospital or did he stay longer?
   a) (If longer) Why?
   b) How did you feel about it?
   c) What about your husband?
2. I know this was a hard time for you. What was your health like during the first few months?

    a) (If difficulties) Did you have any medical help?

    b) From whom and what?

3. What about your husband's health?

4. What about your state of mind? Did you often have feelings of sadness and worries?

    a) What particularly bothered you?

    b) What did you do when you felt like that?

    c) Was there anybody you could turn to for help?

    d) (If yes) Who?

5. How was your husband's state of mind?

6. Did you find that the two of you could talk over your worries or was this hard?

7. When you first came home from the hospital, who took care of X mostly?

    a) Did you have any help?

    b) (If yes) Who? For how long?

    c) Did you have the same kind of help for your other babies?

8. How much did your husband do in connection with taking care of X when he was a baby?

    a) Did he ever change the baby's diapers, feed him, bathe him?

9. In the first few months, did you and your husband ever get a chance to go out together alone, without the children?

If yes

    a) How often?

    b) Who took care of X?

10. Did you find there was any change in your social life from the time before X was born?

    a) In what way?

    b) Why?

11. Now let us talk a little bit about X as a baby. How would you describe him as a baby?

12. All babies cry, of course. Some mothers feel that if you pick up a baby when it cries, you spoil him. Others think you should never let a baby cry for very long. How do you feel about it?

    a) What did you do about this with X?

    b) How about the middle of the night?

13. I know it is hard to remember this far back, but as a baby, was X the kind of child who was happy alone or did he demand a lot of attention?

a) In what way?

b) How did you feel about it?

14. Were you able to spend time with X besides what was necessary for his physical care?

 a) (If yes) Tell me what you did during this time. How much did you cuddle him, sing to him, and that sort of thing?

 b) How about your husband?

15. Now, would you tell me something about how the feeding went when X was a baby?

 a) Was X bottle fed or breast fed?

 b) How did you decide?

16. Did you try to keep to a regular schedule or did you feed X whenever he was hungry?

 a) In what way?

17. How long was X bottle-fed or breast-fed?

 a) When did you start weaning X?

 b) How did you decide it was time to begin this?

 c) How did you go about it?

 d) How did X react to being taken off the breast or bottle?

18. Was X a good eater or did you have problems?

 a) What kind?

 b) Did X have colic?

 c) (If yes) For how long, and what did you do about it?

19. What about X's sleeping?

 a) When did X start sleeping through the night?

 b) Where did X sleep?

20. How about bathing? Did you have any problems about that?

 a) In what way?

21. What about X's health in general?

 a) What kind of problems did you have?

 b) Who took care of X's medical needs?

22. Do you remember when X started rolling over, sitting, crawling, standing, walking?

 a) Because of X's handicap, did he have any special problems with these?

 b) What were the problems?

 c) How did X manage?

 d) Is there anything particular you did, or did you just let nature take its course?

23. Did X have any special problems because of his handicap in reaching for things?
    a) In what way?
    b) Did X have any special ways of overcoming his handicap?
    c) Did you do anything special to help X?

24. What about talking? Do you remember when X first said words like "papa" or "mama"?
    a) Would you consider X an early or a late talker?
    b) In what way?
    c) Why do you think this was so?
    d) Did you do anything special to help X's talking?

25. On the whole, as a baby, did X seem to have average, superior, or below-normal intelligence?
    a) In what way?
    b) Why do you think it was so?
    c) How did you feel about it?
    d) How did your husband feel about X's intelligence?

26. Was there anything X did as a baby that particularly surprised you in view of his handicap?
    a) (If yes) What?
    b) How did you feel about it?

27. Looking back on X as a baby, was he a cuddly, affectionate baby, or did he not like to be picked up that much?
    a) In what way?

28. Do you think that X was very attached to you or did it not seem to matter if someone else took care of him?
    a) In what way?
    b) How was X with your husband?

29. What was X's relationship with his sisters and brothers as a baby?
    a) Did they like to help take care of X?
    b) How did X respond?

30. Was there anybody else who was close to X?
    a) (If yes) Who?
    b) In what way?
    c) How did you feel about it?

31. What about taking X out? Did you find it hard to do so when X was a baby?
    a) In what way?

b) How did you handle the problem?

32. Looking back at these first few months, what did you find hardest?
    a) What worried you most?
    b) Was there anyone or anything that helped you get through it? (If yes) What?

33. Now, I would like to talk more specifically about X's handicap. At the time you brought X home from the hospital, did you consider it very serious or not that serious?
    a) In what way?
    b) What made you think that?
    c) How did you think it would affect X's life?
    d) How did you think it would affect your life?
    e) What did your husband think about it?

34. When X was born, did the doctor give you the impression that there was any medical help for X's handicap?
    If yes
    a) What?
    b) How much would it help?
    c) How did you feel about it?
    If no
    a) Why?

35. Was there anything you read at this time about children with handicaps like X's?
    If yes
    a) What?
    b) How did you feel about it?

36. At this time, did you have any contact with other parents of handicapped children?
    If yes
    a) Who?
    b) What effect did it have on your feelings?
    If no
    a) Would you have liked to?

37. In the first few months, did X have any specific medical treatment for his handicap?
    If yes
    a) What?
    b) Where and with whom?

c) Who suggested it?
d) What did you think it would accomplish?
e) Were you satisfied with it?
f) In what way?
g) What about your husband?

If no

a) Did you plan to find help in the future?
b) What? Where? When?
c) What did you think it would accomplish?

38. How did you first hear of the government's program for thalidomide babies?
    a) From whom?
    b) When?
    c) What did you think of it?
    d) What about your husband?

39. How old was X when you first brought him to the Rehabilitation Institute of Montreal?
    a) How long was X there the first time?
    b) Do you remember your first impression of the hospital?
    c) What did you like most about the hospital?
    d) What did you like least?

40. Who was the person who gave you the most help in understanding X's problem?

41. Was there anyone you found particularly unhelpful?

42. On the whole, how did you find the physical arrangements and the care of the children? In what way?

43. How did you find the doctors?

44. What about the nurses?

45. What about the physical and occupational therapists?

46. What about the psychologists?

47. Was there anyone who tried to help you in your role as a parent of a handicapped child?
    If yes: Who?
    a) In what way?
    b) How helpful did you find (him) (her)?
    c) What about your husband?

48. On the whole, do you think the staff did a good job in explaining to you the nature of the disability and what they could do to help?
    a) What would you have liked them to tell you that they did not?

49. When X was in the hospital, were you able to stay in Montreal?
    a) How often were you able to visit X?
    b) Did you find that the visiting hours were sufficient or would you have liked them changed?
    c) What about the length of hospitalization? Did you find that it was justified or do you think it could be shortened?
       If no
       a) How often were you able to see X?
       b) Did you have any other ways of keeping in touch?
       c) What about the length of hospitalization? Did you find it justified or do you think it could be shortened?
50. (*If X needed operation*)
    a) When did you first hear of X's operation?
    b) From whom?
    c) How did you feel about it?
    d) What about your husband?
    e) Do you think it was adequately explained to you or would you have liked to be told more about it?
    f) Did you have the feeling that you as parents were given the right to choose or that you were being pushed into something?
    g) Looking back at it, do you think the operation was justified?
51. (*If X needed prostheses*)
    a) When did you first hear about the possibility of prostheses for X?
    b) From whom?
    c) How did you feel about it?
    d) What about your husband?
    e) Do you think it was adequately explained to you or would you have liked to be told more about it?
    f) Did you have the feeling that you as parents were given the right to choose or that you were being pushed into it?
    g) Do you think you were given adequate training in the prostheses so that you could manage at home?
52. Do you think the Institute helped you in learning how to take care of X and manage him?
    If yes
    a) In what way?
    b) From whom?
    If no
    How do you think a hospital might help you in this way?

53. On the whole, do you think your contact with the Institute made you feel more hopeful or less hopeful about X?
    a) In what way?
    b) What about your husband?

54. If the government had to set out another program for handicapped children, do you think it would be a good idea to have special centers such as the Institute or would you rather be given the money directly and choose your own doctors?
    a) Why?
    b) What about your husband?

55. On the whole, do you think the government's program helped you or interfered with your role as a mother?
    a) In what way?
    b) What about your husband?

Appendix B

Text of Letter Sent to Parents[1]

Dear Mr. and Mrs. X:

We would like to see your child for a re-evaluation, and an appointment is given to you for ——, —— the ——, ——, at 8:45 A.M.

I do not know if Doctor Décarie had the opportunity to speak to you about it the last time you were here, but one of the things the psychologists have been talking about with some of the parents is a way of profiting from your experiences in order to help you more effectively in the future, as well as other mothers of handicapped children. There has been so much to discuss and plan each time you have come in that you seldom had the chance to sit down and talk at length about the problems you have faced, the solutions you have found, and the ways in which things could be improved. Basically, this time we should like to ask you to help us; by sharing your experiences as a mother with us, you could teach us how we can learn to deal with your problems, and those of mothers like you, in a more helpful fashion.

We are aware of the fact that you are a busy person and we do not want to prolong your stay at the Institute unnecessarily. But, during the time that your child will be re-evaluated by the different members of the Rehabilitation team, a series of interviews has been planned in which you can, if this suits you, talk about these things. Mrs. Ethel Roskies, a psychologist at the University of Montreal, who works with Doctor Décarie and who is particularly interested in the problems of parents of

[1] While this was the letter sent to the largest number of parents, as usual the heterogeneity of the sample made it necessary to change the format of the letter for some of the mothers. In particular, the two mothers whose children were not living at home, and the one family not participating in the habilitation program, were sent individual, rather different, letters.

handicapped children, has undertaken this task and she is very much looking forward to spending some time with you.

As this re-evaluation will last a week, we would like you to consider therefore a stay in Montreal for approximately one week.

May we assure you that the father's presence is always welcome, but the presence of the mother and the child is essential.

Please let us know on the attached sheet, whether or not you are able to keep the appointment scheduled.

Sincerely yours,

M. MONGEAU, M.D.
Chief of Service
Physical Medicine and
Rehabilitation

MM:pc
encl.

Glossary of Medical Terms
(Larousse Medical Illustré, 1954; McNalty, 1961)

Amelia, congenital absence of (one or more) extremities.

Amenorrhoea, pathological absence or stoppage of the menstrual discharge.

Anomaly, a deviation from the normal.

Atresia, congenital imperforation of a normal channel or opening of the body, or pathological closure of it.

Bicornuate, having two horns or hornlike processes or projections.

Coloboma, a gap in one of the structures of the eye, usually due to congenital malformation.

Congenital, dating from birth; existing before birth or at birth.

Dysdactyly, malformation of the fingers.

Dysgenesis, dysgenic; defective developmental embryo malformation.

Dysmenorrhoea, pain occurring in the back and lower abdomen at or about the time of the menses.

Ectromelia, congenital anomaly consisting of the absence or atrophy of one or several segments of a limb.

Hemangioma, an angioma (tumor) composed of dilated blood vessels.

Hemimelia, incomplete or defective extremities.

Horseshoe kidney, a congenital anomaly produced by fusion of the upper or lower poles of the two kidneys so that the kidney assumes the general shape of a horseshoe.

Iatrogeny, iatrogenic; condition involving adverse effects induced by the physician in the care of his patients.

Imperforation, the condition of being closed or occluded; the term is used particularly in relation to structures which normally are open, as the vagina.

Lobulate, consisting of lobes (a globular part of an organ separated by boundaries)

Meatus, a passage; an opening.

Mesenchymal, relating to the mesenchyma.

Mesenchyma, the embryonal connective tissue, derived chiefly from the mesoderm, which gives rise to bone, cartilage, and other connective tissues, as well as to the lymphatic and blood vessels.

Mesoderm, the middle germ layer of the embryo, lying between the ectoderm and the entoderm.

Microtia, abnormal smallness of the external ear.

Palsy, loss of motor function in some part of the body.

Phocomelia, developmental anomaly with hands or feet being attached to the trunk of the body by a single, small, irregularly shaped bone.

Physiatrist, physician who specializes in the branch of medicine that deals with the diagnosis and treatment of disease and disability by physical means. As used at the RIM, the term indicated the medical specialist in rehabilitation.

Physiotherapist, one skilled in the methods of physical therapy and qualified to use these in treatment of disease and disability, usually under the supervision of a physician.

Polydactyly, presence of more than the normal number of fingers or toes on a hand or foot.

Primigravida, one who is pregnant for the first time.

Prosthesis, an artificial part, for example, a leg or arm; artificial restoration of some part which has been lost.

Psychiatrist, physician specializing in the branch of medicine that deals with the science and practice of treating mental, emotional, or behavioral disorders.

Rectovaginal fistula, an opening between the rectum and the vagina.

Rehabilitate,[1] to re-educate a person who has been sick or injured to take his place in the world.

Syndactyly, a condition in which two or more toes or fingers are fused.

Teratogenesis, teratogeny; the development and birth of a monster.

Teratogenic, characterized by teratogenesis.

Tetraphocomelia, phocomelia involving all four limbs.

---

[1] The term "habilitate" is not given in the dictionaries consulted; by analogy, however, it would presumably mean "to educate a person who has been born sick or injured to take his place in the world."

Bibliography[1]

Allen, F. H., and G. H. J. Pearson (1928). "The emotional problems of the physically handicapped child," *British Journal of Medical Psychology, 8,* 212–235.

Armstrong, K. (1963). "Habilitation of patients with congenital malformations associated with thalidomide: medical social aspects," *Journal of the Canadian Medical Association, 88,* 980.

Balint, Alice (1953). "Love for the mother and mother love," *in* M. Balint, *Primary Love and Psychoanalytical Technique.* New York: Liverwright, pp. 109–127.

Barker, R. (1948). "The social psychology of physical disability," *Journal of Social Issues, 4,* 28–39.

Barker, R., Beatrice Wright, L. Meyerson, and M. Gonick (1953). *Adjustment to Physical Handicap and Illness: A Survey of the Social Psychology of Physique and Disability.* New York: Social Science Research Council.

Barsch, R. (1968). *The Parent of the Handicapped Child: The Study of Child-rearing Practices.* Springfield: Thomas.

Bergmann, Thesi, and Anna Freud (1965). *Children in the Hospital.* New York: International Universities Press.

Blakeslee, B. (1963). *The Limb-Deficient Child.* Berkeley: University of California Press.

Boivin, G. (1968). "Nothing like the human hand," *Inter-Clinic Information Bulletin, 7* (No. 4), 17–19, 22.

Bowlby, J. (1960). "Separation anxiety," *International Journal of Psychoanalysis, 41,* 89–111.

Bronfenbrenner, U. (1958). "Socialization and social class through time

---

1 Only works directly referred to in the text are cited here.

and space," *in* E. Maccoby, T. Newcomb, E. L. Hartley (eds.), *Readings in Social Psychology*. New York: Holt, Rinehart and Winston, pp. 400–425.

Brooks, M. B. (1966). "Crisis intervention for the limb-deficient child," *in Industrial Society and Rehabilitation—Problems and Solutions* (pp. 99–100). Proceedings of the Tenth World Congress of the International Society for the Rehabilitation of the Disabled, Wiesbaden, Germany.

Canadian Doctor (1965). "For those who were spared," *31*, 31–33.

Caplan, G. (1960). "Patterns of parental response to the crisis of premature birth," *Psychiatry, 23*, 365–374.

Chodoff, P. (1963). "Delayed effects of the concentration camp syndrome," *Archives of General Psychiatry, 8*, 323–333.

Coughlin, Ellen W. (1941). "Some parental attitudes toward handicapped children," *The Child, 6*, 41–45.

Cowen, E. L., and P. H. Bobrove (1966). "Marginality of disability and adjustment," *Perceptual and Motor Skills, 23*, 869–870.

Danforth, D. D. (1966). *Textbook of Obstetrics and Gynecology*. New York: Harper and Row, Hoeber Medical Division.

Davis, A., and R. J. Havighurst (1948). "Social class and color differences in child rearing," *American Sociological Review, 11*, 698–710.

Davis, F. (1961). "Deviance disavowal: the management of strained interaction by the visibly handicapped," *Social Problems, 9*, 120–132.

—— (1963). *Passage through Crisis: Polio Victims and Their Families*. Indianapolis: Bobbs-Merrill.

Dean, C. (1958). *Lower Extremity Prosthetic Device for Children*. Michigan Crippled Children Commission.

Décarie, Thérèse Gouin (1967). "A study of the mental and emotional development of the thalidomide children and of the psychological reaction of their mothers," *Inter-Clinic Information Bulletin, 6* (No. 4), 8–13.

—— (1968). "The mental and emotional development of the thalidomide children and the psychological reactions of the mothers: a follow-up study," *Inter-Clinic Information Bulletin, 7* (No. 4), 1–7.

—— (1969). "A study of the mental and emotional development of the thalidomide child," *in* B. M. Foss (ed.), *Determinants of Infant Behaviour, IV*. London: Methuen, pp. 167–189.

Denhoff, E., and R. H. Holden (1955). "Understanding parents: one need in cerebral palsy," *Cerebral Palsy Review, 16,* 9–11, 25.

Dimanche Matin (1964). "Les victimes de la thalidomide sont plus intelligentes que la moyenne!" July 12, p. 8.

Eastman, N. J., and L. M. Hellman (1966). *Williams' Obstetrics* (13th ed. rev.). New York: Appleton-Century-Crofts.

Ehlers, W. H. (1966). *Mothers of Retarded Children.* Springfield: Thomas.

Farber, B. (1959). "Effects of a severely mentally retarded child on family integration." *Monographs of the Society for Research in Child Development, 24,* No. 2 (Serial No. 71)

Fishman, S., and H. W. Kay (1964). "Acceptability of a functional cosmetic artificial hand for young children," *Artificial Limbs, 8,* 28–44.

Franklin, A. W. (1963). "Physically handicapped babies: some thalidomide lessons." *Lancet, 1,* 959–962.

Franz, C. H. (1962). "The increase in the incidence of malformed babies in the German Federal Republic (West Germany) during the years 1959–62," *Inter-Clinic Information Bulletin, 2* (No. 2), 2–18.

Gilpin, R. (1963). "Habilitation of patients with congenital malformations associated with thalidomide: prosthetic aspects," *Journal of the Canadian Medical Association, 88,* 973–979.

Gingras, G., et al. (1964). "Congenital anomalies of the limbs" (Part 1: "Medical aspects"; Part 2: "Psychological and educational aspects"), *Journal of the Canadian Medical Association, 91,* 67–73, 115–119.

Goffman, E. (1963). *Stigma: Notes on the Management of Spoiled Identity.* Englewood Cliffs: Prentice-Hall.

Hall, J. (1963). "Habilitation of patients with congenital malformations associated with thalidomide: surgery of limb defects," *Journal of the Canadian Medical Association, 88,* 964–972.

Hall, W. T. (1961). "Family disorganization associated with severity of handicap (by cerebral palsy) of a minor child." Unpublished doctoral dissertation, University of Minnesota.

Hill, Gertrude (1966). "Developmental study of a congenitally tetraphocomelic child." Thèse de licence inédite, Université de Montréal.

Holt, K. S. (1957). "The impact of mentally retarded children upon their families." Unpublished doctoral dissertation, Sheffield University.

—— (1958a). "The influence of a retarded child upon family limitation," *Journal of Mental Deficiency Research, 2,* 28–34.

—— (1958b). "The home care of severely retarded children," *Pediatrics, 22,* 746–755.

Hutchison, J. (1967). "Occupational therapy in the amputee program," *Inter-Clinic Information Bulletin, 6* (No. 4), 19–21.

Inter-Clinic Information Bulletin (1961–   ). Prepared by prosthetic and orthotic studies, New York University Post-Graduate Medical School, for the subcommittee on child prosthetics research and development.

Janis, I. (1958a). "Emotional innoculation: theory and research on the effectiveness of preparatory communications," *in* W. Muensterberger and S. Axelrad (eds.), *Psychoanalysis and the Social Sciences, V.* New York: International Universities Press, pp. 119–155.

—— (1958b). *Psychological Stress.* New York: Wiley.

Jordan, T. E. (1962). "Research on the handicapped child and the family," *Merrill-Palmer Quarterly, 8,* 243–260.

Journal of the Canadian Medical Association (1963). "Habilitation of thalidomide-deformed children," *88,* 488–490.

Kammerer, R. C. (1940). "An exploratory psychological study of crippled children," *Psychological Record, 4,* 47–100.

Kelman, H. R. (1964). "The effect of a brain-damaged child on the family," *in* H. G. Birch (ed.), *Brain Damage in Children: the Biological and Social Aspects.* Baltimore, Md.: Williams and Wilkins, pp. 77–100.

Kral, V. A. (1951). "Psychiatric observations under severe chronic stress," *American Journal of Psychiatry, 108,* 185–192.

Kral, V. A., L. H. Pazder, and Blossom Wigdor (1967). "Long-term effects of a prolonged stress experience," *Canadian Psychiatric Association Journal, 12,* 175–183.

Lacomme, M. (1960). *Pratique obstétricale.* Paris: Masson.

Larousse Médical Illustré (1954). Paris: Librarie Larousse.

Lazure, D. (1963). "Habilitation of patients with congenital malformations associated with thalidomide: psychological and psychiatric aspects," *Journal of the Canadian Medical Association, 88,* 962–964.

Lowenfeld, B. (1964). *Our Blind Children.* Springfield: Thomas.

Lussier, A. (1960). "The analysis of a boy with a congenital deformity," *in* A. Freud *et al.* (eds.), *Psychoanalytic Study of the Child, XV.* New York: International Universities Press, pp. 430–454.

Lynd, H. M. (1958). *On Shame and the Search for Identity.* New York: Harcourt Brace.

McBride, W. G. (1961). "Thalidomide and congenital abnormalities," *Lancet, 2,* 1358.

McKeown, T. (1967). "The community's responsibility to the malformed child." Symposium No. 9: "The cost of life." *Proceedings of the Royal Society of Medicine, 60,* No. 2, Part 2, 1219–1224.

McNalty, Sir Arthur (ed.) (1961). *The British Medical Dictionary.* Toronto: Caxton.

Mead, Margaret (1952). *And Keep Your Powder Dry.* New York: William Morrow.

Michael, J., and Helen Shucman (1962). "Observations on the psychodynamics of parents of retarded children," *American Journal of Mental Deficiency, 66,* 568–573.

Mongeau, M. (1967). "Our experience with thalidomide children: an interim report," *Inter-Clinic Information Bulletin, 6* (No. 4), 3–7, 12.

Montreal Star (1963). "City Institute aids thalidomide baby," December 17, p. 14.

Moreault, P., B. Hébert, and G. Gingras (1963). "Psycho-social and pedagogical aspects of dysgenesis," in *Disability Prevention-Rehabilitation* (pp. 182–187). Proceedings of the Ninth World Congress of the International Society for the Rehabilitation of the Disabled, Copenhagen, Denmark.

Myklebust, H. R. (1966). *Your Deaf Child.* Springfield: Thomas.

Neff, W. S., and S. A. Weiss (1965). "Psychological aspects of disability," in B. B. Wolman (ed.), *Handbook of Clinical Psychology.* New York: McGraw-Hill, pp. 785–826.

Niederland, W. G. (1961). "Problem of the survivor," *Journal of Hillside Hospital, 10,* 233–247.

O'Neill, Monica (1965). "A preliminary evaluation of the intellectual development of children with congenital limb malformations associated with thalidomide." Thèse de licence inédite, Université de Montréal.

Parsons, T., and R. Fox (1958). "Illness, therapy and the modern urban American family," in E. Gartley Jaco (ed.), *Patients, Physicians and Illness.* Glencoe: Free Press.

Prechtl, H. F. R. (1963). "The mother-child interaction in babies with minimal brain damage," in B. M. Foss (ed.), *Determinants of Infant Behaviour, II.* London: Methuen.

Rancourt, Réjeanne (1965). "Evaluation du développement mental de sujets atteints de malformations dues à la thalidomide." Thèse de licence inédite, Université de Montréal.

Rathbun, J. C., and J. K. Martin (1963). "Habilitation of patients with congenital malformations associated with thalidomide: pediatric aspects," *Journal of the Canadian Medical Association, 88,* 959–961.

Redl, F. (1942). "Group emotion and leadership," *Psychiatry, 5,* 573–596.

Reid, D. E. (1962). *A Textbook of Obstetrics.* Philadelphia: Saunders.

Repond, A. (1956). "Les réactions et les attitudes des familles envers leurs enfants anormaux," *Evolution Psychiatrique, 21,* 317–330.

Robertson, J. (1958). *Young Children in Hospital.* New York: Basic Books.

Robson, K. S. (1967). "The role of eye to eye contact in maternal-infant attachment," *Journal of Child Psychology and Psychiatry, 8,* 13–25.

Roe, H. (1952). "The psychological effects of having a cerebral palsied child in the family." Unpublished doctoral dissertation, Columbia University.

Roskies, Ethel (1969). "Abnormality and normality: mothers' perceptions of their congenitally limb-deficient thalidomide children." Unpublished doctoral dissertation, Université de Montréal.

Roth, J. A. (1963). *Timetables.* Indianapolis: Bobbs-Merrill.

Sears, R. R., E. E. Maccoby, and H. Levin (1957). *Patterns of Child Rearing.* Evanston: Row-Peterson.

Shere, E., and R. Kastenbaum (1966). "Mother-child interaction in cerebral palsy: environmental and psychosocial obstacles to cognitive development," *Genetic Psychology Monographs, 73,* 255–335.

Sherr, Marie (1954). "An evaluation of the social and emotional development of the cerebral palsied twin." Unpublished doctoral dissertation, University of Illinois.

Siller, J., and S. Silverman (1958). "Studies of the upper-extremity amputee, VII: psychological factors," *Artificial Limbs, 5,* 88 117.

Smith, H. T. (1958). "A comparison of interview and observation measures of mother behavior," *Journal of Abnormal and Social Psychology, 57,* 278–282.

Smithells, R. W. (1963). *Early Diagnosis of Congenital Abnormalities.* London: Cassell.

Solint, A. J., and M. H. Stark (1961). "Mourning and the birth of a defective child," *in* A. Freud *et al.* (eds.), *Psychoanalytic Study of the Child, XVI.* New York: International Universities Press, pp. 523–537.

Sommers, V. S. (1944). *The Influence of Parental Attitudes and Social Environment on the Personality Development of the Adolescent Blind.* New York: American Foundation for the Blind.

Speirs, A. L. (1962). "Thalidomide and congenital abnormalities," *Lancet, 1,* 1270–1273.

Strasser, H. (1965). *Erhebungen uber die entwicklung einer gruppe gliedmabenfehlgebildeter kinder und ihre lebensbedingunge.* München: Forschungsbeilung der Mental-Health Gruppe.

Tremblay, Francine Bonnier (1967). "Etude longitudinale du développement intellectuel de sujets thalidomidiens." Thèse de licence inédite, Université de Montréal.

Vancouver Sun (1963). August 24, p. 8.

Webb, Jean F. (1963). "Canadian thalidomide experience," *Journal of the Canadian Medical Association, 89,* 987–992.

—— (1964). *The Thalidomide Problem in Canada.* Ottawa: Child and Maternal Health Division.

Webster's New World Dictionary (1958). Toronto: Nelson, Foster and Scott.

Wenar, C., and J. B. Coulter (1962). "A reliability study of developmental histories," *Child Development, 33,* 453–462.

Winnicott, D. W. (1956). "Primary maternal preoccupation," published in *Collected Papers.* London: Tavistock, 1958, pp. 300–306.

Wolfenstein, Martha (1957). *Disaster: A Psychological Essay.* Glencoe: Free Press.

Wolff, P. (1963). "The natural history of a family," *in* B. M. Foss (ed.), *Determinants of Infant Behaviour, II.* London: Methuen, pp. 139–171.

Worchel, T. L., and P. Worchel (1961). "The parental concept of the mentally retarded child," *American Journal of Mental Deficiency, 61,* 782–788.

Wright, Beatrice A. (1960). *Physical Disability: A Psychological Approach.* New York: Harper and Row.

Zuk, G. H. (1959). "The religious factor and role of guilt in parental acceptance of the retarded child," *American Journal of Mental Deficiency, 63,* 139–147.

Chronological Index

Subject Index

341

Library of Congress Cataloging in Publication Data
(For library cataloging purposes only)

Roskies, Ethel.
   Abnormality and normality.

   Bibliography: p.
      1. Handicapped children—Care and treatment—
Canada—Case studies. 2. Mother and child—Case
studies. 3. Thalidomide. I. Title.
HV890.C3R6   362.7'8'43   70-37757
ISBN O-8014-0691-9